To Rosie,
Your 20's are an amazing time to explore the world. But more importantly to explore yourself and figure out what your unique purpose is. Your

**HAP WORKING THE WORLD**

purpose is that thing you do that you are passionate about, when doing it it makes you feel alive and strong, time stands still. So _enjoy_ using your 20's to discover your purpose. Do what u enjoy and do what you WANT. In fact answer this question: "If you had all the money+time in the world and didn't have to worry about expectations, WHAT WOULD YOU DO?" now do it! 😊  HAP 5/11/12

# HAP WORKING THE WORLD

## HAP CAMERON

ALLEN&UNWIN

First published in 2012

Copyright © Hap Cameron 2012

All rights reserved. No part of this book may be reproduced or transmitted in any form or by any means, electronic or mechanical, including photocopying, recording or by any information storage and retrieval system, without prior permission in writing from the publisher.

Allen & Unwin
Sydney, Melbourne, Auckland, London

Level 3, 228 Queen Street
Auckland 1010, New Zealand
Phone:(64 9) 377 3800

83 Alexander Street
Crows Nest NSW 2065, Australia
Phone:(61 2) 8425 0100
Email:info@allenandunwin.com
Web:www.allenandunwin.com

National Library of New Zealand
Cataloguing-in-Publication Data

Cameron, Hap, 1981–
Hap working the world / Hap Cameron.
ISBN 978-1-877505-11-9
1. Cameron, Hap, 1981—Travel. 2. Voyages around the world.
I. Title.
910.41—dc 23

ISBN 978 1 877505 11 9

Internal design by Design by Committee
Map by Janet Hunt
Set in 12/16.5 pt Bembo by Post Pre-press Group, Australia
Printed and bound in Australia by Griffin Press

10 9 8 7 6 5 4 3 2 1

The paper in this book is FSC certified. FSC promotes environmentally responsible, socially beneficial and economically viable management of the world's forests.

To my loving parents,
you were my pillars of strength when everything else was falling down.

To *mi amor*,
words cannot explain how lucky I feel to have you in my life.
I look forward to writing the next chapter together.

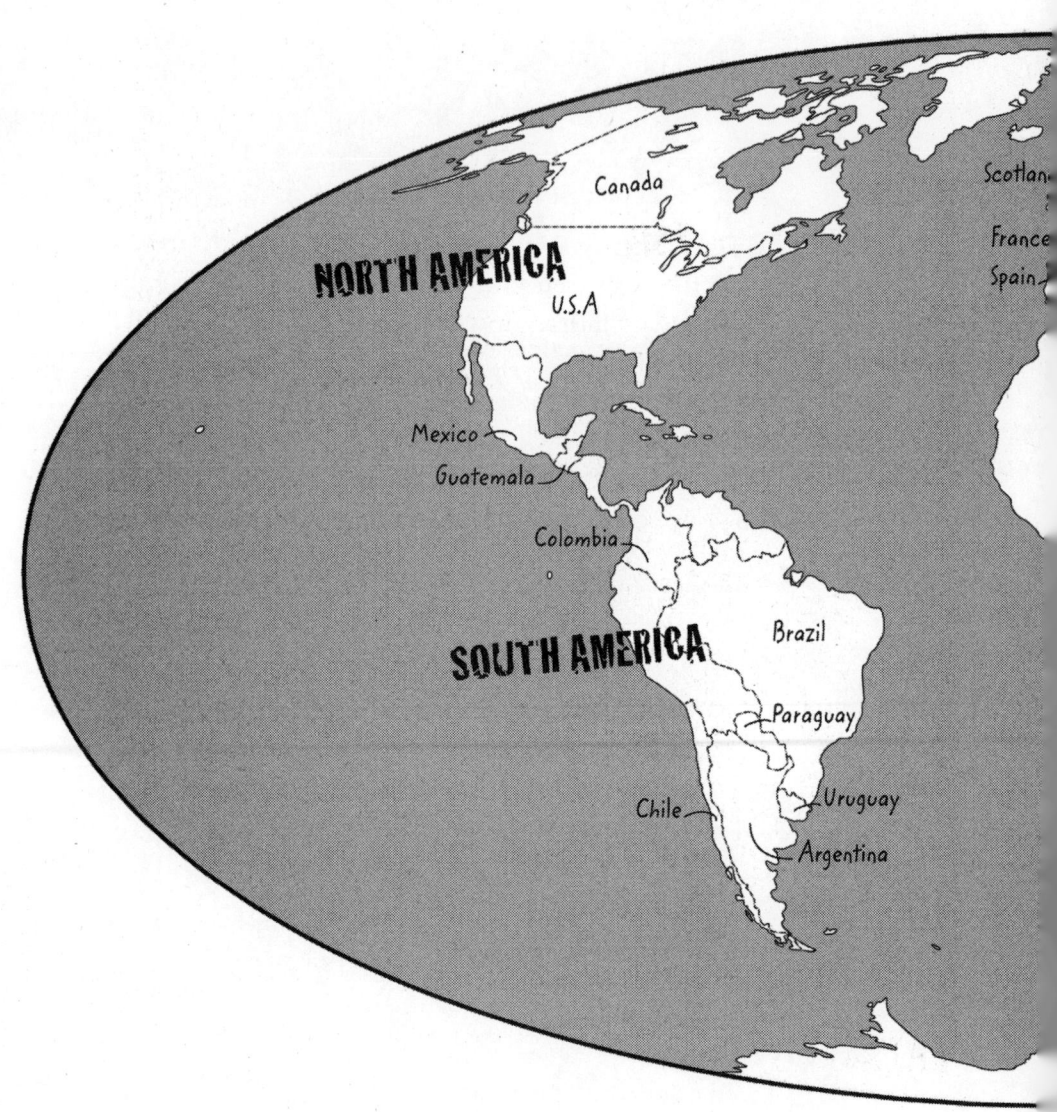

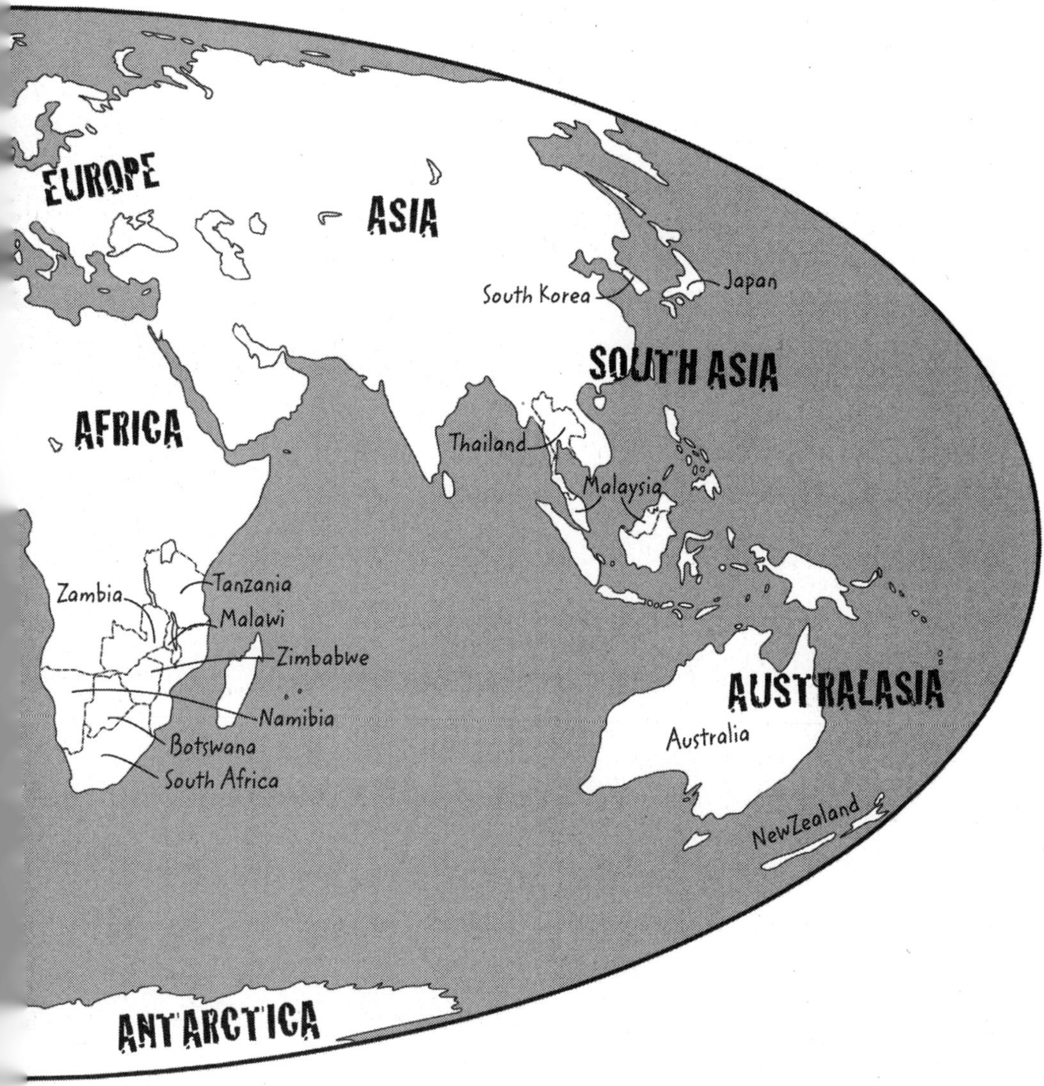
EUROPE
ASIA
South Korea
Japan
SOUTH ASIA
AFRICA
Thailand
Malaysia
Zambia
Tanzania
Malawi
Zimbabwe
Namibia
Botswana
South Africa
AUSTRALASIA
Australia
NewZealand
ANTARCTICA

DISCLAIMER: The names, nationalities and even genders of some characters have been changed to protect their identities, although last time I checked I was still a guy.

# CONTENTS

| | |
|---|---|
| **THE END** | 1 |
| **THE BEGINNING** | 5 |
| **CHAPTER 1:** Glorified Babysitter | 7 |
| **CHAPTER 2:** Life of Luxury | 38 |
| **CHAPTER 3:** The American Dream | 55 |
| **CHAPTER 4:** Erection Specialist | 65 |
| **CHAPTER 5:** Canadian Nomad | 79 |
| **CHAPTER 6:** Homeless Pig | 91 |
| **CHAPTER 7:** The Waiting Game | 116 |
| **CHAPTER 8:** Hope and Hugs | 121 |
| **CHAPTER 9:** American Beauty | 142 |
| **CHAPTER 10:** A Memorable Stopover | 148 |
| **CHAPTER 11:** Falling Off the Long White Cloud | 170 |
| **CHAPTER 12:** Glorified Boy Scout | 183 |
| **CHAPTER 13:** The Heart of South America | 194 |
| **CHAPTER 14:** The End of the World | 206 |
| **CHAPTER 15:** My Everest | 217 |
| **CHAPTER 16:** Preparing for the Final Continent | 237 |
| **CHAPTER 17:** The Dark Continent | 249 |
| **CHAPTER 18:** The Final Continent | 275 |
| **EPILOGUE** | 323 |
| **EPIClogue** | 331 |
| **SHOUTOUTS** | 334 |

## The End

'We going to kill you, motherfucker!'

I hear the *clunk* as all the doors of the car are locked. Then the tinted electric windows start to close, separating me from the African ghetto outside and sealing me into this nightmare. I'm now trapped in a locked car with three gangsters. There is no escape.

In an instant the guy who is sitting beside me in the spacious backseat of the car has changed from being my best friend into a gangster. He pushes me against the door, shouting at me, 'We going to kill you, motherfucker! You heard about the tourists that been killed in Dar es Salaam? That's what we do, we kill tourist motherfuckers like you!' My stranger-danger alarm is wailing like a World War II bomb siren, and all I can think is, *You've cocked up this time, Hap.*

I curse myself as I feel the weight of the money belt around my waist. It feels like an anchor. It contains my passport,

Malawian money and my debit card, which is the only way I have of accessing cash. I curse myself again for going against my usual travel protocol of not wearing a money belt. My backpack is between my legs; it holds my new laptop, which I bought before the trip and which has all my documentary footage and photos on it. Despite the desperate situation, I do a quick mental check and I'm pretty sure I have backed up the majority of the footage.

I weigh up my situation. I'm in a locked car with tinted windows bumping its way down a rough dirt road into the heart of a ghetto in a notoriously dangerous African city. Although I'm scared, I'm also very calm. I start calculating my options. The doors are locked so I can't escape. Three gangsters against one foreigner who has the upper body strength of a ten-year-old girl. But I'm a taekwondo black belt—well I was eight years ago when I was living and working in Korea.

A scary vision flashes before me: I'm being held hostage in a dark concrete room, lying on a thin stained mattress, cockroaches crawling over my sweat-drenched, bruised body, waiting for my family to wire money through to these gangsters to buy my freedom.

Stories of dead tourists go through my mind, such as the 29-year-old Australian who six weeks earlier had been found dead in Nairobi with his bank account records showing his credit card had been stolen. Or the times I thought I would die when I encountered wild animals on my 2500-kilometre bicycle trip through southern Africa.

But here I'm dealing with humans, organised street gangsters. I know what to expect. I know they want my money. I hope they don't want my life. Unlike an animal, I can reason with them. I set myself a single goal: to get out of this car, preferably with all my limbs and organs intact.

I'm brought back to reality as the backseat gangster seems to have read my mind.

## The End

He shouts, 'You want to call for help? You want to call for help, motherfucker?'

The driver opens the electric window, letting in the blinding sun, and the oppressive humid air of the inner-city wraps its sticky film around me in this shrinking backseat world.

'Go on, call for help! Everyone here fears us. They're scared of us. No one cares about you.'

I make eye contact with the disinterested faces of the shantytown locals who are walking along the side of the dirt road, going about their everyday business. My eyes are as wide as saucers as I try to telepathically tell them I'm in danger. They look through me. I'm a *mzungu*. A white man. In a black man's world. To them I'm a rich tourist passing through; they live here. They know if they interfere, their lives will be made a living hell. Fair enough.

I agree with the backseat gangster that nobody is going to help me and he gets the driver to close the window.

He shouts at me again. 'Give us your money, motherfucker!'

Ironically I think to myself, *He really should tone his language down.*

He grabs my bag from between my legs and passes it to the intimidating hulk of a gangster in the front seat. The stony-eyed giant opens it up and takes out my laptop. He then pulls out my Swiss army knife. The knife is engraved with my name and the number 1994, the year my aunty gave it to me for my twelfth birthday. Just six days earlier I had celebrated my 30th birthday; the knife was in my pocket, the knife that has been to all seven continents.

Now the gangster in the backseat reaches over me and grabs at my pockets, turning them inside out. He seems annoyed that I only have some small change.

'Where's your money, motherfucker? Is it in the hotel? Don't fuck with us.' My money belt feels glaringly obvious underneath my sweat-soaked shirt, but I toss up whether to give it to him. I decide not to. Will this be my second poor decision of the day?

# HAP WORKING THE WORLD

In an apologetic manner I spread my arms out, showing the palms of my hands. Hoping like hell I'm convincing, I pour everything into my words: 'Look at me, I haven't shaved or had a haircut in six months. Do I look like I have money? I'm not a rich tourist driving around in a 4WD; I told you I'm riding my bicycle through southern Africa. I've been volunteering here in Africa, trying to help your people. I was setting up a sustainable bicycle workshop and making an independent documentary about it. When we first met I told you that I was off to the internet café to report my lost credit card. I have no money, I told you that.'

Unfortunately the gangster in the back is good at his job. He reaches over again and pats down my torso. His strong hands tear open my shirt to reveal my money belt.

'Motherfucker, you lied. We going to fucking kill you!'

So after nearly nine years of working the world, this is how it's going to end—killed by gangsters in an African ghetto.

My mind drifts away from this nightmare to remember how my dream had started.

## The Beginning

The past nine years had all come about from a pretty unimpressive start. I hadn't had a life-changing moment. I hadn't been diagnosed with cancer. I hadn't won Lotto or sold a multimillion-dollar business.

I had a textbook happy childhood. I am the youngest child of a nuclear family, Mum, Dad, sister and me. My birth certificate says my name is Mark, but I have been called Hap for as long as I can remember. People believe that I'm called Hap because I'm always happy, but the opposite is true. As a baby, my father described me as a 'grizzly little bugger'. I was always crying. In the way of nicknames, he called me Happy and over the years this got shortened to Hap.

When I was a kid, weekends were always spent playing sport and enjoying the outdoors. I lived in the same house and walked the same way to school, from kindergarten (although Mum walked with me then) through to high school, my whole life. After school I worked at the local department store and in summer holidays I worked picking fruit. In my final year of high school I was voted head boy, then, the following year as an 18-year-old, I left my hometown to attend university. Two years later the seed of my goal was planted.

It all began in 2001–02, an era when Facebook, Twitter and YouTube were just vague ideas floating around in some soon-to-be-rich teenagers' minds. Back then I'd had an email account for only two years, reality TV had just taken off with the *Survivor* series, we listened to CDs instead of iPods, and when I rang a mate I used a landline because I didn't have a cell phone.

It was at this time, as a 20-year-old, that I went over to Australia's Gold Coast during my second-year university holiday and worked 60-hour weeks in a dusty, sweaty factory making timber shutters for houses. It may not sound like the stuff that dreams are made of, but I loved working with guys who had gained a wealth of knowledge from a lifetime in that job, and being a part of the camaraderie, the workplace banter, the jokes.

I loved living in a place where I was an unknown entity, where I could be whoever I wanted to be. To me, that was true freedom. Everything was new, exciting and an adventure. I began to think that if I enjoyed living and working in Australia, imagine what the rest of the world could offer me.

I believed my twenties were for living life, a time when there were no expectations, the perfect time to make a dream a reality. Years 0–21 had been about education, and 30 onwards would supposedly be about having a career and a mortgage, getting married and having kids. I saw no rush.

After my Australian working holiday I came back to New Zealand and entered the third year of a marketing and management degree, with my previous plans of post-graduate study out the window.

I wanted to travel the world.

But I wanted to truly experience the world, and I wanted to see the whole world, every continent. I was $30,000 in debt after university so I would have to work along the way to fund my adventure. Therefore, I came up with the plan of dedicating my twenties to working the world.

I finished university in November 2002. Then, during an Outward Bound course in January 2003, at age 21, I committed myself to the goal of living and working in every continent of the world before I turned 30.

I had only two things on my mind: to live life with no regrets and to have a good time along the way.

Little did I dream that this innocent goal would end up consuming my life, changing my life, becoming my life.

The one thing I have learnt from working the world is that everyone has a story to tell. From the Filipino waiter on an Antarctic cruise ship to the little Mexican orphan to the millionaire European businessman to the hardened Canadian oil-rig worker to a remote African villager with AIDS to you, the reader. We all have a story, and here is mine.

# Chapter 1
# GLORIFIED BABYSITTER
### ASIA: Seoul, South Korea, 7 April 2003–12 July 2004

I was waiting at Christchurch airport, and the agent who had organised a job for me in Korea and had my air tickets was nowhere to be found.

It seemed as though someone didn't want me to go. In fact, did I want to go? The front page of my local paper had featured articles about the SARS epidemic that was infecting Asia, and to cheer me up there was a little side article about North Korea and South Korea being 'on the brink of war'. What I didn't know at that point was that they had been on the brink of war for more than 50 years, and that the media was never a good indicator of what was actually happening in a would-be travel destination.

The airport speaker system broke from its continual round of *This is the final boarding call for flight blah blah blah*, to *Could Hap Cameron urgently come to the airport information desk.*

# HAP WORKING THE WORLD

'Hi Hap. I'm so sorry, I got stuck in traffic. Here's ya tickets. You better hurry up and check in as you don't have much time. Someone will be waiting for you in Korea. If you have any problems, give me a call. Good luck.'

I stood there with the tickets and the agent must have seen the look on my face, like that of a three-year-old who has lost his mother in a busy shopping mall. 'OK, I'll take you to the check-in counter and get you checked in.'

And I was planning to live and work in every continent of the world?

'ANNNN YOOOONG HAAAA SAAAEEEE YO,' I said, while bowing with all the enthusiasm of a 21-year-old in a foreign country for the first time, trying to make a good initial impression on his new boss. The clean-cut Korean man who, to my unworldly eyes, looked like all the other Korean men in the airport except for the piece of paper he was holding with 'Hap' written on it, grunted at my welcome and turned on his heels. I hoped I hadn't just told him to get fucked, or maybe he was grunting because, like me, he thought five syllables to say 'Hi' was a little over the top. Regardless of what I thought, he was my lifeline in Korea so I followed him.

The conversation on the ride from the airport to my new school was non-existent. Considering I was still trying to remember the five syllables of hello and my new boss could only manage grunts, it wasn't surprising.

Conversation wasn't essential as I was transfixed with what was outside the window. We were on a twelve-lane highway passing row upon row of apartment buildings draped in a smoggy haze.

Everything was completely different from Nelson, the small town of 50,000 at the top of New Zealand's South Island where I grew up. In Nelson in the 1980s and 1990s, an Indian running the corner shop was something you'd only see on *The Simpsons*;

## Glorified Babysitter

Asian food consisted of a spring roll from the local fish 'n' chip shop and taxi drivers' first language was English. I felt I had been pulled out of the grassy hills of *The Sound of Music* and thrown into *The Matrix*.

Judging by the grunts and gestures my new boss made, I assumed that we had arrived in my new neighbourhood, Bucheon. My new home away from home struck me as one big construction site. Cranes were busy constructing more twenty-storey buildings to keep the current ones company. Like water pouring onto the ground, the spreading puddle of Korea's capital city Seoul had no clear city limits. My visitor's introduction book told me that the population of Seoul and its surrounding cities totalled twenty million people. I suppose that shouldn't have been surprising considering you can drive from one end of Korea to the other in five hours and 50 million people call that space home.

However, I got the feeling that my boss didn't know where he was. We had been driving around the same block for some time now and he was looking up at the buildings, every inch of which was covered in signs and billboards, even the windows. There were a lot of things about Korea that I never really understood and this was one of them—covering your windows with advertising so you couldn't see out . . . why have windows?

Now I was sure my boss was lost, as he was on the phone impatiently spitting out Korean. I didn't pick up any *ann yong ha sae yo*s. He hung up, grunted and tapped the dashboard of the Hyundai executive-styled sedan, which I took to mean we would wait here.

I looked to my left and there was a 2-metre-high metal fence surrounding a construction site and on the other side was a barber shop that had two spinning red, white and blue striped poles. At this point my mind started to wander. Why doesn't my boss just take me to my school or new apartment? Maybe the English teaching contract I had signed was just a cover up? Maybe I was going to be chained to a mafia-run brothel bed wearing a pretty little pink dress to meet the sexual desires of twisted businessmen? I suppose this scenario wasn't totally out of the question as I was as much an English teacher as I was a male prostitute. I hadn't taught a day in my life, but for the Koreans it was enough that my passport said I was from a native English-speaking country and that I had a university degree.

In the rearview mirror I saw another gleaming black, executive-styled Hyundai sedan pull in behind us. My boss gave a grunt then got out and went to talk to the driver of the other car. I waited patiently, still totally clueless as to what was happening.

The passenger side door opened and the expensive-suit-wearing driver of the other car greeted me with a big, game-show-host smile. After a prolonged double handshake followed by a shoulder rub and a rehearsed introduction—'Hello, I'm Mr Kim. How are you? OK'—he held his left hand in the air signalling me to wait while he reached into his pocket. He hit speed dial then rapid fired orders into the phone. Then, with his game-show-host smile and a few more 'OK, OK's he passed me the phone.

'Hello,' I said hesitantly.

A cute, giggly Korean voice on the other end replied, 'Hello Hap, I'm Catherine, your Korean co-worker. I'm so sorry but we thought you were coming tomorrow and the driver doesn't know where our school is. Mr Kim is the school director, and he will take you to your apartment where you can sleep. We will come and get you in a couple of hours and bring you to school.'

Mr Kim flashed me more smiles, slapped my back with more 'OK's then went about trying to get my pack out of the car in a way that a health and safety manual would advise how *not* to pick up a heavy object. I followed him across the side street and entered a twenty-storey building, my new home. The elevator took us up twelve storeys of OKs and smiles, and I thought to myself, *How does this guy run a private English language institute with only the one word—OK?*

## Glorified Babysitter

Mr Kim seemed very proud of my new apartment, and from the elevator and corridor I thought rightly so. It was very modern, although everything in this neighbourhood was modern as everything was still being built.

We entered the apartment, and despite Mr Kim's charades indicating I was the first person to live there, I didn't quite believe him as he cleaned up the ashtrays and takeaway boxes. But he was right; I couldn't have asked for a nicer apartment as the first place to call my own.

Mr Kim gave me a quick tour of the apartment. The toilet and shower were squashed into what would normally be barely enough space for a toilet. The laundry and kitchen merged into the compact living area and a mezzanine sleeping area that had a 1.2-metre clearance between the floor and ceiling. The grand finale to the tour included Mr Kim instructing me how to use the wall-mounted air-conditioning unit which he clearly didn't know how to use. He waved and smiled goodbye and pointed to the mattress on the floor, gesturing for me to sleep by putting his head on his hands and closing his eyes.

I lay on the light-green fitted sheet covering the mattress, with the buzz of construction work on the one side and the twelve-lane road on the other. I myself was also buzzing; everything that I had seen throughout the day was just so different to the previous reality of my first 21 years on this planet. Korea was known as the land of the morning calm, but from what I had seen and heard—the traffic, the smog, the toilets, the language, the apartment buildings, the noise—there was nothing calm about Korea.

Little did I know at that point, as I lay awake on my first day of working the world, that Korea was going to be my longest chapter, and the lack of calm was going to be the thing I would love about it.

What Korea lacked in beauty and space it would make up

for in its colourful, friendly, vibrant, wacky pulse, which would satisfy any culture junkie's addiction.

## Culture shock cock

People talk of culture shock, but I just felt like a pig in shit. It was my first time in a foreign country, I didn't know anyone, and everything was completely different from my home town.

I was literally fresh off the boat in Korea. It was the first time I had to do my supermarket shopping by looking at the pictures on the packages, trying to figure out if the photo of a baby meant it was milk powder or washing powder. It was also my first time using chopsticks, negotiating a subway system, having my own cell phone, and ordering food in a foreign language.

I was loving learning this new culture with all its quirky goings-on, such as men holding hands, businessmen stumbling around the streets at 7 p.m. looking like they should be at a university keg party, mothers letting their little kids go to the toilet on the footpath, wearing rubber slippers when using the squat toilets, and eating the national dish of super-spicy fermented cabbage, which is an accompaniment to breakfast, lunch and dinner.

Once I had mastered chopsticks and the five syllables of hello, and added *goodbye, sorry, excuse me* and *thank you* to my vocabulary, I was ready to take on uncharted cultural territory.

I'm a sucker for hot baths and I'd heard that bathhouses were a big part of the Korean culture.

With vague directions, I set off on my adventure. I walked down the footpath of the twelve-lane road, marvelling at all the neon lights like a five-year-old seeing fireworks for the first time. After fifteen minutes' walking, I spotted a building with a fire symbol that supposedly represented the bathhouse, accompanied by a jumble of Korean signage. Out of the jumble, I saw the number 8 and guessed that was the floor on which I'd find the bathhouse.

## Glorified Babysitter

The *bing* of the elevator announced my arrival on the eighth floor. The doors opened to reveal an IKEA-decorated foyer that was trying to pull off a plush feel with the use of mirrors and plastic plants.

Under the inquisitive eyes of two relaxed-looking businessmen sitting in the foyer, I slipped off my worn skate shoes and placed them among the polished black leather shoes. I approached the expansive reception desk and got the usual giggling and mouth covering from the Korean woman behind the counter. I was halfway through my 'I'm here because I want a bath' charade when I realised that Koreans may not even use the baths for washing. And so in caressing my body, pretending to rub soap all over it, I probably just came across as an unco-ordinated stripper.

The receptionist, still giggling from my stripper impersonation, came around to my side of the counter. The first thing I noticed was that she was attractive and obviously indulged in the new fast-food culture instead of sticking to rice and kimchi for every meal. The second thing I noticed was that she was showing more skin than her fellow conservative countrywomen.

Uncharacteristically for a Korean woman, she surprised me by clasping my hand in hers. It shouldn't have been that surprising as I did seem to be in the land of hand holding.

From my obvious lack of knowledge of the Korean culture, she clearly thought I needed to be walked to the door of the men's bathhouse. She was right; I didn't have a clue what I was doing and there was no use telling me where to go as I wouldn't have understood. Like it was my first day at school and she was my mother, the confident beauty led me down a corridor that resembled my university hall of residence, with doors lining the walls.

We stopped in front of a door, and she ushered me into a room, signalling that I was to get changed and then she would be back. At least that was my interpretation. She shut the door in the self-assured way of a girl who knew I would like to have sex with her.

With the door shut, I took in my surroundings. There was a shower in the corner, and a double bed with a heart-shaped pillow lying on it. I sat on the bed and then everything started to make sense. Although I was in a culture where everything was foreign and new to me, even I knew that being escorted to a room with a double bed and heart-shaped cushion by a skimpily dressed girl holding my hand was a bit weird . . . I was in a bloody whorehouse!

A wave of panic hit me. I didn't want to have sex with a hooker. I couldn't speak the language. I was in a room sitting on a bed that had seen more action than Bruce Willis. All I could think of was getting to the safety of the neon lights and street smells outside.

I rushed out the door, down the now obviously pay-for-sex mood-lit corridor and headed straight for the elevator door. I hit the ground floor button with the intensity of a crackhead ringing his dealer's doorbell.

Ronald McDonald's scantily dressed love child came rushing from behind the counter as I waited for the elevator doors to open. Her self-confidence was smashed as she explained with her hands that one of her co-workers would be servicing me and that she was just the receptionist. It didn't matter, I needed to breathe the sweet smell of rotting rubbish on the street.

As the elevator slowly made its way up the floors I tried to explain in my Korean vocabulary of *hello, goodbye, thank you* and *excuse me* that I thought she was beautiful but unfortunately I wanted a bathhouse and not a whorehouse. As the receptionist took off back down the corridor—presumably to look for another co-worker—the experienced pay-for-sex businessmen laughed at my panicked state.

Thankfully I heard the welcoming *bing* of the elevator opening before the receptionist had time to find my love slave.

# Glorified Babysitter

As the doors closed on the IKEA sex kingdom, a rush of relief swept over me. It was time for a beer.

On the street, I found one of the ever-abundant Korean bars that was named 'Free Beer' and ordered a *makchu*, which my pocket phrasebook told me was beer. The Korean owner saw this as a great opportunity to practise his elementary English and came bounding back with two glasses and a 3-litre pitcher of pink bubbling, smoking beer that resembled the contents of a witch's cauldron.

This was my first experience with a Korean wanting to practise his English, and I loved it, especially as I got free beer. I didn't know that by the end of my Korean chapter I would be trying to avoid these 'free English lessons' and the elementary-school exchanges: 'How are you? Do you like chicken?' or 'I'm fine, I like chicken, goodbye.'

With the pink beer bubbling away in my stomach and my travel motto 'You lose much by fearing to attempt' bubbling away in my head, I asked Mr Kim, the Free Beer proprietor, where to find a legitimate bathhouse. After making sure I had the correct directions and Mr Kim reassuring me that this was his local bathhouse and the best in Korea, I walked off into the neon jungle to find it.

## Dong chim!

'Teacher! *Dong chim*!'

These were the words I heard just before feeling a seven-year-old's fingers rammed up my bum for the first time. I regret to say that it wasn't the last time I was violated by a minor's finger.

'Jerry! In the corner, NOW!' I yelled to the small-fingered bum bandit as my classroom exploded into laughter.

What I had just experienced was my first *dong chim*. If you ask anyone who has taught English in Korea, or any Korean, about *dong chim*, they will know what you mean. *Dong chim* is a supposedly funny game that Korean kids play. Instead of the game of pinkies which I played growing up, where you slap the other person's bare leg with your hand and try to leave a welt, the Korean kids stick their fingers up an unsuspecting child's bum while shouting '*dong chim*'—*dong* meaning shit, and *chim* I suppose something to do with fingers up bums.

My visions of angelic little smiling Korean children were well out the window before my first *dong chim*. Korean kids are like kids anywhere else in the world—they are kids. And when they attend six hours of normal school, and are then sent off by their well-meaning parents for a further two to five hours of lessons at various private institutions known as *hagwon*, it is kind of understandable why Korean children aren't as angelic as you would think.

The un-angelic behaviour of the kids wasn't helped by the fact that I didn't have a clue what I was doing. I had no teaching qualifications and my only classroom experience was a week of volunteering at a kindergarten in New Zealand when I found out I would be working with kids in Korea. And despite having a university degree, my knowledge of English was embarrassingly poor, to the point where I couldn't answer my student's question of 'Why do you say "an orange" and not "a orange"?' I was basically just a white guy who could speak English and hold a textbook. When people ask me what it was like teaching English, I always say 'Try to explain the difference between "would", "should" and "could". Now try to explain it to ten-year-olds who have trouble introducing themselves in English.'

As with anything, you either sink or swim, and I decided to swim. What followed was a crash course in English teaching: first, I had to learn about the language that naturally flowed from my mouth, and second, I had to learn how to teach.

I learnt how to teach from an experienced Canadian teacher at my *hagwon*. I taught myself grammar by reading all the children's textbooks that I would be using in the classroom and re-educating myself on what nouns, adjectives and gerunds were, and about the various tenses. I also learnt what not to do from my mate Dave. I'll refer to him as 'Dave Teacher' because in Korea you are called by the position which you hold in society. As in all Confucian societies, there is great importance placed on family and an individual's position within society. When addressing someone you do not call them by their given name, but rather by their position within the family or society. For example, you would address an older woman working in a shop as *ar-ju-ma*, meaning older married lady. Like me, Dave's position in society was related to the kids, who operate in both Korean and English culture, so he was addressed by his English given name and then his position in Korean society.

Dave Teacher was one of a bunch of players from my university soccer team who had come over to Korea while I was there. If Korea thought SARS or North Korea were a threat, they hadn't met my university soccer team. The future of Korea was not bright with my fellow team mates in the classroom.

Dave Teacher was a good-looking athletic guy who got likened to Brad Pitt by the giggly Korean girls. All foreigners are given movie-star names but for some reason my curly brown hair and underdeveloped body reminded them of Tony Blair, the English prime minister of the time!

Dave Teacher had an unorthodox approach to teaching. His classroom usually resembled a university party as he always played drinking games such as Ship Came into the Harbour or the Clap Game. The only difference was that the students were not forced to consume large amounts of alcohol.

It wouldn't have been uncommon for a Korean teacher to go past Dave Teacher's classroom and look in the window, thinking, *He he he, Dave Teacher is playing with the kids again and pretending to sleep. Look how hard they are working. And doesn't he look like Brad Pitt, he's so cute. He he.* Little did they know that Dave Teacher was sleeping off his hangover. The reason the kids would be concentrating so hard was because they were looking for a word in their Word Find that Dave Teacher had added to the list but not to the puzzle of jumbled letters. It was a good trick. I was guilty of using it too—'Hap Teacher, I no find banana in Word Find'.

## Taekwondo or torture?

When I first arrived in Korea I wanted to experience life as a local would. I joined the local soccer club, where I was treated like a superstar, travelling with them to play away games against neighbouring teams. I became a member of the local gym and bath house. I studied the Korean language, and taught myself to read and speak.

Every day my younger students would run into class wearing their taekwondo *dobok* (uniforms) and practise their groin kicks on me. So I took up Korea's national sport. I decided to set myself the goal of getting my black belt. But things didn't start too well.

Taekwondo academies are like rice in Korea; they are everywhere. Considering it's the home of taekwondo, that should not be surprising. I asked a team mate at my soccer club to recommend a good local academy. He went a step further and arranged for me to turn up to a class. At this point I had been in Korea for only five weeks.

At 8 p.m. I entered the fluorescent-lit academy which was crawling with miniature *dobok*-clad Bruce Lees. They stopped mid-kick and a murmur of *'waeguk'* alerted the room that a foreign guy had just walked in. The Grand Master barked at his pupils and they returned to their rhythmic chorus of chants to the sound of bare skin slapping against rubber pads.

The Grand Master approached me. He was short and stocky with a melon-sized head. His baby face had a warm smile that looked just on the edge of laughter, and he had massive tree-trunk legs the size of my torso. These legs I would later see break three baseball bats and his head smash through ten layers of stone.

He stopped about a metre away, the smile disappeared, then he saluted me, barking out something in Korean, and bowed. When he came back up from the bow his smile had returned. I was thankful—this was not a guy you would want to make angry. He kindly explained to me that I was to do what he had just done every time I entered the *dojang* as a sign of respect.

The Grand Master shouted out a command. The two other masters dropped what they were doing and arrived at his side. They welcomed me with the same saluting and bowing routine. The Grand Master pointed to the gorilla-sized master with a slicked-back Elvis hairstyle and said, 'Big Master.' He then pointed to the younger of the two, an attractive sporty type who would have been every young girl's heart-throb and said, 'Small Master.' We shook hands and greeted each other in polite Korean. I addressed the Grand Master as *kwanjangnim*, meaning the owner of the taekwondo institute or grand master. And I would call the other masters *kun sabomnim* and *chagun sabomnim*, respectively meaning big master and small master, due to their size not rank.

I liked these guys.

When the current class had finished, I took the floor with the new class of 12- to 15-year-old boys who were shyly looking me up and down. What followed was an unco-ordinated ordeal that left me feeling as though I had consumed horse tranquilisers for dinner. My legs wouldn't move as fast as my mind thought they should be able to. In that first lesson I found out that taekwondo is not about kicking things as hard as possible but rather the power comes from speed and technique.

Finally the Grand Master shouted, signalling the warm down. We gathered around, sitting cross-legged in rows three deep.

I, prematurely as it turned out, congratulated myself on surviving my first lesson. How wrong I was.

If the stretching session that followed had taken place back in Roman gladiator days, it would have been known as torture. You know the method where your extremities are strapped onto a wooden machine and stretched to snapping point? Well, I am not sure if Korea ever got the memo about torture being a crime against humanity but, excuse the pun, it was alive and kicking in that taekwondo *dojang*.

As *chagun sabomnim* came up behind the first boy in the row, the fourteen-year-old drew his heels into his groin to attempt a stretch, much like I had done many times at soccer training on the grassy fields back home. Then Small Master crouched behind him as though he was going to give the boy a bear hug. But instead, he crouched over him, placing his left palm on the boy's left knee and right palm on right knee.

Small Master's hairless athletic arms tightened as he pushed down on the boy's knees. He continued to do this with a gentle bouncing action on the boy's spring-like knees, each time putting more weight into the downward movement. Slowly the boy's knees assumed greater flexibility; soon he would be doing those head kicks with miraculous ease.

Then, after twenty seconds of this, Small Master's feminine body-builder arms flexed like an axe-wielding executioner's arms going in for the decapitating swing. All of Small Master's weight came down on the boy's knees, slamming them to the padded floor underneath, stretching them as though he was ripping the wings from a chicken carcass. The boy fought back the tears. Small Master moved on to the next boy in the line.

Eventually Small Master arrived at me. Four boys of the sixteen had cried. To say I was tense would have been an understatement. Did I have health cover in Korea? As Small Master bent over me, he kept saying 'Relax, relax.'

To my horror, after I had been violated by Small Master, Big

## Glorified Babysitter

Master, having seen I had the flexibility of a rubber band that had been left in the sunlight, shook his head like a disappointed father who used to be a football star and has just realised his son is fonder of poetry than football. Big Master was going to make me flexible; he wanted to 'help me'. Noooooooooooo!

Some of the kids stayed behind, joining Grand Master as he watched his new foreign asset (having a foreigner at your academy is like having a national representative play at your local club). I sat on the floor in front of his other prized asset, Big Master, who I later found out had been the Korean heavyweight champ five years previously.

The hulky frame of Big Master sat down directly in front of me, very delicately for a man of his size, sort of like an elephant doing a curtsy. I unfolded my chicken-wing legs, which were the size of Big Master's wrists. He gestured for me to spread my legs, and he also spread his legs in the same pose right in front of me so together our legs made a diamond shape. He then wiggled closer to me on his bum as though we were performing some kind of weird mating ritual.

He wiggled up until his outstretched feet were pushing on my outstretched ankles. Then he kept pushing, spreading my matchstick legs wider and wiggling his genital area closer to mine. At this point I was glad of my inflexibility; if I had been capable of doing the splits then there would have been an uncomfortable groin-on-groin moment.

Big Master, who had been doing this his whole life, was looking totally nonchalant, and oblivious that he was dealing with a guy who made using the squat toilets look painful. The master kept pushing my ankles further apart and the sound and vision of snapping branches filled my head.

Grand Master was watching and kept saying 'Happuh, relax, relax.' But as he had only spoken in single English words and not sentences that first night, I wondered if he knew what relax meant.

I tentatively put my hands out so now I looked like some kind of pained zombie yoga reject. His heavyweight hands swallowed up my feminine ones. To my horror, he then started to lean back while casually laughing and smiling. In my head the alarm bells were going off like an overexcited kid on a drum kit. Slowly the tears started to well in my eyes; my future ability to walk literally lay in Big Master's hands. Would this Elvis-haired torturer not be happy until he had torn me into a hermaphrodite?

I think he got the idea when his smiles and laughter were met with distressed grunts and teary eyes. In this country of status and supposed honour, where the type of car you drive is directly related to your place in society, he knew making me cry would shame this new foreigner who held high status because of his teaching position and because he came from an English-speaking country.

He finally let up. I slowly rose to my feet, keeping my face to the ground while wiping my long sleeve across my face to remove the moisture from my eyes. He slapped me on my back, nearly sending me down onto the padded floor, and cheerily said, 'OK?'

The next morning I got up fifteen minutes early and stretched—something I would do until my black belt test.

## The language of love

Growing up, I had always been the nice guy or the funny guy. I wasn't the oh-my-god-I-want-to-have-passionate-no-strings-attached-sex-with-him guy—probably from the girl's fear of breaking me in half. But as any English-speaking foreigner in an Asian country will tell you, you automatically become more attractive when you set foot in Asia. Maybe that is because you are attractive, but more likely it's because you are different, new meat on the market, worthy of bragging rights, or maybe your passport is seen as a potential ticket out. Having sex with you might be seen as a good way to get a free English lesson, or maybe it's just love. Whatever the reason, I wasn't too concerned. I was going to make the most of my Tony Blair good looks.

On one particular Saturday night, I was extremely hung-over from the night before, when Wendy the Canadian English teacher and her boyfriend, Caleb, somehow managed to get me to emerge from my pounding *soju*-induced slumber to go for 'just one beer'.

The three of us would always venture a little further each time we went out in search of a new bar. We found a suitable bar and ordered the usual 3-litre pitcher of beer. The cute girl with the big eyes behind the bar seemed to find my Korean endearing and was quite interested—maybe because there were only two old drunken Korean men as my competition. It always amazes me that you find the things you want when you aren't looking for them.

With Wendy as my wingwoman, we ended up inviting Sang-Mi, the big-eyed beauty, to a singing room after she finished work. I wasn't so sure that the singing room was a good idea as I hated singing, and for very good reason—I make a strangled albatross sound harmonious. So as far as trying to impress a girl, and a Korean girl who has been brought up singing at that, it wasn't the best idea.

However, my Tony Blair good looks must have outweighed my singing ability because Sang-Mi and I ended up staggering back to my apartment as the sun was coming up and doing something that loosely resembled putting a marshmallow in a coin slot.

In the morning, without the help of alcohol for communication and the dimmed lights to push my Tony Blair looks into the Tom Cruise realm, the goodbyes were awkward and somewhat inconclusive. Sang-Mi went home and I was left wondering if the goodbye I had just engaged in was a 'We will never see each other again' or a 'Let's meet up again' or 'I know I'm a conservative Korean but that was bad sex.'

## HAP WORKING THE WORLD

The following week on my way home from an international film festival, my bus dropped me off close to Sang-Mi's bar. She had been on my 21-year-old male mind, as a good-looking girl usually is, for the couple of days since we hooked up. I spent five minutes walking up the stairs to the fake wooden entrance of the bar only to walk back down again, cursing myself for being the equivalent of a ten-year-old who is too scared to send a love letter to his crush.

So with my travel motto 'You lose much by fearing to attempt' still buzzing in my brain, I pushed open the bar door. Sang-Mi's immaculate doll-like face blushed and the smile that she couldn't suppress quickly reassured me that I had made the right decision. I walked through the dimly lit, empty bar and our conversation unravelled, flowing with miscommunication.

Sang-Mi, in her softly spoken voice, said, 'Hello, Happuh, how are you?'

In my droning Kiwi accent and nervous voice I quickly blurted out, rapid fire, 'I'm fine, I have just been to a movie and thought I would pop in and say hello.'

To which she replied, 'OK, I go to movie with you, when?'

'Ummmm yeah, movie, ummmmm this Saturday?'

'OK, here my number, call me.'

On Saturday we managed to meet up, which was nothing short of a miracle considering our painful phone conversations had been spoken in words not sentences. I quickly learnt what my university communications lecturer meant when she said that communication was 85 per cent non-verbal.

Sang-Mi ran up and hugged me. She had a confidence about her, was older than me at 28 and dressed with a style that expressed her artistic interests. I was 21 and happy to be on a date with Korean Barbie. Dave Teacher and my mates were great but weren't that keen to lie in bed with me and watch DVDs on a rainy Sunday.

## Glorified Babysitter

I was eager to make a good impression and had got my Korean teacher to ring up the movie theatre and make a booking for two. We clumsily entered the dark theatre after the film had already started, and I attempted to direct Sang-Mi to our allocated seats. Then my cell phone rang. Yes, I was that guy. I panicked and pulled the battery out of the phone as I hadn't worked out how to put it on silent. It was the first ever cell phone I had ever owned and the instructions were all on Korean.

I slumped into the seat, doubting that Sang-Mi was so proud to be with her foreign trophy. Our first date had started off awkwardly but I was glad to be in the safety of the theatre, and keen to let the film save me from further embarrassment and allow my brain to relax, not having to come up with words to fill the long silences.

My relief was short-lived as the movie unfolded. The film was in some sort of Scandinavian language with English subtitles, so Sang-Mi could not understand it. This was probably a good thing. Although the scene where the 40-year-old son pleasures himself while watching through a keyhole as his mother gets dressed was self-explanatory in any language.

From this experience, I learnt never to pick a film based on its screening time, although that's all I had to base my choice on as the synopsis was in Korean. I think the film was called *Careful*, as afterwards Sang-Mi's first question was, 'What "careful" mean?' On the way back to my apartment I taught Sang-Mi that careful did not refer to pleasuring oneself over a family member. I think she understood me.

Back at my apartment, we had three hours to kill before meeting up with Dave Teacher and my mates. Like any one-track-minded, red-blooded male, I was determined to pull out all my charm so I could have a shot at putting in a good performance.

I slid into first base effortlessly but struck problems advancing to second. As my hands were caressing the porcelain skin beneath her thin shirt, Sang-Mi seemed to think it was a great time to start up with the English lesson again.

'Happuh, careflee.'

Being the patient I-will-do-anything-to-have-sex-with-you kind of young male, I quickly explained, 'You pronounce it care-ful, not care-flee.' A couple of minutes later it seemed this game of bedroom baseball had stalled between bases until the English lesson was over.

Sang-Mi kept saying 'careflee', and I kept explaining that the movie we watched was called *Careful*. As you would in any relationship where there was a lack of a common first language, I pulled out the English–Korean dictionary. It was here that I learnt my first lesson in Korean. In the Korean language there is the one character that represents the sound for *r* and *l*. Instead of trying to say 'careful', Sang-Mi was trying to say 'carefree'. I was rather impressed by this new word, especially because she had so much trouble comprehending 'careful'. I laughed and explained carefree to her, using me as an example, 'I am carefree,' while quickly resuming my bedroom baseball game.

'Happuh, careflee,' Sang-Mi said again, but this time pointing between her legs to home base.

As I'm rounding second base with thoughts of carefree sex in my head, Sang-Mi thumbed through the dictionary and said another word 'breed'. Now, with my thoughts confirmed, I was running as fast as I could to the home base that wanted to breed, thinking that I had better not take any chances with the condom that'd been in my wallet since leaving New Zealand, but to use the new one I had strategically placed under the mattress for this very moment.

Then in a weird flash my mind flicked back to the bottom shelf of the family bathroom cupboard, to the box of Carefree branded tampons. Then to the *R/L* Korean lesson I had just learnt.

It looked like baseball was cancelled due to field conditions.

Sang-Mi said, 'DBD, OK?'

I sighed. 'OK, DVD.'

**Glorified Babysitter**

## Soju and a SHITuation

A few days later I was paid an impromptu visit by my mates Rob and Tommo who lived two hours south of Seoul in Kwangju. They had just arrived back in Korea on the night flight as all their money had been stolen and they'd had to cut their Thailand holiday short after only a week.

The usually bouncing, smiling duo were in low spirits after a holiday that had promised so much but delivered so little. They greeted me. 'Hey bro, we need to get pissed.'

At the supermarket we purchased a bulk 3-litre bottle of *soju* (Korea's chemical version of saké). Back at my apartment we started a drinking game with another friend, who was also happy to help out his mates in their time of need.

We were very successful in our endeavour and the number of shots being consumed directly correlated to the slurring of our words; Thailand, along with reality, was fast becoming a distant memory.

A while later a blurry vision of Sang-Mi appeared in front of us and upon seeing the state of me and my friends, the first thing she said, with a confused and disgusted look on her face while pointing at the bottle of *soju*, was 'Why you drink cooking *soju*? Drunk persons only drink that.'

So that explained why it was in a 3-litre container, was so cheap and tasted moderately more like paint thinner than usual.

As Sang-Mi made her way up the ladder to my mezzanine bedroom, one of the boys power-spewed all over my table, covering it in a sea of Pad Thai. This kicked off the Spewing Olympics and we all ran to my tiny bathroom. Me and my weak stomach barely made it to the door and I projectile-chucked all over the bathroom floor. Then the four of us took turns standing in the kitchen at the entrance to the closet-sized bathroom, adding to the growing communal pool of vomit, a scene that reaffirmed why our parents always said binge drinking was a bad idea.

Once we had emptied the contents of our stomachs, I reached

over the toilet, grabbed the showerhead and attempted to wash the vomit down the plughole. Due to the consistency of the mixture, it clogged the plughole and the lake of vomit threatened to overflow the doorway into the kitchen.

Deciding to flag brushing my teeth, I called it a night and stumbled off to bed, leaving the boys to clean up the table. Smelling of cooking *soju* and the sweet aroma of spew, I slurred out an apology to Sang-Mi, who seemed to be enjoying the entertainment more than anything.

At 6.30 a.m. I woke to a bulging stomach, a piercing headache, the taste of fermented vomit in my mouth and vague memories of drinking copious amounts of cooking *soju*. I carefully made my way down the precariously steep ladder to the living room where cushions lay on the floor with a note on top of them that read *Bro, you snore like a train, we couldn't sleep, got early bus, Cheers.*

I walked to the toilet and as I opened the door the smell hit me, and then the memories. Not being able to face cleaning up the mess at this early hour on a Sunday, I just stood in the kitchen and, like a five-year-old, aimed for the toilet bowl.

Then I ascended the ladder, hit my pounding head on the 1.2-metre-high ceiling and collapsed onto the mattress beside Sang-Mi's warm body.

Sang-Mi rolled over, her big eyes, usually immaculately made-up, looking like they had been kept open all night by the unrelenting sound of a freight train that she had been too polite to stop. She propped up her naked body on one arm as though she was going to say good morning. I was so hung-over, the last thing I felt like doing was having a morning conversation in broken English and Korean. I just wanted sleep to take me to that beautiful place where I wasn't feeling so crap.

Then in the same tone as she would normally say good morning, she calmly said the words that every 21-year-old male world traveller has nightmares about. 'Happuh, I have baby!'

## Glorified Babysitter

She now had my full attention.

I attempted to collect the remaining brain cells that hadn't been drowned in cooking *soju* and stammered out, 'My baby?'

'Yessuh.'

The following half hour was spent consulting the Korean–English dictionary and discussing the future of our baby. Considering abortion was illegal in Korea, you could say its future was bright.

Sang-Mi left and I began cleaning the bathroom, ankle deep in vomit, and contemplating my situation. After I had finished cleaning, I sat on the fold-out couch I had salvaged from the roadside. My life flashed in front of my eyes as I wondered how I was going to explain my looming fatherhood to my family. My working-the-world goal was hanging by a thread and the life of an unborn child was in my hands. Having a baby was not really part of my plan. That was something I was going to do when I had reached my goal, had a stable job and was in a financial position to give it the best life possible.

What was I thinking? Having a baby with Sang-Mi was not even an option. Our relationship was based more on the language of love-making as opposed to the language of love and we didn't even speak the same language! Her policeman father didn't even know about her foreign boyfriend, and that was for a good reason. The only people who knew about me were her mother, who was in hospital faking an injury so she could sue the person who had crashed into her, and Sang-Mi's cousin who slept on her bedroom floor.

I rang Dave Teacher, who was always a good source of advice in low moments.

'Hap, mate, as you know abortion is illegal here in Korea but there are plenty of clinics that do it.'

Needing a shoulder to cry on and someone to help make sense of this crazy situation, I rang my Korean teacher at school, who was nothing short of an angel. She came around and shared a female perspective on it, agreeing that I had got myself in a 'SHITuation'.

We spent the afternoon searching the web for clinics. There was no shortage of the life-ending clinics that would breathe life back into my travels at the expense of a new baby—but was this murder? Could I actually do this? Was there another option?

Finally I rang Sang-Mi and asked her to come around as we needed to talk. She seemed surprised at my request, but came anyway.

I sat there wallowing in what was one of the worst days of my 21 years on the planet so far and pondered how I was going to discuss the future of our baby, aided only by the Korean–English dictionary. I had always supported abortion—not strongly, but I never saw merit in bringing up an unwanted child in a love-deprived environment. Never did I think I would have to actually make that decision myself.

Sang-Mi arrived wearing her high heels and Pink Panther fur coat that I no longer found so sexy. She looked at me and, with the innocence of a little girl who has unknowingly fed her pet mouse rat poison and wonders why it is sleeping so much, asked me, 'Happuh, what wrong?'

'What's right?' would have been an easier question.

Holding the dictionary, the words *baby, future, abortion, what you want* feebly dribbled from my mouth.

Sang-Mi just looked at me like I was a silly-billy. 'Oh Happuh, I joke. No baby.'

My reply wasn't so feeble. 'A joke! You no have baby? Why are you telling me you have a baby?'

'I joke. He he, you think I have baby. He he. No no, joke.'

A mixture of rage and relief swelled inside me. Sang-Mi then left to meet her friends, laughing at what a silly-billy I was, and I met up with my mates and celebrated my new freedom.

So I found out the hard way that the language of love was not English.

# Glorified Babysitter

Sang-Mi and I slowly drifted apart. I realised I was in it for the wrong reasons and that we had nothing in common. She was beautiful, petite and cute, but she got puffed walking up the stairs and couldn't leave the house without applying a truckload of make-up. I loved her beauty, but there was more to a relationship than physical attraction. Plus, I wasn't that fond of her jokes.

## The pigeon and the statue

My father always told me that in life sometimes you're the pigeon and sometimes you're the statue, meaning that sometimes you do the shitting and other times you get shat on. In Korea I found out the true meaning of this.

My one-year teaching contract was coming to an end. Like a ship in safe harbour, life was comfortable. I was still playing soccer with my local Korean soccer team and I was now being trained to use nunchucks after achieving my black belt in taekwondo. And to top it off, I had just fallen in love. I don't mean a superficial Sang-Mi-type love, I mean real love.

Her name was Mi Kyong, and she was beautiful, had a heart of gold and loved me back with her whole being. To this day, I can still remember how she would wait for me at the subway station and her face would break into a smile as I appeared at the top of the steps. She would then bound towards me and hug me as though I was returning from war and we hadn't seen each other for years.

Life was good, so I decided to renew my contract for another six months. I had been thinking of going to Spain and learning Spanish, but the plan was still pretty vague, plus Mi Kyong still had six months left in Korea before she was going to live her father's dream of learning English in Australia. After that she would return to help run his furniture company. Why is it that some parents feel the need to pressure their children into what to do? Mi Kyong's dream was to be a dancer. She had such an adventurous spirit and would bubble with enthusiasm and passion when she talked about dance in her mix of English and Korean. But sadly, in Korean culture the expectation is that you get a good job and please your parents, even if that means unhappiness—so her dream was crushed.

Renewing my contract was not going to be easy. It should have been simple: fly to Japan with papers from my *hagwon*, get my Korean teaching visa and fly back to Korea the same day. The hard part of all this was Mr Kim, the *hagwon* director.

Mr Kim had turned out to be full of hollow promises. We were promised staff trips away only to be phoned while we waited with our bags and told that we would not be going. Catherine, the giggly Korean voice on the end of the phone who had first welcomed me all those months ago, had quit. While crying, she had told me, 'Mr Kim, bad man.' She was just one in a long line of Korean teachers I saw come and then leave crying because of Mr Kim. He even got me to tell Wendy, the more experienced Canadian teacher who had trained me, that she didn't have a job and had to move out of her apartment. I was told by the Korean teacher at my school that this was a cultural thing and that Mr Kim didn't want to lose face in front of her. Where I'm from it's called being a coward.

The *hagwon* was doing badly, to put it mildly, which was no surprise considering we had Mr Kim at the helm. For the whole year I had been there we had never once had enough students to break even. Mr Kim only turned up to eat his lunch. He didn't even know what books we were using in the classroom, probably because he couldn't speak English! But Mr Kim's lack of interest in running the *hagwon* made my job a breeze. I was essentially my own boss, so why not renew my contract for six months until I sorted out my next working-the-world chapter? It would also allow me to spend some more time with Mi Kyong.

I approached Mr Kim with another new Korean English teacher to translate for me. Mr Kim was surprised—not that

## Glorified Babysitter

I wanted to renew my contract, but that I was only contracted to work for a year. This was because Catherine had organised everything when the *hagwon* had started up, including my standard one-year English-teaching contract. He needed me; an English *hagwon* without a native English speaker is like McDonald's without Ronald.

Long story short, I tied in a visa run with a long weekend in Tokyo. As it turned out, Mr Kim had given me the wrong paperwork, so I couldn't get a work visa. When I tried to re-enter Korea on a tourist visa, immigration wouldn't let me in as I only had a one-way ticket to Korea; I did not have onward passage showing that I would be leaving Korea within the three-month period of the tourist visa. At this point of my travels I didn't know the trick about buying a refundable ticket, so I spent US$600 on a ticket to leave Korea, so I could enter Korea.

Mr Kim was not too happy about my arriving back with no working visa. I was also not so happy with Mr Kim. He still owed me two months' salary, totalling US$4000.

Things started to get heated in his office as we both shouted at the poor innocent Korean English teacher who was translating. I hoped that she was translating what I was saying into something a little more polite.

I was wary of not getting my outstanding pay, and did not want to end up as another teacher at another struggling *hagwon* who had not been paid for six months, but was still there because the director was always promising to pay 'next month'. We reached a standoff: I would not teach on a tourist visa unless he paid me and organised my new work visa, and the enraged Mr Kim would not pay me unless I worked.

Mr Kim proceeded to pull out all his dirty tricks. First came the bullshit trick, with him saying that my outstanding salary had gone on paying both my tax and the unsuccessful visa run. Next came the guilt-trip trick. He said that if I didn't teach on the tourist visa, the *hagwon* would have to close down. Then the blackmail trick. He would only pay me the money if I signed a new one-year contract. This didn't really seem the best grounds on which to start a new contract, but I decided to sign so I would get my money.

Mr Kim came back from the bank with a large stack of notes. Large because the highest denomination in Korea is a 10,000 won note, which is equivalent to US$10. You could imagine my monthly 2,000,000 won pay cheque which I got in cash each month.

But the stack of money that Mr Kim had with him was a fraction of the size of my usual pay. I found this suspicious because he was meant to be paying me for two months. He only had US$1000 and said that he would have the rest of the $4000 next week if I continued to work on my tourist visa until he could get me to Japan for a new visa.

I agreed and signed the same grammatically incorrect and mistake-ridden contract I had signed a year ago. But then I asked the translator to tell Mr Kim to 'stick his job, I quit.' She spoke in the low tone all Korean women use with men and people in higher positions; it didn't sound like the tone with which 'I quit' should be delivered, but it did seem to have the desired effect. Mr Kim's eyes bulged, his smooth, soft skin pulled taut over his cheekbones and there was no sign of the game-show-host smile he had welcomed me with a year before.

The teacher translated back to me that I was to be out of my apartment in two days, and then she apologised profusely for Mr Kim on behalf of all Koreans.

When I rang up the labour department that protects teachers in Korea, I was told I was entitled to the outstanding $3000 as I had fulfilled my contract to the stated terms. However, as the hagwon had fewer than six employees Mr Kim did not have to pay me! I found out the hard way that contracts don't hold the same obligations in Korea as I had grown up believing.

I had definitely learned what it felt like to be the statue.

**Glorified Babysitter**

## Things happen for a reason

So there I was, homeless and jobless in Korea. One of my soccer team mates picked me up and drove me to the other side of Seoul to Dave Teacher's place, where he had a spare room.

Dave Teacher lived in Machon-Dong, at the end of the purple subway line on the outskirts of Seoul. It was totally different to where I had lived in Bucheon, with its 24-hour mega supermarket, twelve-lane highways, two-storey bathhouses, nightclubs and apartment buildings. Machon had narrow, poorly constructed streets which meandered below a bird's nest of electrical wires. The only supermarkets were small local shops and outdoor market stalls that sold everything: fruit, veggies, fish, meat, rice and pigs' heads. The smells were enough to make you vomit, but I loved it.

I picked up work at a *hagwon* 40 minutes from Dave Teacher's place on the subway, teaching Monday to Thursday in the afternoons and evenings. Things were pretty hectic, with some classes having upwards of thirty kids—a far cry from Mr Kim's where at one point we had only thirty kids in the whole *hagwon*.

Then I saw another advert for an urgent two-week position as an English-speaking business teacher for a teenage boy. I applied for the job and got it. It was perfect. I could teach the boy in the morning then go to my normal job at the afternoon *hagwon*. As fate would have it, getting that job was going to be a pivotal moment in my working-the-world goal.

On my first day I turned up a little early to the five-star hotel where the teenage boy was staying with his mother. I was escorted up to the room by a tuxedo-clad Korean Ken doll wearing white gloves. At the door, I was met by Mrs Malikov, a bright, bubbly, smiling Korean woman. Her attire was casual, yet she looked elegant—not at all like the normal conservative Korean style.

Mrs Malikov apologised for her son not being ready and knocked on a bedroom door and pleaded in Russian for him to hurry up. Bradley appeared from his room with all the energy of a bear who had overhibernated; in fact, he even looked a bit like a bear. He was a solid seventeen-year-old; his baggy white pyjamas rested on his belly and his greasy, slept-on straight black hair framed a round face. The hint of Korean in him could easily be mistaken for a tan. He gave me a lacklustre welcome and then made his way to the shower in a manner that made walking look extremely arduous.

While Bradley was in the shower, Mrs Malikov filled me in on everything. Her husband was Russian and they lived in Spain. She had been in Korea on business when she had got the phone call from Bradley's private school that he had been expelled. She had flown him out to Korea, as his Russian father was in America on business, and needed a tutor for Bradley so he could keep up with his studies.

Bradley Bear appeared from his shower and Mrs Malikov left us to get acquainted. It was clear from the start that Bradley was very intelligent but, like a lot of teenagers, didn't know what his passion was and therefore lacked motivation and direction. He was more interested in partying. The only way I could get Bradley working was to bribe him with Korean barbecue. I would set him goals each morning and if he achieved them we would drink *soju* and eat Korean barbecue for lunch.

I was as much a rent-a-friend-come-tour-guide for those two weeks as I was a teacher. Mrs Malikov really just needed someone to entertain Bradley in the mornings while she was attending to her business.

We had lived totally different lives. The life Bradley talked about back in Spain was a life of luxury. He was one of those kids who had been born into a world of opportunities—opportunities that 99 per cent of us don't have—but he was at the age when he didn't appreciate it, or maybe just didn't realise it.

The two weeks came to an end and we celebrated with a little farewell dinner. Bradley constantly pestered his mum until she said he could go out for one drink if I chaperoned him. The problem was she gave me enough money for a whole night out, not just one drink. It was 6 a.m. when I got Bradley safely home. We embraced by the taxi and said our goodbyes. As I hopped back in the taxi, Bradley said, 'I'm going to get you to be my teacher in Spain.' I just laughed it off and told him he was crazy. I shut the taxi door and told the driver to get me to the airport as fast as possible as I had to catch a flight to Japan to renew my Korean work visa.

With a head full of *soju* and suffering sleep-deprivation, I managed to make it to Japan, negotiate the Osaka train system, arrive just in time at the immigration building, fall asleep on a bench, get woken with my visa, then get back on the train to the airport and eventually fly home to Korea.

A couple of weeks later, Bradley a distant memory, I received an email from Mr Malikov. He said that Bradley had told him I was the best teacher he had ever had and Mrs Malikov had spoken highly of me. He wanted to fly me to Spain to live at their mansion and prepare Bradley for his high-school exams—which Bradley had failed the previous year.

After experiencing what it was like to be the statue with Mr Kim, and finding out the hard way that contracts mean nothing in Korea, I decided against my morals that I was going to be the pigeon with my new *hagwon*. I collected my last pay cheque from the afternoon *hagwon* and called in sick the next day. A hysterical Mi Kyong took a taxi with me to the airport. For the rest of my life I will never forget waving goodbye to Mi Kyong. She stood there with tears running down her face, landing on my oversized hoody I had given her. Through the automatic doors of the departure gate, her quivering voice shouted, 'I love you.' Then the doors slid shut on my Korean chapter.

I cried all the way through immigration and customs.

# Chapter 2
# LIFE OF LUXURY
### EUROPE: Alicante, Spain, 12 July–19 November 2004

Suddenly I found myself in Alicante, Spain, feeling lonely, missing my mates and girlfriend, and experiencing reverse culture shock. I would go to talk to the Colombian maid and only Korean would come out. I was still bowing when meeting people, shaking hands the respectful two-handed way.

Alicante is located two hours south of Valencia—golden beaches sprinkled with topless, bronzed local beauties and crispy-red beached whales, in town from the United Kingdom on cheap package deals. It wasn't a place you went to experience the Spanish culture (you could, you just had to try harder to find it) as there was such a big tourist scene. But this meant one thing: plenty of sun and plenty of options for night-time fun. I was 22 years old now and couldn't think of anything better.

Compared to the concrete jungle of Korea, I found myself in

## Life of Luxury

paradise, living the life of luxury. I lived on the Malikov family estate, outside of Alicante. The family lived right by the ocean in a massive four-storey house that they had built. It was like a well-designed sandcastle that moulded into the peninsula, with manicured gardens tumbling off the cliffs into the turquoise water of the Mediterranean. It had breathtaking 360-degree views without a neon sign or twelve-lane highway in sight, an amazing swimming pool, a jacuzzi, a sauna, an underground bar with a banquet table and a temperature-controlled walk-in wine cellar containing more than 10,000 bottles.

The maid and gardener, a husband and wife from Colombia, lived with their daughter in a comfortable house at the back of the property and I had the two-storey guesthouse. The semi-private beach was not on my doorstep, but rather a one-minute walk away. Life was tough.

### Meeting Mr Malikov — the Godfather

On my first morning, I woke up to the beautiful Spanish sun, on the continent of Europe. But working was the last thing on my mind as I made my way through the maze-like Malikov house with melancholic American country music droning on the house-wide speaker system.

I could tell I was heading the right way as the strong smell of Cuban cigars filled my nostrils. I wondered if maybe there was a Cuban cigar bar housed somewhere in this fantasy mansion.

I arrived at the source of the cigar smoke—a hulk of a man in his late sixties with balding grey hair and a pencil-thin moustache. If it wasn't for his baggy white sleeveless T-shirt and beach shorts, he could have easily passed as a high-ranking Russian officer in a war movie. Although he had the demeanour of a colonel, he didn't need a military uniform to intimidate—he just did. The man was on the phone and waved his half-smoked cigar to the black, recently polished, high-backed office chair in front of his desk, which was bigger than my family's dining table.

Mr Malikov looked relaxed, although he sounded annoyed and angry as his deep voice bellowed into the phone, or maybe that was just because he was talking in Russian. As the palms of my hands started getting sticky on the black leather seat, I wondered if I looked relaxed. I could feel Mr Malikov eyeing me like a would-be punter does a racehorse.

I have always found Russians intimidating, maybe because of the old war movies I used to watch or the harsh tone in which they speak. Mr Malikov's presence took that fear a step further. He hadn't even talked to me but I felt I had to be playing my A game. I was no longer an English teacher who could bullshit his way out of not knowing something by saying, 'Oh, we just say it that way. You have to remember that learning English is not a science, it's an art.'

To calm myself, I took in the surrounds of the office. Behind the chairman-sized desk was a single porthole window that looked underwater into the pool; it was like the set of a James Bond movie. Below the window was a conference table on which the new season's line of upmarket leather products was carefully laid out: handbags, wallets, briefcases, cigar holders, laptop bags, planners and ashtrays. This was Mr Malikov's business; this was how he had made his money. A loan from his mother to buy some cheap leather key chains and have them printed with logos had led to a multinational leather goods company.

*Click.* Mr Malikov put the phone down and turned to give me his full, godfatherly attention.

'Hello, Hap, is it? I hear a lot about you. You call me Mr Malikov. Come, we go outside now.'

Although I am six foot tall, I felt like a twig following a 200-year-old tree trunk as we walked to a sheltered outside sitting area, which looked over the cloudless blue horizon that effortlessly fell into the waveless blue ocean. The scratchy cane of the outdoor chair was a welcome relief from the sticky leather office chair.

'Hap. I send Bradley to best private schools money can buy. He has so much opportunity. You know what he is like from your time in Korea. He very unmotivated. I don't say I was best father, I make mistakes, I spend much time building up my business. I bring you here to Alicante because you and Bradley do well in Korea and Mrs Malikov speak highly of you, that you were motivated and organised. I think he learn from you. It cost me a fortune to send him to private schools, and I pay you only a fraction of the money to do the same thing, makes sense, no?' He laughed the last bit out.

I was beginning to fall under his spell. I liked this Godfather figure—after my experience with Mr Kim I appreciated his straight-talking and no-bullshit approach, and it *did* make sense.

Then he gave me some car keys and told me to take Bradley into Alicante to sign him up for a computer course. I opened the garage door and before me were several gleaming cars: a Jaguar, a limited-edition Rolls Royce, a Jeep and two Mercedes. Shit! If only Mr Malikov knew the last car I had driven was a Toyota Starlet that had been passed down from my grandmother to my mum to me, and that I had never driven on the right-hand side of the road!

I should have been reassured we were taking the 'old' Mercedes, but I wasn't. As we slid out of the estate security gate, Bradley put on his aviator sunglasses, opened the sunroof and turned up his R&B full volume, pretending he was cruising the streets of LA. What R&B Bradley didn't know was that he wouldn't be feeling so gangster in six weeks' time when he and his mate took the Mercedes for a joy ride and wrapped it around a billboard at 100 kilometres per hour, writing off the car.

I, on the other hand, focused intently on driving on the correct side, trying to avoid driving into the rumble strips next to the road. All was going well until we came into Alicante.

# HAP WORKING THE WORLD

I hesitantly manoeuvred the Mercedes, which felt like a tank after the Starlet, through the narrow cobblestone streets, looking for a park.

*Don't double park.* Mr Malikov's words rang in my head.

Bradley wanted to look at a watch—a watch that cost more than the Starlet and all my worldly assets put together. (Admittedly a twenty-year-old granny car and a backpack of shitty clothes don't cost much.)

'Park here.' Bradley impatiently pointed to a parking space outside the jewellers shop, one that meant he only had to walk 5 metres to the entrance of the shop. The fact that I would have struggled to parallel park even the Starlet in the space didn't matter.

With Bradley's impatience growing and his nagging increasing, against my better judgement and Mr Malikov's advice, I took Bradley's word that double-parking was fine. After all, the whole damn street was double-parked.

We spent twenty minutes with the jeweller, who was extremely attentive and made sure that Bradley passed his regards on to Mr Malikov. Even though the air-conditioning was a welcome relief, I couldn't relax knowing the car was double-parked across the plaza, just out of sight. Finally Bradley finished up, after I had pestered him about his class starting and the double-parked car. The armed guard checked the footpath outside and pushed the button on the safety door for us to exit.

As we crossed the plaza full of old men chilling out before going home for their siesta, we saw the Mercedes rolling off into the distance. Not because I had forgotten to put on the handbrake, but because it was on the back of a tow truck. I had never seen Bradley run so fast; in fact, I had never seen him run. As the police tow truck rounded the plaza, the driver looked at our frantic faces with the aloofness of a strip-club bouncer watching Candy's routine for the hundredth time.

We were both willing to do anything to avoid the feared

# Life of Luxury

phone call back to Mr Malikov. I was trying to make a good first impression and Bradley didn't have too many get-out-of-jail-free cards left.

Bradley rang the police station, but as it was nearing siesta time they were more useless than usual. To get the car out would cost in the vicinity of 200 euros and probably wouldn't be possible until the following day. And the worst news of all, the owner of the car had to pick it up. Shit.

Bradley, God bless him, made the dreaded phone call to Mr Malikov. They spoke in Russian, and I imagined the conversation went something like this: 'Hi Dad, Hap double-parked the Mercedes and it got towed and I have missed my computer class.' When he got off the phone, Bradley said that Mr Malikov had told us to sit tight, he would ring some people—some good people, no doubt.

We sat in the plaza, which the old men had now deserted. I wished I could join them so I didn't have to deal with the rest of the day.

Mr Malikov rang back and when Bradley got off the phone he had a grin on his face that said 'The Godfather has got it sorted.' The car was ready. We just had to go to the police pound and ask for a high-ranking officer who would be expecting us.

We arrived in a taxi and dropped the name of the police officer to the guard at the front gate. An overweight, balding man in his fifties wearing casual clothing appeared and ushered us through while explaining something to the guard. He took us to the Mercedes, where the police inspector gave us the all clear with a slap on the wrist and no mention of the 200 euros.

On the 40-minute drive back to the Malikov estate, I felt lucky we had the car back. With the sunroof down, arm out the window and the Spanish sun glistening across the Mediterranean, we cruised the coastal highway homeward bound. Once we were safely parked next to Mr Malikov's covered Rolls Royce,

Bradley slipped up to his room and I prepared to see to Mr Malikov.

I entered the smoke-filled office. Mr Malikov seemed in a jovial mood, happy with himself. Bradley always said that his moods depended on how his shares were going, and from his mood it looked like he had had a prosperous day.

'Have a seat, Hap,' he said in a way that a mafia don would to his son.

'I want you to learn something from today. It's important that you know the right people in the right places . . . OK, I'm off for my massage. Oh, and don't double-park again.'

I liked this guy.

### Lady luck (lack of)

After six weeks of living the life of luxury, eating the best food and having my laundry done and house cleaned, I needed freedom. The novelty had worn off and I felt caged in. The only people I knew in Spain were the Malikov family, the maid and the gardener. Bradley was my only ticket to a social life in the real world but I always had to play the chaperone.

My lack of freedom and friends contrasted with the previous thriving good times I'd had in Korea and continually watered my loneliness tree. The tear-filled phone conversations with Mi Kyong in the evenings were the fertiliser; I missed her little laugh and excitable ways. With her tears and my tears I felt like I was drowning the happiness out of her, and it weighed heavily on my mind. I had asked Mr Malikov about getting her a job, but Mi Kyong's father wouldn't have a bar of it. She had to learn English in Australia and go into the family business.

It was time for a change before I became like the lifeless trees in the barren, arid landscape that lined the highway into Alicante. Mr Malikov was supportive of my idea to move into the centre of town, and even bought me a scooter so I could do the 40-minute commute.

I answered an ad I'd found at the institute where Bradley did his computer classes and where I studied Spanish. I met up with Ted, the house owner—a 31-year-old Irishman with a receding hairline and a wit to make up for it. Like all Irishmen I was going to meet in my travels, I got on with Ted like a house on fire from the get-go.

There was one other flatmate who we called Doc Hollywood, a laid-back 26-year-old Californian with all-American good looks, who was in Alicante learning Spanish.

I enjoyed the friendship of Doc and Ted, and the chance to leave work behind when I scooted past the Malikov's security gate. Ted was a laugh, not just because of his Irish sense of humour but because of his obsessive-compulsive cleanliness. Doc Hollywood and I would push the swivel sink tap to one side, sit at the kitchen table and await Ted's arrival. With a 'Hi guys,' Ted would go straight to the kitchen sink, move the tap to the centre of the sink and we would burst out laughing. We would get a barrage of 'Fook you guys' and then Ted would join in laughing at himself.

Ted also had an obsession with unplugging all appliances when he turned them off. For example, I had to plug in the TV first before turning it on, same with the microwave, jug, and toaster; the only appliance spared was the fridge.

Ted told me this story, which I think sums him up wonderfully. He was backpacking through South America with his mates and had just had a night of love-making with a luscious Latina. 'Back when I had a full head of hair,' he would add. Ted, being the clean-conscienced man that he was, didn't want to leave the condom at her house, so he double tied it and put it in his pocket to dispose of later. He said his goodbyes to his lover and made his way quickly back to the hostel to brag to his mates and collect his bags before catching the morning bus to a neighbouring country.

In all his post-sex euphoria he forgot about the condom filled with future Irish doctors and lawyers in his pocket. He only remembered it when he was filling out the customs form at the border; one of the questions was 'Are you carrying animal semen?'

How would you explain to a customs officer in Spanish that the condom in your pocket was full of your own semen and not that of an animal's—I'm not too sure which was worse. After a lot of sweating—sweating was another thing that Ted did well—over whether to declare it or not, he decided against it. Luckily he didn't get searched and disposed of Ireland's future generation in a rubbish bin on the other side of a South American border town, probably to be eaten by stray dogs.

With all Ted's talk of sex, thoughts of Mi Kyong drowning my heart, and the need to improve my Spanish, I went on a mission. A mission that would kill all three birds with one stone: find a local Spanish girlfriend. I award Alicante the prize of having the most beautiful women. They were beautiful in a generic way that would have you swearing you had seen them in a bikini on the front of one of those men's magazines at the petrol station.

So I started my mission by adding, '¿*Cuál es tu número de teléfono?*' to the list of phrases I was learning. Looking back now, I laugh. I don't know what my plan was for taking the conversation from saying hello to asking for a telephone number. God forbid if I had actually got a number, and had to ring one of those women.

Motivated by fantasies of sex with a local model, I hit the bars. I loved the Spanish bars. I would set my alarm for 10 p.m., get up, have a shower and walk down the street in the warm evening air to the old quarter. These pedestrian-only cobblestone lanes had the highest concentration of bars I had ever come across. Then around 2 a.m. I would make my way down to nightclubs on the marina and finish by walking home as the sun was coming up.

In Korea, the fact that I had a 24-pack of ribs didn't matter because I was white and could speak English. In the eyes of Korean girls I was in the same pedigree as an English prime minister. In Alicante I was not a novelty. I was just another annoying English-speaking tourist, in town to get drunk, turn red on the beach, stare at all the topless sunbathers and try out my cheesy pick-up lines. '*Hola, guapa.*' (Hello, beautiful.)

Ted would always tell me, 'Hap, mate, you can't expect to pick up chicks when your opening line is "Where are you from?"' It was one of the first sentences I had learnt at Spanish school.

For some weird reason they always answered 'Alicante' or just blatantly ignored me and turned towards the wall for a more fulfilling conversation.

Unfortunately for me the local girls had standards. So I changed tactics. I turned my attention to a confident Argentinean girl in her late twenties who always wore mini-skirts and was studying English at the language institute where I was studying Spanish.

We met at a beachside bar for an *intercambio*—an opportunity to try out our new-found language skills—that we had organised after class one day. She was probably solely there to practise her English, but like most sex-deprived young males, my priority was not just to practise my Spanish. I had ulterior motives. On the third *intercambio* I gave her a ride home on my scooter. With her hands clasped around my waist, her mini-skirt hitched up and the warmth of her Latina loins pressed against me, I was praying she wouldn't ask me, 'Hap, why your scooter have gear stick?'

On a hung-over Sunday afternoon with the living room blinds pulled down, Ted and I lay on each of the couches, going through our phones for potential girls to meet up with. I came across the mini-skirted Argentinean and with the overconfidence brought on by my hung-over daze, I slowly typed a text message in Spanish, asking if she wanted to meet up that evening. Ted was very encouraging, as all mates are in these situations—not so much because I might find love, but because she might have a girlfriend for him or at the very least he would get to see me do something embarrassing but entertaining. I got to the end of the text and ran it by Ted who spoke fluent Spanish, albeit with an Irish accent. He suggested I sign off with '*un beso negro*'. *Why not*, I thought, *all Spanish people sign off texts with* un beso, *a kiss*. Then I sent it.

My sense of accomplishment and excited mood were short-lived when Ted looked at me with the alarmed expression he usually reserved for finding out that I had forgotten to unplug the TV after I had turned it off.

'You didn't send it, did you? You didn't write "*un beso negro*", did you?'

'Yeah, why?' I replied, my sense of achievement fading and taking on Ted's more alarmed mood.

Then he started laughing in a way that meant he knew he wouldn't be meeting any girlfriend of my Argentinean friend, but that I had succeeded in embarrassing myself.

I innocently replied, 'It just translates to *black kiss*, doesn't it? Kind of romantic, I thought, a kiss under the night sky or something, eh?'

'It means to kiss the anus . . . to give a rim job!'

Let me just say that things didn't go well with the Argentinean, and I received a text back that loosely translated to *don't contact me again*. Fair enough, I had only met her three times. We hadn't even kissed and I was asking her if she wanted a rim job. Cheers, Ted.

Since I was having no luck with the Spanish-speaking ladies I now moved my attention to the English-speaking foreign girls at my language school. There was a Canadian woman who was there learning Spanish, and it just so happened that her daughter was coming to visit. Perfect. Judging by the mother's looks, I hoped the daughter wore the same genes.

She did. Nineteen years old, blonde, beautiful, English-speaking, two arms, two legs—she fitted the bill. I took her

### Life of Luxury

out for a night on the town and on the walk home we sat in a park and flirted. The conversation moved to the local nudist beaches and I made her a drunken promise that I would take her there tomorrow on my scooter. I got her number and we parted ways, me with thoughts of us lying naked together on the beach. With a head full of booze, I focused on the fantasy side of us being naked and blurred out the awkwardness of being sober and getting naked on a packed beach full of naked people with a chick whose mother had entrusted me with her.

The following morning good ol' Ted encouraged me to text her, so I did.

*Hey I'm going 2 the nudist beach at 1pm, txt me if u wnt 2 go.*

With butterflies in my stomach from making this bold move, I took the scissors while Ted wasn't looking and went into the bathroom to trim my overgrown bush below. I was delighted with the result as I gained an inch of penis I never knew I had.

I never got a reply and it wasn't until Monday when I bumped into her that I nervously enquired about the text I had sent. She replied, 'Oh, I don't have a phone yet—that number I gave you was Mum's.'

### Time not money

No more girls. It was time to focus on my work.

Work was going well, I had Bradley on track for his exams, and life was good. I still missed Mi Kyong and we emailed regularly, but she was off to study English in Australia. I also had a life of my own now. I would ride out in the mornings to the Malikovs', blue skies overhead and the ocean on my right. I would go up to the guesthouse that had been my home for the first six weeks of my time in Alicante and there I would prepare the day's lesson. I had set up the classroom with a whiteboard and study posters on the wall. Afternoons were spent taking Bradley to the gym or playing tennis with him before he went to his computer classes.

## HAP WORKING THE WORLD

Twice a week, I would teach Mrs Malikov English while Ted taught Bradley maths. Ted was in finance and accounting so I had hired him to teach Bradley. It was always entertaining doubling Ted on my scooter back into Alicante at the end of the day. Every time, I would arrive with two sweaty handprints on my abdomen and one tense, perspiring Ted.

One day an annoyed Mr Malikov called me down to his office and told me, 'Hap, the crew on my boat, I fired them. I want that you and Bradley fly to France with me next week and help crew it back.'

So the following week Bradley and I were disembarking from Mr Malikov's private jet at a small airport in Toulon, southern France. A driver welcomed us and drove us to the boat. When I say boat, I mean super yacht.

The best part of the trip was running into a storm and the captain deciding we needed the shelter of a port. And what better place to shelter from Mother Nature than Ibiza, the party capital of the world! For the three days we were there, it was beautiful sunshine, and the captain and I spent our time cruising the island on motorbikes during the day and sampling the clubs at night.

The best part about this week at the office was that I was getting paid for it!

But it also got me thinking.

I had always said that I wanted to be a millionaire, back in the day when a million dollars was a lot of money. If someone had told me that I would be living in a mansion on the Mediterranean with a maid, a private jet, a 30-metre super yacht and luxury cars, I would have thought it sounded like my dream. In Alicante I got to live the dream, but for me the grass was not greener on the other side. I found out my previously held belief that being rich made life easier was not so.

I still believe that money helps, and I would much rather be rich than living in a cardboard box shining shoes. But from my

## Life of Luxury

experiences, I learnt that money is not everything. As the old cliché goes, money doesn't buy happiness.

From what I saw during my time with the Malikovs, having money brought more options, therefore it could cause a whole lot more stress. Mr Malikov, for example, had told me he regretted buying the super yacht. Before this he had a smaller boat, but as always when you have more money you want bigger and better things—I suppose we all live to the limits of our income. He had been content with his previous yacht which he was able to captain himself, with minimal crew and less maintenance, and because of its size he was able to stop in most ports. Now he pumped a million dollars a year into the upkeep of the new boat. It cost him more than the average person's annual income to fill up with fuel. Something that was supposed to bring him happiness had brought nothing but stress.

The other lesson I learnt living this dream was how lucky I had been growing up with my family. We had a comfortable lifestyle. Instead of a super yacht we had a 14-foot yellow runabout boat that we had used to spend summers water-skiing and fishing. We didn't have a holiday house, but we would take the family tent and go camping every Christmas, or go hiking during the year. We didn't have a maid, but I learnt the discipline of doing chores, looking after myself and earning pocket money. I didn't get sent to the most expensive boarding school, but rather walked to school every day and Mum would take the day off work if I was sick. My education wasn't handed to me; I paid my way through university. If I screwed up it was my money I was throwing away. I learnt the value of money and the unfortunate lesson of what it was like to be $30,000 in debt at the age of 21, like most university students. My father was not a multimillion-dollar man with an international empire. He was my dad. He taught me soccer and cricket, coached my soccer team and helped me with school work.

I had just gained my first lesson in the university of life. I was now beginning to understand things a little more. Mr Malikov had spent his life building up this empire so his family could reap the rewards and have a secure future, but in doing so he had made certain sacrifices. I now understood my parents' philosophy; children should have time spent on them, not money.

## Adios

It was a couple of weeks out from the start of Bradley's exams. We had covered all the course material and I was confident he would do well. For me, Bradley's exams would mark the end of my time in Alicante. After Alicante I was going to do a quick trip through Europe for three weeks and then go backpacking in Brazil with Dave Teacher and another mate from Korea. After Brazil, I wasn't sure where in the world I would be working next. As it happened, I didn't have to think about what was after Brazil as Mr Malikov had plans for me.

Once again I was summoned to his office. There he offered me what I now believe was the biggest opportunity of my life: a position in his American business. I would do a three-month trial in the United States, and if I liked it he would then send me to work at the Russian company. After learning the Russian side of the company, I would return to the corporate world and live the American dream.

After nearly five months of living and working in Alicante, I picked up Bradley from his business exam, the exam in which I would later find out he had gained his highest mark. We went for lunch at a bar overlooking the marina. With the hard work and frustrations behind us, and a cold beer in hand, we reminisced about our time together and talked about the future, about our roles in the Malikov business.

I dropped him off at the Malikov Estate, hugged the ever-smiling Mrs Malikov and shook Mr Malikov's hand. He had a knowing look in his eye that said, *I remember when I was 23, carefree with not a worry in the world. Make the most of Europe and Brazil.* He would see me in the States at the start of February.

The next day, after my goodbyes to Ted and Doc, I went for a walk with Jayne, a girl I had met on my birthday and who I had been seeing the past couple of weeks. Our travel romance had been the icing on the cake. She was an English traveller who had arrived in Alicante to learn Spanish and had just returned from backpacking through Brazil.

In Alicante, where nobody knew us, it was no-strings-attached passion; we didn't have to worry about what our work colleagues thought, or meeting the parents. She was just starting her time in Alicante and I was leaving to travel. We were taking different paths. Maybe if we had both settled down, had careers, were living in the same city back in the real world, our relationship may have flourished into something else. But that is the beauty of travel romances, you both know where you stand, and you take it for what it is: a travel romance. The fire burns intensely, you skinny dip together, you walk under the full moon, you pamper each other, you massage each other by candle light, you put your all into the limited time you have together.

I made the most of the warmth of lying next to a beautiful girl and being held in her arms, to feel love, not knowing the next time I would feel it. So when we had our last kiss in the plaza outside the bull ring in the mid-morning sun, it was a passionate kiss with feeling, knowing we had shared a special couple of weeks together and knowing we would most probably never see each other again.

I walked to the bus station with my pack on my back containing almost all the possessions I owned in the whole world. Because I had been so emotional leaving Korea and Mi Kyong, I had missed out on the feeling I had now. A sense of achievement, of finishing a chapter of my life, of ticking off a continent. That feeling was something I would never tire of while working the world.

# HAP WORKING THE WORLD

Looking back at when I first arrived, I couldn't speak Spanish, I didn't know anyone and Alicante was a foreign place. Now I could get by in Spanish, I had a friendship with Ted, had had a wonderful romance with Jayne, and Alicante had become my home for those five months. I knew the quickest way to get to the beach on my scooter. I had my favourite back-alley bar, found behind a nondescript door, and inside had people packed between its graffitied walls and served the best mojitos from a giant teapot. I had a full bank account and I had two months of backpacking through Brazil with my mate Barney. (Dave Teacher had gotten all his money stolen in Thailand so he had to forfeit meeting up in Brazil to return to Korea and get back out of debt.) Little did I know that in Brazil, Barney and I would become best mates and he would play a major part in my working-the-world quest.

But for me, life could not be better; I had two months to get travel out of my system before the corporate world and my dream job consumed me.

# Chapter 3
# THE AMERICAN DREAM
### NORTH AMERICA: Columbus, Ohio, USA, 26 January–17 April 2005

The bored hotel receptionist handed me a jug of hot water. As I walked out of the automatic doors, the grey clouds and early morning cold hit me. My long curly hair had been laid to rest on a Brazilian barber-shop floor the previous week, and I hunched my shoulders up, hoping the collar of my jacket would ward off the burning cold. I walked across the car park, avoiding the deeper patches of snow so that my new shiny black business shoes didn't leak and let my holey socks, which Mum had bought me four years earlier, get wet. As I poured the hot water over the iced-up windscreen of my work car I thought back to just last week.

It seemed a lifetime ago that I had been lying on the beaches of Brazil with Barney. Getting dressed had involved pulling on a singlet over my shaggy shoulder-length hair and slipping on boardies and jandals. As the ice melted, I had a yearning to be teleported back to Brazil, to the passion, energy and affection of the generations of good-time people. The idyllic beaches, the bustling cities, the parties, the dancing, the sun, the beer, the jungle, the wetlands, the bikinis! It was the time of my life. I was 23 years old, backpacking with one of my best mates, no worries in the world, no mortgage, no wife, no kids, no expectations. Just exploring and enjoying living life with no regrets.

Now winter in Ohio was my reality, and a generic chain hotel with the token suburban sports bar across the car park my home.

The following week I found a room in a bachelor pad in Columbus's trendy Short North district, which lay between the unimpressive downtown skyline and the Ohio State University campus. My flatmates were two guys who worked with an Indy 500 pit crew. They were away a lot which meant I had the eight-person hot tub and extensive home entertainment system to myself.

Life was a complete contrast from Brazil. The *beep-beep* of my alarm would wake me up, I would pull myself out of the king-sized bed, shower, and button up the pressed business shirt and pants that Mr Malikov had got me to buy on the first day I arrived. I would then shave and gel my respectful short-back-and-sides haircut. I would drive down the snow-lined highway to work where I would sit in my windowless office in front of my computer. It was a tough transition from Brazil, but this was going to be the greatest career opportunity of my life.

## I'm a somebody!

Not only was I living the American dream in my three-storey bachelor pad, but my future was looking brighter than the Brazilian midday sun.

On the first day of working the world in America, I found

## The American Dream

myself sitting in front of Mr Malikov's desk. The surroundings were not quite as plush as the Spanish estate. The light grey walls had no porthole window looking into the pool, and while Mr Malikov's desk was still larger than your average desk, it was not made from the finest timber but rather assembled from a business furniture catalogue. The other big change was that there was no smell of cigar smoke, much to the annoyance of Mr Malikov. Ohio had just brought in legislation banning smoking in the workplace.

He said to me, 'This is why I no live in America, too many rule! In Spain if I want to smoke, I smoke.'

After we had caught up, he presented his plan to me. He had the same air about him this day as he had when he told me about regretting buying the bigger boat. He told me how things could be going better for the US side of his company; this particularly pained him as this was the company he had first started up. He was now 66 years old, but had been driven out of retirement to save this company. He could have just shut it down, but how could a man who had built up an international empire shut down the first company he had started from the spare room of the house he had lived in 30 years ago? He could run the business from Spain with the occasional trip to the US to oversee things, but he needed someone on the ground who he could trust. Bradley was too young at this stage. And that's where I came in—he wanted me to be his right-hand man.

I had studied management and marketing at university, and as I had lived and worked at his Spanish house under his eye, Mr Malikov knew he could trust me. I would be the assistant marketing manager, but this was just a title. My job was to learn every facet of the business, and to know it better than everyone else, as he believed this was the only way you could lead. Even though everyone else wore casual clothes, he required me to wear business attire and to always have polished shoes. Mr Malikov believed that you could tell a lot from a person's shoes. Basically, I was his protégé; I had to set an example.

The plan was that after working three months in Ohio, and then learning the Russian side of the business, I would come back to the States and sign a two-year contract.

Finally, in society's eyes, I would be a somebody.

## Money or the bag?

'Have you had unprotected sex with multiple partners?' the attractive nurse asked me.

Was I dreaming? I wanted to answer 'No' in the hope that another sexy nurse would appear behind her. Then in unison they would reply, 'Well, best we see to that, sir.'

Unfortunately for me I was not in a fantasyland; I was lying firmly on my back in a hospital. The nurse, a real nurse, a goddamn university-qualified, legitimate nurse, was doing her job.

I sighed and answered truthfully, 'Yes.'

This answer might have been received with laughs and cheers if I was with a group of macho males, but I was not. I was in the Ohio State University Hospital emergency room, and the nurse told me in that medical tone of voice, 'Sir, we will have to test you for HIV as well.' 'As well' meant they were going to test me for meningitis and a whole bunch of other diseases which I had always thought other people contracted, not me.

This was the moment in my life when I realised that I was responsible for my actions, that the decisions I made affected my life. Up until that point I had been fancy free, with the beautiful happy-go-lucky nature of someone in his early twenties.

How had I ended up in the ER wondering if I had meningitis or HIV?

I had woken up on a Saturday morning with a mega-headache. I put it down to going for after-work drinks the night before

## The American Dream

with the Russian immigrant workers in the storeroom, which turned out to be a mistake as they had an unhealthy appreciation of vodka. I lay on the couch and when I couldn't take the headache anymore I made a desperate trip to the pharmacy. I stumbled out of the pharmacy with my head spinning from standing upright, clutching a container of generic ibuprofen. I went back to the couch and ate them like candy while watching a movie. By the time I had finished watching the movie I was considering sticking them up my bum as suppositories; they were doing nothing. I went to bed hoping sleep would cure me, only to wake up with diarrhoea, vomiting and the intensity of the headache turned up.

It was now apparent that I was more than hung-over. The only other time I had felt such pain with a headache was when I was living on the outskirts of Seoul with Dave Teacher. The freshly graduated doctor at the third grade hospital in the rundown area of Machon-Dong had seemed more interested in practising his halting English and had diagnosed me as having the flu. It was not until later, after enduring the sickest three days of my life with an unrelenting pain behind my eyes, unable to sleep, unable to eat or hold down food or water, that I managed to make it to a modern foreigner's clinic where the doctors spoke English. There I was told I could possibly have had viral meningitis, although the doctor could not be certain. She also told me what I already knew—that if I had had the bacterial form of meningitis it could have been fatal. I remembered being warned at school not to share drink bottles, after a couple of people in the region had died from the highly contagious bacterial meningitis. She said that I had been through the worst and confirmed what I already knew, 'You get very very sick.'

Now, here I was in the US, nine months later. I was paranoid that I had the deadly meningitis and that my flatmates would get back from the Indy 500 to find me dead on the floor in a pool of my own vomit. Scared, I had driven myself to the hospital, battling to concentrate on driving on the right side of the road and obeying the road rules.

When I reached the safety of the hospital I told the young nurse checking my symptoms the only time I had felt a headache like this was in Korea where they suspected I had had meningitis. With the mention of meningitis I was treated like someone who had a contagious disease. Fair enough, I probably did.

Then the nurse came in with a doctor and they performed a spinal tap. This is a procedure where they stick a needle into your spine to extract fluid that can be accurately tested for meningitis. There was another nurse taking blood for my HIV and other miscellaneous tests.

The doctor came back and confirmed that I had meningitis, but they had to send the spinal fluid off for further analysis to see if I had the potentially fatal bacterial strain or the viral version. I was wheeled through industrially cleaned corridors and taken up in an elevator into an isolation room.

For the next sixteen hours I just saw faces looking through the small glass window of the isolation room door. Every now and then a nurse or doctor wearing a mask would come and take further blood tests and ask me more questions. It was at this time, when I was lying on my back staring at the ceiling, that I began to think about life and what I wanted from it. I was on the other side of the world where no one knew what was happening to me, waiting on test results that could change my life—perhaps end my life. Death felt a little closer. I was scared. At that moment the answer was clear as day: I wanted to be happy, to do what I wanted to do, to live life with no regrets—the reasons I had set myself the goal to live and work in every continent.

With the headache still pounding like a tribal drum in my head and my eyes closed trying to rid myself of it, I thought about the American dream I was living. Yes, it was a perfect job. If you had asked me at university in my first year, I could not have dreamt of a better situation than to be involved with

# The American Dream

a small multinational company with nothing but opportunities ahead of me. In a month's time I would be flown to Russia to learn about the company and there was already talk of other opportunities such as a trip to China to see the production side of the business.

I was enjoying the work and learning the business. I got on well with everybody; I liked office life, playing little jokes on the administration girls, hiding the IT guy's car, having the office ladies bring me cookies, learning how to say hello and goodbye in Russian from the workers who assembled our products in the stock room, and being able to drink as much coffee as I wanted. My plan was to sign the contract and then leave after two years to travel. I would then be 25.

Lying on the hospital bed, I knew that I had been kidding myself that after two years I would leave the job. Deep down I knew that as soon as I entered the Malikov business it would be hard to walk away. The lure of more money, promotion and moving countries would reel me in.

With this new-found understanding of the importance of my happiness, I realised that living the American dream in Columbus, Ohio, would not make me happy. Columbus had a population of over one million, but the life had been sucked out of the downtown area by supermalls in the suburbs. It snowed in Ohio, but there were no mountains for snowboarding, and it was a twenty-hour drive to the beach. I wouldn't be happy calling this place home for two years. At that moment I made the decision that as soon as I was out of hospital I would email Mr Malikov in Spain thanking him for this amazing opportunity but telling him that I would be going at the end of my three months. Where to, I didn't know, but I would be leaving.

Then there was a knock at the door and a greying, masked doctor walked in with a clipboard. He declared that I was lucky, that my spinal tap had come back as viral meningitis, and my blood tests showed I was HIV negative.

However, he wasn't finished. 'But . . . Mr Cameron, here at Ohio State University Hospital we like to be thorough. I am going to give you a genital and rectal examination.'

Fortunately, I was used to these examinations. I come from a family that is plagued with stomach problems, and I had had doctors' fingers up my bum since I was sucking my thumb. Having a doctor spread my cheeks and rearrange my meat and two veg didn't worry me. But the thing that was weird about this situation was that the doctor had three students with clipboards standing behind him! I suppose this shouldn't have surprised me; I was in a university hospital after all.

As I lay there with my hospital gown pulled up, the doctor's latex-gloved hand lifted my meat and began to exam it under the watchful eye of the students. All I could think about was that it would be a really bad time to let my concentration slip and start thinking about the sexy nurse. As *cold mince, cold mince, grandmother, faeces, dead sheep, parents having sex* went through my mind, the doctor told me to turn over for my rectal examination. With my face pressed into the pillow, he gave me the thumbs up . . . literally speaking, that is. Everything was all OK. I thanked him and farewelled the students, hoping they had enjoyed the show.

There I sat, alive, king of the world. I had my own isolation room, I mean suite, and didn't have to worry about sharing a ward with the common sick folk. I had my own TV, an en suite, three meals a day and a very attentive doctor and nursing staff.

I was about to learn another valuable lesson.

All up I was in the isolation room for 24 hours. Now if you have had to use the privatised health care system in the United States, you know that it is costly. With all my tests, scans and room charges my bill came to just under US$12,000. It so happened that the previous week I had been telling my father that I wasn't going to renew my travel insurance because I never used it, that it was a waste of money. He told me I would be a fool if I didn't renew it. I hadn't renewed it, but luckily it didn't expire for two more days! The following day, from my bed in the bachelor pad, as well as emailing Mr Malikov, I also renewed my travel insurance.

## Goodbye

I spent two out of my last four weeks in Ohio recovering from meningitis.

I went back to work for my last week and everybody knew I was leaving. In my working-the-world quest it was always something I grew to love, leaving a job. Why? First, the change; I never stagnated in a job. Second, as anybody who has left a job on good terms knows, you get showered in compliments that you would never get if you weren't leaving. Even the fat, angry, pitbull-faced cleaner, who you thought was plotting to kill you and never laughed at your bad jokes, will come up and say they will miss you.

In my remaining six and a half years of working the world, I would have more than my fair share of going-away parties. My Ohio farewell party was spent in the staffroom. The motherly ladies, who had given me sheets and blankets when I first arrived, baked me a cake and everybody had put in and bought me a T-shirt with an American flag on it. I thought about my father who was from the loyal employee generation and had worked the same job all his life; he would only get to experience these compliments and farewells when he retired. Why is it that we don't compliment more often? After all those compliments, I was left wondering if I had made the right decision. I had.

My most special moment came when I was saying goodbye to Mr Malikov, who was over from Spain at the time. I arrived at his hotel room, in a much more luxurious hotel than the one I had stayed at three months earlier. He was in the suite with an attached boardroom.

We sat at the smokeless boardroom table. 'So you leave, Hap.' He paused then continued, knowing that I didn't know how to take the rhetorical question. 'I no think you like Columbus.' He paused again. 'Now you know why I no live here.' And he laughed.

I still liked this guy.

Mr Malikov made sure that I was certain I wanted to leave by asking me one last question. 'My CEO is leaving, and I have to find someone else and pay them US$120,000. Are you sure you don't want to stay here in Columbus?'

I was sure.

# Chapter 4
# ERECTION SPECIALIST

**NORTH AMERICA: North Carolina, Kentucky, New Jersey, New York, USA, 1 June–26 August 2005**

After Columbus, I flew to Europe on the first-class plane ticket Mr Malikov had bought for me a month earlier. But instead of getting a connecting flight to Russia, where I should have been going to learn the Russian side of the business, I boarded a budget airline, where the excess baggage charges cost more than the taxes and ticket, and headed for Scotland.

Looking back, I find it all quite symbolic: leaving first class for the budget ticket I had bought myself. I had given up job security for an unknown future; I had given up riches for my still-intact credit-card debt. I had given up suits and briefcases for jeans and a backpack. I had given up the American dream for my dream of working the world.

After two flights, a twelve-hour stopover and a train trip, I arrived late at night in a cold, overcast Edinburgh. Still feeling the effects of the meningitis and now jetlagged, I welcomed even the thin mattress that I shared with the vacuum cleaner and shelves of unclaimed treasures from previous flatmates in my sister's hallway cupboard.

After I'd recuperated, celebrated my sister's birthday and caught up with uni mates, my sister and I left the castles, cobblestone streets, friendly locals and atmospheric smoky bars and headed to Nice in the south of France. We were in Nice to meet our parents, and aunty and her partner. This was our parents' trip of a lifetime, which they had been working towards for years. It was their first time out of Australasia.

We spent a couple of weeks at a villa nestled among vineyards, with the six of us catching up on the past two years since we had been together. There was lots of laughter, eating and drinking. However, it soon came time to leave. My sister headed back to work in Edinburgh and I hopped on a plane to London from where I would fly back to the United States to start another chapter of my life.

## Back in the US of A

Here I was back in the States, about to start my new chapter as an erection specialist. I had touched down in one of the greatest cities in the world, New York, a city that felt strangely familiar, mostly because of growing up with images of it on TV. It was a sensory trip just walking the streets. I was totally entranced by the constant honking of yellow taxis gridlocked in traffic, steam rising from underground subway systems, people of every colour, creed and race hustling and bustling past you on the packed footpaths, beggars and buskers, businessmen and bums, gangsters and goons, and a skinny guy from New Zealand. I spent a couple of days checking out the sights: Ground Zero, the concrete old lady in the bay, Central Park, and the breathtaking views from the top of the Empire State Building.

## Erection Specialist

Feeling on top of the world and content with my life, and filled with the energy of the city, I made my way to the downtown Greyhound bus station to catch the midnight bus to Louisville, Kentucky, where Jimmy was waiting for me.

I didn't know anything about Jimmy or the work I would be doing. Barney, the mate with whom I had travelled through Brazil, was going to work for Jimmy at the US Open. I didn't know if it was the golf, tennis, swimming or motocross open, all I knew was Barney's stepbrother had worked for Jimmy while living in Louisville. Since I had had no plans after leaving Mr Malikov's corporate world, I had emailed Jimmy from my Ohio office asking if he needed an extra hand. While I was in Europe with my family, Jimmy had confirmed that he would need someone for two jobs for wealthy clients at the US Open.

And that was why I was now shaking hands with a fella in his early thirties who was possibly skinnier than me. He had a firm handshake as you would expect from someone who uses his hands for work. During the next couple of months I would hear Jimmy say many a time in his put-on, redneck accent, 'Happa, I'm African-American, bruuuuther.'

And, yes, he was African-American, but he was a rare breed of pale albino African-American who would get sunburnt queuing under the fluorescent lights in McDonald's. Jimmy was Zimbabwean, and when he picked me up from the bus station he was wearing a South African rugby shirt along with a cheeky smile, and speaking in his thick Zimbabwean accent that he still hadn't lost after twelve years in the United States.

Jimmy and I hopped onto the front benchseat of his big red beat-up, pickup truck, which he affectionately called the 'Red Baron'. We went back to Jimmy's warehouse and prepared some equipment for the next day's departure to North Carolina where we would be working. Jimmy then dropped me at a hotel and left me the Red Baron, as I had to pick up Barney from the bus station at 5 a.m.

## HAP WORKING THE WORLD

In the early morning darkness, amid the smell of day-old hotdogs at the rundown bus station, I welcomed Barney. We embraced each other in the way that two guys hug when they have shared the best six weeks of their lives together and know everything about the other: their greatest fears, biggest regrets, aspirations, dreams and darkest secrets.

The last time we had seen each other was at the airport in Brazil when I was going off to enter the corporate world. In the four and a half months since that time, Barney had been teaching English in northern Brazil and still had the suntanned glow to show for it.

We went back to the hotel where Barney showered, before Jimmy and the others picked us up in the mini-van. The rest of the team was made up of local boys from Jimmy's rugby club. Jimmy was a source of great laughter, and the laid-back nature of the other guys told me that I was going to enjoy this chapter of working the world. As we drove along Ben Harper's voice poured out of the mini-van stereo system, singing about Nashville, Tennessee. At that moment I looked out the window and saw the highway sign announcing that we were passing through Nashville, Tennessee.

That's what I love about being in America—all the places that are spoken about in Hollywood movies and song lyrics start to become real. From that moment on, every time I heard that song it would take me back to that mini-van, sitting next to one of my best mates, the Tennessee sun shining in the blue sky outside, surrounded by friends I was yet to get to know.

### So, what ya'll do?

'So, what ya'll do?' drawled the waitress in her fifties as she took our orders. Jimmy took the floor with his deadpan face. In his fake redneck accent, which was done in a way so as not to be offensive, he exclaimed, 'We're erection specialists, daaarlin'.'

# Erection Specialist

We were erecting a tent village that would hold 500 corporate clients a day for the 2005 US Golf Open. All up, we would be spending three weeks in Pinehurst, North Carolina, the small town that was hosting that year's tournament. While the Open was on we would park clients' cars and provide security at night, patrolling the tent village. After the tournament was over, we would take it all down.

For those three weeks, my body didn't know what had hit it. My white skeletal figure slowly bronzed and developed growths, growths that were deposits of meat attached to the bone, known as muscle.

Jimmy loved to act the fool and give the crew a laugh. Sometimes you would look up and see him waddle past like a sumo wrestler with his shorts pulled up his bum, blinding you with his snow-white chicken-leg thighs. Other times he would go berserk with the sledgehammer, pounding in a metre-long stake and then roaring with triumph when he had finished like he had just won a carnival prize.

The one thing Jimmy loved more than having a laugh was hard work. He always talked about the old days when he had worked with three other Zimbabweans going from event to event putting up tents.

'Back in my day, we just wore bare feet, slept on the grounds and could put these tents up in no time at all,' Jimmy explained with complete sincerity.

The reality was, he was a hard worker and expected nothing less from us. We earned every cent he paid us. There was no such thing as walking; everything you did, you did at a run, and I mean sprint. If Jimmy wanted a hammer, you ran like your life depended on it, and sometimes it did when the crew was holding up the large beams. People would tell us we looked like a well-disciplined military team the way we erected a tent.

Safety gear was non-existent: my safety boots were the old running shoes Jimmy had given me; my reflective vest was the sun shining off my sweaty chest (ribs); my hard hat was a baseball cap from the local hardware shop—shit, the Village People had more safety gear than us. I knew no different—that's just how it was.

There was a lot of stress making sure the tents were erected in time. As you could imagine, the 500 corporate clients who had bought their expensive tickets would not be happy eating their five-course lunch in the scorching heat instead of an air-conditioned tent. Plus it was Jimmy's livelihood; he relied heavily on the US Golf Open and the PGA Tour, so he had to perform.

But there was no greater feeling than sitting back in a deck chair with the rest of the tenting crew and a cooler of ice-cold beer, looking over the completed tent village we had worked so hard to put up. A beer had never tasted so sweet and an erection had never felt so good!

## Nocturnal watchmen

Barney and I, 'the Kiwis', were assigned the night-time security work while the Open was on. Why, I'm not sure; maybe it was because New Zealand's national bird, the kiwi, is nocturnal, or maybe because nobody else wanted to work at night. The rest of the crew parked the clients' cars during the day, answered questions and guided guests to the shuttle bus that ran to the golf course.

Barney and I were pretty useless security guards to say the least. Both of us were exhausted and the twelve-day erection had taken its toll on us, not to mention the big night out to celebrate the completion of the tent village. The spongy artificial grass of the golf simulator proved too much of a temptation for us. We grabbed a couple of mothballed moving blankets that the banquet tables had come wrapped in and went to sleep.

I was woken by Barney shaking me and saying in a hushed, tense voice, 'Bro, there's someone here.'

All of a sudden our job didn't seem so cruisy. This was

## Erection Specialist

America; if the burglars were serious, they would be armed. We, on the other hand, quickly realised how unarmed we were. For starters, it was pitch-black inside the tent and we had no flashlight, so we equipped ourselves with the simulator's golf clubs and the dim light of Barney's cell phone. As we made our way towards the noise, I was thinking to myself that I was going to get shot for some lousy TVs.

To this day I'm not too sure what our plan was for confronting the thieves. As we bumped our way past the tables in the banquet tent, we were relieved to find that the noise was a disgruntled guy emptying the portaloo trailer.

Barney and I weren't the only Kiwis working at the Open. On the last day of the tournament, Jimmy gave us two day passes so we could experience this major sporting event. As most of the clients were already at the golf course, we had the shuttle bus to ourselves. The elderly driver picked our accents straight away and said, 'Your boy Michael Campbell's doing well. Him and Tiger Woods are playing to win as we speak.' We had kind of heard that Michael Campbell was doing well but didn't know he was doing *that* well.

We found out what hole Michael and Tiger were playing and, jandals in hand, ran through the sea of polo shirts. Needless to say, we stood out in our board shorts and singlets.

We arrived at the 13th hole and followed Michael and Tiger all the way to the 18th. It was a memorable moment when Barney and I found ourselves up a tree like a couple of monkeys at the packed 18th hole to watch Michael Campbell win the 2005 US Golf Open, one of New Zealand's greatest sporting moments on the world stage.

Still on a high, we ran barefoot down the fairways to get a shuttle bus back to the tent village to start pulling it down. With gravity on our side, and the adrenaline of seeing Michael's win still pumping through us, we worked through the night with ease. The boys were eager to get the tents down and back to

Louisville to their loved ones. Barney and I were going to tag along like a couple of stray dogs.

## A cultural experience

You don't think you're going to have a cultural experience in Kentucky unless you're a bourbon-drinking KFC pilgrim. But I did, the peak of which came on the Fourth of July, America's Independence Day.

With all the tenting boys back with their loved ones, Barney and I took the Red Baron down to the river for an Independence Day concert. We weren't expecting much as we set up on the grass in front of the stage in the late afternoon sun, with our warm, cheap dozen of Milwaukee's Finest.

Soon the ground around us was littered with stereotypical happy families. They had their rugs and Walmart picnic chairs that resembled fold-out living rooms complete with leg rests, cup holders, tables and coolers. I remembered back to a conversation I'd had with some New Yorkers at the Open. They had described Kentucky as a shithole, the compost heap of America. I couldn't agree with them more; Kentucky *was* like the compost heap of America, not because it was a shithole, but because it was so damn down to earth. I loved it.

The country music started up, and the sun started going down over the river, along with the beers. Then and there I had one of my most memorable cultural experiences, most probably because I wasn't expecting it. I wasn't in some Indian temple praying to Buddha, hanging out with natives in the Amazon or living with a tribe in some remote African village. No, I was happily drinking cheap beer, surrounded by what some people would describe as redneck Americans, but who I would describe as fun-loving, warm-hearted folk.

These families took the two guys from New Zealand under their wings and, along with the little kids, had us up dancing.

We sang with everyone else at the top of our voices in our thick Kiwi accents 'I'm proud to be an American' and the Bruce Springsteen classic 'Born in the USA'. They were all proud to be American, they were all united, and they were celebrating it. It wasn't arrogance; it was raw balls-to-the-wall patriotism. They were just having a good time with their families and passing on their sense of pride to the next generations.

On the drive home in the Red Baron, Barney and I were in a contemplative silence. I was thinking back to when Mr Malikov had offered me the job in his American business, and how I had automatically thought that I didn't want to go because I believed all Americans were loud and arrogant. The States was a place I had never really had any desire to go to when I left on my working-the-world quest.

I find it quite funny looking back. If I said the kind of things I had said about Americans about a minority ethnic group, I would be called a racist. But because I was saying it about Americans, it was fine, it was accepted, everybody thought the same, or at least no one would disagree. Now, when I hear people make those types of comments about 'bloody Americans', I ask if they have been there.

Of course all countries have their fair share of dickheads. I come from a country of just over four million people, so let's say 10 per cent of the population are dickheads; that would mean that New Zealand has a grand total of 400,000 dickheads. In America, that equates to 30 million dickheads—the population of Canada.

All I'm trying to say is that, yes, some Americans may speak a little louder, they may not travel as much, they may have an ex-president who is one of the most hated people in the world outside of the US Bible Belt, but at the end of the day, they are just friendly, hospitable people.

## Feeling lucky in Kentucky

Barney and I had a new job helping one of the tenting boys with his landscaping business. We crashed on his couch, then, come morning, we would jump in the tray of his pickup truck along with the lawn mower and landscaping tools.

After a week of partying every night—everyone seemed to being using the two Kiwis in town as an excuse to get on the booze—sleeping on the couch and working hung-over, Barney and I doubted if we could keep this up for another month before we got shipped out to the next tenting job.

Our break came after a day out with the tenting boys. We were heading back to town with Jimmy and his girlfriend when he got a call. Jimmy turned to us and asked, 'Can you guys paint?'

Barney and I looked at each other knowing we didn't have a bloody clue, but painting wasn't rocket science and we replied in unison, 'Yup.'

The man on the other end of the phone was Jack, a guy in his sixties who was mad about rugby after spending a year in New Zealand on an exchange when he was in his twenties. Jack required some extra hands for an upcoming job and had got word that Jimmy was harbouring some Kiwis.

On the first day of work we met Jack, a man whose reputation as being a caring, good-bastard family guy preceded him. Nobody had a bad word to say about him. He stuck his hand out and said, 'Bloody Kiwis.' Straight away he felt like a father figure.

He then went on to explain how the job required painting a highway overpass bridge. It would take about three weeks, working every day to paint the 80-metre-long bridge in the red and black of the Louisville Cardinals, the local university football team. Two workers had pulled out on him and he'd thought he was going to have to throw in the job until he heard about us.

We were going to be working with Timmy, a guy Jack

described as 'a fucking fat bastard, but he's incredible on the end of a long roller. He's done plenty of jobs for me, but he's too fat these days; he will be supervising you guys.'

Jack was right, Timmy was a fat bastard. He looked like he was well overdue, with a pregnant gut hanging over his grey trackpants. This guy made breathing seem hard, and I almost felt he was in danger of keeling over at any time.

The job was rather daunting, especially when taking into account the size of the bridge and because Barney and I didn't really have a clue what to do. But Jack had faith in us; well, Jack had faith in Kiwis. He ran us through the controls of the cherry picker while cruising around the Cardinals stadium car park. He then showed us the part of the bridge that went over a railway track and before leaving us to it said, 'If you see a train coming, you get the fuck out of Dodge; I don't need no smashed-up Kiwis.'

With those last words, Jack got the fuck out of Dodge and left us with Timmy.

Supposedly Timmy was good at the end of a roller, but I would never know. All he did was sit in his truck below the cherry picker and watch us paint. Sometimes he would beep the horn and shout instructions. One time Barney whispered to me, 'Don't answer him, pretend we can't hear him.' Timmy struggled to pull himself out of the truck and hobbled underneath the cherry picker. Then, out of breath, he proceeded to call us like you would a dog: 'Pssssss, pssssss.' Barney was fuming. Then he started with our names: 'Hey Barney, hey Hap, I'm going to use the restroom and pick up some paint. I'll be back soon.' An hour later, he was perched in his truck with the suspension slightly relieved after the restroom stop. He never seemed to have any paint, but always came back with McDonald's so he could eat while enjoying the painting show.

After a couple of days, Jack took him off the job as he probably realised Timmy served no purpose apart from cutting into his profit margin and keeping the local McDonald's in business.

Then life fell into place: we moved into a basement apartment underneath Jimmy's office. In real estate they say it's all about location. Well, this was the perfect house for a couple of young guys, right on Bardstown Road where all the bars are. The fact that the flat had no doors, apart from the front door, no ceiling (all kinds of wires hung from overhead) and no furniture didn't matter. We grabbed some old mattresses from Jimmy's rat-infested warehouse and stole a butter knife from a diner to spread jam on our sandwiches.

I had everything I needed: a job, a place to sleep, good people to hang out with and a great mate to share it with. I felt lucky in Kentucky.

### Two half-naked guys in a cage

As I mentioned, everyone used us as an excuse to party, and Barney and I would turn up to our painting job in varying states of self-inflicted sickness—something that you only seem physically capable of in your younger years, and something you come to realise in your later ones is not worth the pain. One particular night, after a barbecue spent throwing horseshoes around a peg in the ground with all the Louisville rugby and tenting guys, I went home at some point when the sun was up and climbed into bed. Immediately the alarm went off. Then, in the process of stumbling to the toilet, I fell through my newly acquired bedroom door, as I had forgotten it had no hinges and was just leaning against the doorway.

Unfortunately we had to get to work, as Jack needed the job done. Most people would have called in sick—it was a Sunday after all—but we didn't want to let Jack down. I pulled up at the house where the barbecue had been. Barney had not finished partying and stumbled out the door, wearing some oversized Dame Edna glasses, beer in hand.

'Let's go paint, fucker,' he slurred.

# Erection Specialist

He was in party mode, so we turned the stereo up. On the way to the bridge, I stopped off and bought a couple of buckets of coffee and enough caffeine pills to have even Timmy raving all night at a dance party.

The first couple of hours were rather fun. I painted *I Love Barney* on my bare chest, and at one point we extended the boom of the cherry picker to its full height and started dancing. This must have been quite a show for the Sunday morning motorists, as our cherry picker basket came level with the cars on the overpass. The motorists would have seen two half-naked guys covered in paint, dancing in the middle of the sky like they had been transported from a full-moon party in Thailand. All we needed were the glow sticks and psytrance bass lines.

The afternoon wasn't so lively. Productivity dropped, to say the least. Actually, productivity wasn't that high in the morning either, but energy levels were. With the caffeine pills having no effect and our hangovers in full swing, motorists were in for another show. Barney was in a bad way and the inevitable happened: he started spewing.

Now, as you know from Korea, I have a really weak stomach and will spew at the smell of a bad fart. It's also a common occurrence for me to dry retch while brushing my teeth, just because the brush's hit the back of my throat. The problem was that when you are in a 1.5-metre-wide cage, 6 metres in the air, you can't escape the sight and sound of someone else spewing. So Barney set me off as well.

Now the show was two half-naked guys leaning over the side of a mechanical boom basket, sending fountains of last night's keg and sausages over the car park below. We left our mark on Kentucky in more ways than one.

Life carried on like this—minus the spewing—until the bridge and the white bathroom walls of our dungeon apartment were covered in the colours of the Louisville Cardinals. It was time to move on. After four fun-filled weeks in Kentucky, the bridge was painted and it was time to find another erection.

Next thing I knew I was at the wheel of the Red Baron, heading down the highway out of Louisville, in convoy with Jimmy and the tenting crew on the twelve-hour drive to Newark, New Jersey, for the PGA Tour.

## Going out with a bang in NYC

We arrived in Newark and it felt like we had driven onto the set of *The Sopranos* or *The Godfather*. I couldn't believe people actually talked like that: 'Gimme a cwoffee.' This PGA tent job was the same as the job we had done in North Carolina for the US Golf Open. The only difference here was that after we had finished, we were able to jump on the train and be in downtown New York in 30 minutes. Not a bad place for an after-work beer.

Three weeks later the tent village had been erected, cars parked, security work completed, then the tent city pulled down and put on the trucks to lie dormant in Jimmy's Louisville warehouse for another year. The US chapter was coming to an end.

Jimmy and the boys were heading back to Kentucky early the next morning, so we had a few beers with them. Then Barney and I got the train into New York to celebrate. We had worked nearly every day for the three months we had been in the States.

After checking out of the hotel, Barney and I went to the famed Jersey Shore for a couple of days. Then we boarded the Greyhound bus that would take us to the next destination, 100 hours and numerous bus stops away, on the opposite coast of the continent.

# Chapter 5
# CANADIAN NOMAD

**NORTH AMERICA: Vancouver, British Columbia; Banff, Alberta, Canada, 26 August 2005–17 April 2006**

Barney and I arrived in Vancouver, having survived on a diet of dried-out hotdogs during our 100-hour Greyhound bus marathon.

Once again it was time for the process familiar to a Western nomad setting up roots in a foreign city: find a job, a place to stay, and transport.

We could tick transport off the list right away as my good mate Bugz, who I had grown up with, was waiting in Vancouver in our van. I say 'our' van as Barney and I had gone thirds with Bugz in the $900 Plymouth Voyager. As with most cars in this price range, it came with certain characteristics: peeling blue paint, rust, leaks, missing hub caps and unpredictable headlights that needed a 'kickstart'.

It seemed like half the world was trying to find an apartment in midsummer Vancouver. When you are three itinerant guys in your early twenties living in a van and looking for a one-bedroom or studio apartment for only three and half months, you find the property managers aren't busting down your rusted van door to sign you up.

Out of desperation, we moved into a basement apartment in the suburbs that was rented out by an Indian family who lived above. They must have been shocked on moving day when we pulled up in our junkyard van with only one headlight flickering and two stained world-map-patterned mattresses, that we had just scavenged from a dumpster, tied to the roof. The rest of our furniture consisted of Bugz's camping gear, two deck chairs, a cooler, and miscellaneous cooking pots and utensils. No need to mention that the apartment felt as homely as a crack den, but it was our space and it beat the hell out of paying through the roof for hostels or sleeping in the van.

With me and Barney finding tenting jobs, and Bugz mowing lawns and flipping burgers, we were all now employed. We weren't the happiest of campers in our suburban Indian basement and wanted to be closer to town. With limited options, we packed up our camp, put the mattresses on the roof, and moved into a one-bedroom flat on the sixteenth floor of a block in English Bay.

No doubt we had the neighbours talking: three guys in a one-bedroom apartment in the heart of Canada's most densely populated gay area.

We loved it in comparison with our basement campsite. We were two blocks from the ocean with views over downtown Vancouver, complete with pool, sauna and a downtown price tag. We were living the high life, and we even found a couch (actually a cushionless couch frame from the dumpster) and a coffee table (a scrap of plywood resting on borrowed milk crates).

To make our new downtown shoebox more homely I had

volunteered to take two days off work to drive to Banff and collect some furniture and other creature comforts Bugz had stored there since the previous snowboard season. These things would make our one-bedroom apartment a home—especially the laptop for us to play music on.

I departed Vancouver after work, but only made it five hours into the twelve-hour journey to Banff before the transmission blew up. I spent the night in the van on the Trans-Canada Highway, the buzz of passing trucks keeping me awake. The following morning I got a tow truck and laid the van to rest at the local scrapyard; a mechanic told me a new transmission would cost more than the van. I grabbed all that I could carry out of the van and started hitch-hiking back to Vancouver. You can imagine the looks on Barney's and Bugz's faces when I arrived back with no laptop, no household comforts and no van! We all bought Vancouver public transport passes, and didn't look back.

Life soon got into a routine. Vancouver had all the ingredients of a great city: ocean, mountains, parks, a busy downtown, friendly people, diverse cultures and heaps of good, cheap food. Two thumbs up to summertime Vancouver. Then in November, along with the winter rain, came my 24th birthday. For my present to myself that year I got two sinister looking thieves tattooed onto my lower back representing my favourite quote: *Regrets over yesterday and worries about tomorrow are the twin thieves that rob you of the moment.* (Little did I know at that point in my life that I would come to understand the true meaning of this quote in six years' time when I was celebrating my 30th birthday on the 11/11/11.) But now, like the nomads we were, with the relentless November rain signalling the change of season, it was time for Bugz, Barney and me to pack up our belongings and move camp. The next camp happened to be Banff.

## Ski bum life

There is no doubt about it; Banff is a tourist town, and a beautiful one at that. Every day the buses unload their cargo of high-paying 'tourons' to take in the amazing natural beauty, wildlife, world-class ski-fields and buy overpriced souvenirs from the OK Gift Shop.

Anyone who has lived in a popular ski town knows the first obstacle is finding accommodation. Luckily Bugz had a contact from his previous year living in Banff which saw us land a three-bedroom apartment. The second obstacle in a popular ski-resort town is that accommodation costs don't reflect the minimum wages paid. The only way to make accommodation affordable is by packing as many minimum-wage-earning mates as humanly possible into the space provided.

Once again, in authentic Western nomad style, we filled the three bedrooms with hand-me-down mattresses, constructed a shonky bunk bed of which I got the bottom bunk, acquired a fold-out couch and pimped out the closet with a custom-fitted mattress for our most vertically challenged and daring flatmate. In total we ended up with eight rent-paying flatmates, but the apartment took on an asylum-seeker feel to it as there was always a hitchhiker, a friend in need, a drunken friend unable to drive or walk, an evicted mate, or a visiting friend who took up the limited free floor space. At one stage it reached capacity at fourteen—you had to feel sorry for the one female flatmate using the only bathroom.

To get us all to the Lake Louise ski resort each day, our extended family of eight paying flatmates 'invested' in another $900 car. It was a 1989 Mercury Sable complete with stylish, faded maroon interior and the all-important front bench seat. The Sable was like a once-glamorous runway model whose years of drug abuse, smoking and living off lettuce leaves had caught up with her. We gave the Sable a makeover so she would feel good about herself, which included a collage of snowboard stickers, and two thick black spray-painted racing stripes. The racing stripes were the only things remotely racy about the Sable, and when it was packed to capacity with people and snowboards, it only had two pedals: a brake pedal and a noise pedal.

But the Sable was the give that held the family together, and it would have been fitting to call it 'The Stable.' Like a loving golden Labrador, it was always there for us, waiting obediently to be taken along with excited little kids for a day's snowboarding.

So we had crossed off accommodation and transport from the Western nomad set-up list, now the most important: work. At the start, this consisted of minimum-wage temping work, doing all the jobs that nobody else wanted to do: cleaning hotel rooms, labouring on frozen construction sites, climbing up 20-metre silos running electrical cable, setting up events, collecting laundry, and so on. Then I made a career move and started the weirdest job of my working-the-world quest.

## Toilet boy

I had seen a small ad in the local paper that read something along the lines of 3 x 4hr nights a week, $13/hr, cleaning nightclub toilets. Now that may not seem so appealing, but $13 an hour was a lot of money in Banff, considering all the other jobs I had worked up to that point had been paying around $8.

I rang the number and spoke with John, who explained to me that the job involved sitting in the 'washroom' (that's toilet to you and me) from 11 p.m. to 3 a.m., keeping the toilets clean and handing out paper towels to the nightclub patrons. This I wasn't so keen on; I wasn't sure I could handle being known around Banff as the guy who worked in a toilet on his Friday and Saturday nights.

But I knew someone who would be interested. Bugz's work visa had run out and he needed under-the-table work, so he ended up taking the job. Like all good friends, I took great pleasure in Bugz's misfortune that his only option in life was to work in a toilet cleaning up poo and spew. But Bugz had the last laugh when he came home with pockets bulging with tips.

A week later, a job came up in another nightclub toilet. So like a good mate, Bugz put in a word for me. I handed in my CV (finally, something I was qualified for), got the job and had to eat my words.

My normal day as a toilet boy would go something along the following lines.

Arriving back from snowboarding, I would walk over the pile of clothes on the bedroom floor, left by its three occupants, and have a quick nap on my rickety bottom bunk. My alarm would go off around 8 or 9 p.m., depending if there was a party to go to earlier. I would start drinking with whoever was crashing on our couch or lounge-room floor at the time. Pre-work drinks were a necessary part of the job. If you don't believe me, then you try sitting in a toilet talking to drunk guys all night and cleaning up their spew.

I would then pull on my jacket and walk down the snow-covered streets with the hair in my nostrils freezing with every breath. I would stop off at the convenience store and buy spray deodorant and a bulk load of condoms. I was probably the young male store attendant's idol, coming in every Tuesday, Friday and Saturday night and buying a teenager's yearly supply of condoms each night.

At the nightclub the ear-piece-wearing bouncers would acknowledge me with a raise of the eyebrows and I would skip the queue as though I was the resident DJ.

I would then go and set up in my office which comprised three toilet cubicles, four wall-mounted urinals and a row of hand basins, where I would sit with the paper towels, my tray of condoms, cologne, deodorant and mints. Apart from the fact that at some point during the night I would inevitably have to clean up someone's spew, there was no such thing as a usual night working the toilet. Over my four-month period of being the toilet boy, the following things happened:

I had guys spill the beans about their lives and start crying.

I had gay guys hit on me.

On Tuesday nights, the girls would always come to the men's toilet due to the larger queues at the female toilets. It was ladies' night, the busiest time of the week, and the night all the workers came out. I hated it as it was full of Aussies and Kiwis which meant no tips for me, as no right-minded Aussie or Kiwi is going to tip a fellow countryman to hand him a paper towel. Though they didn't tip, they always provided entertainment. When one of the girls tried to jump the line and use the male toilets, one of the waiting fellas would invariably shout to the delight of the other drunk males waiting, 'If ya wanna piss show us ya tits' or 'You have to piss standing up'. They actually had better aim than some of the men, and no male ever complained about having to wait for a female.

I was constantly fed drinks. Bar staff would bring me shots and patrons would buy me drinks because they felt sorry for me.

I would have police come in every night and look over the cubicle doors for people doing cocaine.

I had people constantly asking me, 'Toilet boy, keep an eye out for me' as they ducked into the cubicle to powder their nose. When leaving they would say, 'Toilet boy, left you a surprise in cubicle two.'

I had to break up fights.

Some arsehole crapped on the floor, literally.

Every night I would have to push chunks of someone else's vomit down a hand basin plughole.

I had to call ambulance crews to come in and deal with unconscious clientele.

I had couples come in to see if they could rent my cubicle off me for sex.

I spent the New Year's countdown in the toilet!

## HAP WORKING THE WORLD

I was that guy around Banff. I was toilet boy, the guy who worked in a nightclub toilet on a Tuesday, Friday and Saturday night. People would come up to me in town and ask me, 'Where do I know you from?' Most nights I would have people feeling sorry for me offer me a new job, but I would always refuse as I had grown to quite enjoy the quirkiness of toilet life. It had its advantages. I earned more money working twelve hours a week than my mates working 40-hour weeks up the mountain. Best of all, I got to snowboard every day.

### Packing fudge

I could have survived easily on the 'dirty' money I was getting from the washrooms, but my grandmother wasn't too well, so I decided to earn some extra money for a trip home. After all, it had been three years since I had left New Zealand.

I became a fudge packer. It involved standing in the window of a main street chocolate shop wearing a chef's uniform. I would stir fudge in a massive bowl that resembled a witch's cauldron with my metre-long wooden spoon.

Onlooking Asian tourists would video me as I stood in the shopfront making fudge and other goodies like caramel popcorn, toffee apples, and anything chocolate you could think of. I would also man the cash register, and of course I would pack the fudge.

The best fringe benefit of my fudge-packing job was that it gave me an invaluable currency to trade in. Because all us workers were on minimum wage, we all helped each other out and operated a black-market barter system. With my chocolate currency, I was able to get my snowboard waxed for free, trade pizza with the guys next door, and get a staff discount at the booze shop. I was working in a brown-gold mine.

## Do the hokey-pokey

On one particular Saturday evening, as per usual I was working at the fudge shop before going to my toilet boy job. I was being shown the finer art of making hokey-pokey (honeycomb toffee in local parlance) in the shopfront cooking area by head fudge packer, Tim. Tim was a fellow Kiwi who was an airplane mechanic in real life but, like me, wanted to do a snowboard season in Banff, so he packed fudge.

On this evening Tim had to leave early, so I assured him that I could finish the hokey-pokey myself as I had plenty of experience in the front window making fudge. The owner was rather strict about front-window standards as you were so obviously on display to the customers and anyone walking past. The owner was very passionate about chocolate and all things caramel. It was an art. To be sure, I was ready.

Tim ran me through the remaining steps: I would turn off the heat when the buzzer signalled that 1 hour 31 minutes of cooking time was up, wait for the mixture to cool down to 275 degrees Fahrenheit, then finally add baking soda. I would then enlist the help of the cash register girl, Sarah, to lift the cauldron mixing bowl and pour the hokey-pokey into the wooden troughs on the marble display table. Tim left feeling confident that I would be fine and told me to ring him if I needed anything.

To be honest, I was feeling pretty damn relaxed. It was nearing the end of my 10-hour shift in the chocolate shop and my mind was wandering to where I would go for a beer before work in the toilets at 11 p.m. The sound of the cooking timer buzzed, breaking my train of thought and signalling it was time to turn off the heat. I turned off the big Bunsen burner knob, placed the thermometer in the mixture and went to get the required amount of baking soda.

I brought back what looked like a lot of baking soda—which it was. I rechecked the note Tim had left me, just to be sure I was adding the correct amount.

# HAP WORKING THE WORLD

As the mercury of the thermometer reached 275 degrees, I started to sift in the baking soda with a group of excited Japanese tourists videoing me. I decided to add a bit of spice to their holiday videos, which I thought probably consisted of unsmiling Japanese men standing in front of various monuments, and started to do my impersonation of an overly enthusiastic Spanish chef. As I was sifting the baking soda I started doing a *cha-cha-cha* dance, pretending the sieve was a maraca. I was getting a great response from the Japanese, they were getting more and more animated, and this in turn made me more and more flamboyant with my dance moves, and I started shaking my hips with closed eyes. What I didn't realise was that their rapid-fire Japanese and finger pointing wasn't from excitement brought on by my performance, but rather by alarm.

My *cha-cha-cha* hokey-pokey dance was interrupted when I heard the flame of the cooker go out. I cut my performance short and looked down. My joyful mood was thrown into a panic as I saw what had put out the flame: the industrial quantity of hokey-pokey that was pouring out of the cauldron with surprising force and with seemingly no end in sight.

Those who paid attention in science class know about the lethal rising capabilities of baking soda, and now unfortunately I did too, but even more unfortunately I had learnt my lesson with commercial sized portions. All I could think was *My boss is going to kill me*. As the hot mixture started to pool around my shoes I snapped out of my stupor and yelled to Sarah to come and help me pour out the contents of the mixing bowl, as it was so big and perilously full that it required two people. Hearing the shit-has-hit-the-fan tone of my voice, Sarah left her customer mid-sale, pulled on an oven mitt and came to my aid.

My cooking show now had all the customers' attention and a window full of new onlookers! As Sarah and I waddled with the weight of the cauldron over to the display table where I had arranged the containers to pour out the hokey-pokey to set, the lava-like mixture started to cover the floor, similar to the effect of pouring concrete into the foundation of a house. With great difficulty we managed to pour all the contents of the cauldron into the containers while spilling it all over me. I was now left standing there with the gooey hokey-pokey setting like concrete making me look like a bronze statue. One Japanese man who had been videoing was laughing, giving me the thumbs up, saying 'very good, very good'. He then passed the video camera to his wife and he came around into the cooking area to get a photo with me, only this time I was the one in the photo not smiling!

Now I had to start cleaning up the mess, which was similar to dealing with an overflowing toilet bowl. There was golden-brown hokey-pokey everywhere. My relief turned to anxiety again as I realised the hokey-pokey was starting to set like concrete. I'm pretty sure Charlie would have made the chocolate factory pillars from hokey-pokey.

Like a teenager trying to clean up after a party before his parents got home, I tackled the thick coat of hokey-pokey that covered the entire floor of the display kitchen. I set about with a bucket of boiling water trying to melt it off, and then just resigned myself to chiselling away at the mess covering the stone tiles. The whole time I was worried that my boss would come in and see what I had done to his prized front-window cooking area. Luckily the only person who interrupted me was an Irish tourist who popped his head in the door and said, 'I'm not going to buy anyting, I just wanted to 'ave a laugh at ya. What da fook did ya do? Looks like a giant shat himself in here.'

I stayed after closing, chiselling away for two hours, but had to leave to go to work in the toilets. I rang Tim to tell him what had happened and to see if he could come in early the next morning and clean up the rest of the carnage before the boss got in. As I was telling him what had happened and how I had thought there was too much baking soda, and how fast it had expanded, he started to laugh. Tim explained, 'Sorry bro, I totally forgot to tell you that the recipe was for a double batch, but we only ever make a single batch! The pot isn't big enough for a double batch, but it sounds like you found that out the hard way.'

## Bye-bye Banff

My weeks were my weekends and my weekends my weeks. On the weekends when the mountains and the town were overrun with tourists, I would be cleaning spew in the toilets by night and packing fudge by day. Then come Monday it was time for my five-day weekend, except Tuesday when I worked ladies' night.

The Sable held on valiantly to see the season out, but unfortunately it went to join our Vancouver van in car heaven, one week before I left. With the snow melting and our valiant Sable laid to rest on the side of the road awaiting a tow truck, my time as a Western nomad was coming to an end.

After three years of working the world, I had earned enough money fudge packing to buy a ticket home to see my sick grandmother for a month and recharge the family batteries.

# Chapter 6
# HOMELESS PIG
## NORTH AMERICA: Red Deer, Alberta, Canada, 17 May–21 November 2006

After visiting my grandmother in New Zealand, I was ready to hit the ground running back in Canada. The goal was for Barney and me to earn enough money to attend the 2007 Cricket World Cup in Jamaica, and then travel through South America.

With three months left on our one-year Canadian work visas, Barney and I were headed for the Alberta oil fields where we had heard there was plenty of money to be made if you had two arms and two legs. I just hoped they didn't discriminate against my ten-year-old-girl arms.

With a Canadian track record of two cars in eight months, we didn't want to make it three. However, with only $1200 between us to spend on a car, we were pushing shit uphill. While crashing at Barney's girlfriend's house in Calgary, we test-drove Canada's future scrap metal.

## HAP WORKING THE WORLD

Our oil field chariot came in the form of a maroon 1991 Chevy Lumina sedan with 191,000 kilometres on the clock. The second-hand car dealer assured us it was in great condition. We haggled him down to $850. This seemed all too good to be true, and, yes, it was. A couple of months later, we had to take it to the mechanic to check out a noise coming from the brakes. In the mechanic's words we were 'lucky this thing even stops'. Twelve hundred dollars later we had fully new front and rear brakes!

Once we had our car, we were in need of work, so like the gold miners of yesteryear, we headed north from Calgary to the oil boomtowns of Red Deer and Nisku. These oil towns are the hub of souped-up pickup trucks with lift kits that would make it impossible to use a fast-food drive-thru. Everyone seemed to have tattoos, and all the young guys walked around with an arrogance that comes from being able to leave school at sixteen and jump straight into an $80,000-plus job.

Unfortunately getting work on the oil rigs wasn't as easy as everybody had made out, even though there was a massive labour shortage in Alberta because of the oil boom. The newsreader on the local radio station would report that within the coming ten years there was going to be a labour shortage of 100,000 people. Then there were the recruiters adverts offering competitions to win between $500 and $3000 worth of prizes just for submitting your CV. There were also all the stories from Fort McMurray in northern Alberta where the oil sands project had taken off and the average income for a 29-year-old was $100,000. Even 24-hour outlets couldn't stay open due to a lack of labour. McDonald's was flying people in to work at their restaurants. Despite all the news and hype about the labour shortage, no one would consider us as we didn't have oil and gas industry experience.

Finally we got a lucky break; a mate from Red Deer gave us the contact details of the drilling company he worked for. We

went in to meet two easy-going managers who, reclining in their office chairs, told us to do the relevant courses and then come back and see them.

With the little bit of money left over from the car, and our credit cards, we paid for the courses, which left us with nothing. So much nothing that Barney ended up buying underwear from the Salvation Army op shop. I bought socks.

Little did we know when we bought our car that we were also buying our home. The couple of weeks we spent job hunting and doing the courses, we slept in our car. We soon fell into a routine: at the end of our day we would go to the river, which all the farmland backed onto, and jump into the freezing cold waist-deep water with a cake of soap, gasping, and quickly wash 'back, crack and sack'.

We would cook our budget sausages in the public park which had fire pits with free cut wood. Afterwards we would wash the dishes in the hand basin of the public toilet and then brush our teeth. We would drive somewhere inconspicuous and like a married couple we would take our side of the bed. I would raise the steering wheel and recline the driver's seat while Barney would hang up our towels to keep out the light and recline the passenger's seat. Come morning we would pack up the blankets that were hand-me-downs from Banff and drive to our course, or hand out our CVs to uninterested employers.

We spent a lot of time at the local library, usually before dinner, because we could relax on the couches and use the free internet. We got to know the friendly, motherly librarians. When filling out our library card forms we admitted we had no address because we were living in our car, and they went into a motherly frenzy. They rang around the local homeless shelters, which had no available beds, but said we could get free meals there. Our ears pricked up at the thought of not eating jam sandwiches for breakfast and lunch and sausages for dinner.

The first time going to the homeless shelter I was nervous,

probably because I felt as though I was an intruder. I didn't belong there. But in reality, I was homeless with no money; I needed a helping hand until I got my first pay cheque.

This was a time in my life during which I developed a deeper appreciation for my upbringing. As I sat at the table and looked around at my fellow diners, I couldn't help but think how lucky I was. For me this was just a chapter of my life, but for them this was their whole book. There were haggard ladies as skinny as frail 90-year-olds, but who were only midway through their book. And there was a battered, barefoot man whose feet were so black they looked like he had been standing in a fire pit.

After completing our courses, we rang back the drilling company. Barney was standing in the public phone booth beside me, straining with nervous anticipation to hear what the manager was saying to me. We were both anxious; so much was riding on this phone call. If they no longer needed us or had changed their minds, we had nothing else to fall back on. No other company had shown any interest, and we had visited them all, every single one in Red Deer, and further north in Nisku and also back in Calgary at their head offices.

The phone call turned into elation, high fives and hugs. The news was good—we had a trial at the workshop on Monday. What better news to get on a Friday afternoon before Barney's 26th birthday weekend.

## Barney's homeless birthday

That Saturday night we celebrated Barney's birthday in homeless style. We drove our maroon mobile home to a park close to the nightclub area. We had a birthday meal of baked beans and had splashed out on a cheap bottle of whisky. Spotting the only other people in the crappy little park, Barney and I went and joined them at their picnic table. The two girls were sisters; the younger sister was secretly visiting her older sister in Red Deer behind her parents' backs. They were from a Hutterite community, a religion that thrives in the North American prairies and has rules such as not using technology and living a traditional lifestyle (from what I could see, similar to the Amish). The older sister had left the community, and therefore had been kicked out of her family. The reason she left was because she had fallen in love with a disabled Native American man called Wheels when she was his carer.

Later on, Wheels, with a long, styled mullet and wearing dark glasses and a baggy hockey shirt, came down to the park on his motorised wheelchair. Wheels was a character. He talked a lot of shit, but I liked him, plus he kept the other homeless people from coming to ask us for a drink. There must be a law among the homeless that you can't beg from disabled people. The more of our whisky he drank, the more he revealed about his life. He had apparently been a hit man for a local gang, and a champion car racer.

At some point in the conservation he asked about Barney and me. I jokingly said that we were gay lovers. Wheels didn't pick up on my sarcasm, and started to tell us how he and his best mate had experimented sexually when they had travelled together. I tried to tell him that I was only joking, but he just reassured me that he understood.

'It's cool man, I understand, I did the same thing. Things are different on the road.'

I looked at Barney, and he just blew me a kiss—best I not drink too much whisky tonight.

Wheels and I then got into a drunken deep and meaningful. He had found out that I was a Scorpio like him, and I told him that I was born on 11/11. He then told me he was a psychic and really wanted to read my palm. Why not? Surely my future couldn't be any worse than being homeless and drinking whisky in a park. He held my hand and went on to tell me that I had been really sick, which was true. I then told him that the ring I was wearing on my index finger was a ring that I had bought after getting out of the Ohio hospital to remind myself of that time in my life. He then took the ring off my finger, and swapped it for his ring, a ring that had a scorpion engraved on it. He said that I was going to feel more pain in my life, and that he would wear my ring so he could take the pain for me. He told me that he could handle pain, he was used to it. He had lost his legs in a racing accident, in a drag racing car, when apparently the parachute didn't open. He also told me that I would marry a Scorpio, and when I proposed to her I had to give her the ring. I thanked him. I may have even had a drunken tear in my eye. (As I type this, five years later, I am still wearing Wheels' Scorpio ring.)

Barney broke up our Oprah hour with: 'Come on, fuckers, it's my birthday. Let's go party.'

Wheels was keen to come out and reckoned he knew of a good nightclub. The Hutterite girls didn't drink so therefore didn't want to come out with us. But Wheels' girlfriend was supportive of us taking Wheels out, so much so that she slipped me $20 for drinks.

We hugged the girls goodbye, thanked them for a memorable night and wished them well.

Then Wheels said to Barney and me, 'Jump on, I'll give you a ride.'

Barney and I looked at each other. 'What do ya mean, on your wheelchair?'

'Yeah, one standing on the pegs at the back, and one on my lap.'

Barney kindly pointed out that I was the skinniest so should go on his lap—I was just hoping that Wheels was paralysed from the waist down!

As we puttered along at a fast walking speed, Wheels apologised for his wheelchair. He explained it was a rental as his own was being repaired. He was proud to say that his usual wheelchair was the fastest in Canada. The reason it was at the

## Homeless Pig

repair shop was because his girlfriend had the nice thought of washing it, so had put it on the back of the car and it had gone through the car wash!

So there we were, three fully grown men cruising along at a walking pace down the verge of a busy road on an electric wheelchair. Wheels was laughing, Barney was shouting, 'Woohoo!' at the top of his lungs and I was doing warrior fighting calls as though we were about to go into battle.

We got to the nightclub, which had a massive line snaking out of it. Wheels just said, 'Don't worry,' and gunned it—in an overladen motorised wheelchair that isn't the fastest in Canada kind of way—up the disabled ramp. The bouncer seemed to know Wheels and opened the door for us.

The nightclub was your usual oil-town shithole bar/nightclub, with non-descript dark-grey décor and neon beer signs. I bought us drinks and the three of us danced with other random people, Wheels twisting his wheelchair and pumping the air with his fist. Then the night slowly distorted into fuzziness and, along with it, the legend of Wheels.

I woke the next morning with the sun beaming through the driver's side window. I had a dehydration headache and could have drunk straight from a puddle. But we had no water. I turned to Barney, who had his shirt off and draped over his eyes, trying to fool himself that it wasn't blindingly sunny and we weren't in full public view.

'Happy birthday, bro.'

We drove to the soup kitchen, which was serving lunch that day. We both really wanted to freshen up; after all it was Barney's 26th birthday lunch. So we pulled into the gas station car park opposite the soup kitchen. Barney walked in first with a bundle of clothes in one hand in which he had his toiletries and my shaver. He asked the owner of the gas station for the toilet key, and then walked to the end of the chip aisle and unlocked the toilet door located by the ATM.

## HAP WORKING THE WORLD

Barney was taking forever—well, forever in terms of how long it takes the normal person to use a gas station toilet. But considering he had to crap, brush his teeth, wash his face, do back, crack, sack and shave, he did well, re-emerging twenty minutes later.

Then it was my turn. Feeling really awkward because we weren't buying anything (trust me, we would have liked to), I approached the owner. I too had a bundle of clothes in my hand, and I felt as though the owner was suspicious of these two guys with accents who had pulled up in a car, waiting for the soup kitchen to open.

I made it to the safety of the toilet then started to rush through my cleaning routine as quickly as possible so I could get the key back to the owner without raising more suspicion. Unfortunately, setting free last night's cheap whisky and baked beans took a bit longer and was a little messier than expected. So I stripped down to give myself a more thorough clean. I began the gas station toilet wash, where you take your old sock, get it soapy and use it to wash, then with the other sock you dry off; wax on, wax off. Just as I finished up, I felt the urge to pee again.

As I was standing there, just shaking the last dribbles out of the old fella, I heard a key in the door and it flew open. I spun around, dick in hand, butt naked to see the wide-eyed face of the owner. He hastily shut the door, apologising. No doubt he was expecting to find another soup kitchen junkie jacking up heroin, but instead came across what he thought was a naked guy jacking off! If I thought it had been awkward asking for the key, it was certainly more awkward doing the walk of shame to the counter and handing back the key.

As we sat down to Barney's birthday lunch at the homeless shelter we had a laugh about me getting caught. Then and there, Barney and I held up our cups of watered-down cordial and proposed a toast: to our new jobs and to never having to shower in a gas station toilet again.

# Homeless Pig

## First impressions count

Barney and I wanted, well, needed, to make a good first impression at the drilling workshop on Monday. It wasn't hard to do as the work ethic at the workshop was relaxed to say the least. The attitude was not unlike that of unionised road workers: one-hour lunch breaks and a lot of standing around. The idea was that we were here to do repairs on the rig equipment, but the workshop manager was as organised as a two-year-old in a playpen.

The other reason no one was motivated to do anything at the workshop was because this was not the 'real' rig work. People only worked here if they were waiting to get sent up to the oil and gas fields in northern British Columbia. When they were back in Red Deer, they wanted to relax and be on holiday. If they came into the workshop, they were under the impression that they were doing the company a favour, even though they were still being paid a pretty penny.

Barney and I, on the other hand, were ecstatic to be working. The best part was that the staff room had free coffee and tea, and every Friday the company bought everyone pizza. We worked hard because we were used to Jimmy's work ethic. Plus it was paramount that we made a good impression because, like everyone else, we desperately wanted to get flown up north to do the real work.

For the next week and a bit, things carried on the same. We would finish work and go do our back, crack and sack routine in the river, which was warming up now that summer was arriving, though I never saw anyone swimming in it. We would eat dinner at the homeless shelter or cook sausages on the fire pit in the park. Then we would park the car at a dog walking area around the corner from the workshop.

Sleeping in the car was getting rather uncomfortable by now. It was like sleeping in economy class with a steering wheel. Plus it was getting warmer but we had to keep the windows up as

## HAP WORKING THE WORLD

Barney's pet hate was mosquitoes. Barney was the guy who if he could hear a mosquito in the same room he was sleeping in would have to turn on the light and hunt that bloodsucking scum down till its death. Waking in the morning covered in a clammy film from a night of sweating became part of the routine.

The following week we got called into the office, where the two laid-back young bosses told us that we were flying out the next day on a job. You would have thought they had just told us we had won a trip to Disneyland. We had a charter flight out of Edmonton airport, two hours north of Red Deer, leaving at 7 a.m.

Barney and I decided it would be best to drive the car up to the airport and sleep in it there. We checked our emails at the library and told our librarian mothers that we would be away for a couple of weeks as we had finally got work on the rigs.

We arrived at Edmonton airport in the pitch-dark on a miserable night that was pissing down with rain. The dashboard clock said it was just before midnight. We were both dog tired and wanted to find somewhere to park the car where we wouldn't be hassled by security guards. Our headlights found the perfect spot—a grassy green empty lot beside a high-fenced secure long-term car park.

We pointed the headlights up the curb and down into our grassy haven. I was nearly asleep at the wheel. The next thing we knew, the car was sliding, the wheels spinning. We were in mud. I tried to keep the car's momentum going, hoping to get to firmer ground, but no.

'FUCK!' we both said in unison.

Even though all we wanted to do was sleep, we knew we had to get out of the bog that night. Because we were going to work on the rigs, we had all our wet weather gear and gumboots in the boot of the car. We pulled them on and trudged out of the mud and into the rain, heading back to the main road where we had spotted a truck stop. After a couple of hours walking from place to place asking people with tired faces eating their midnight dinners in the lifeless road houses if they could pull us out, we gave up. We went back to the car and let sleep take us away.

After a fitful night's sleep, due to an uncharacteristically cold night for that time of year, I woke before the alarm.

Barney turned over and said, 'You going to ring him, bro?'

It was our only option; I had to ring our supervisor who we were meeting at the airport in an hour's time. Hopefully he could swing past and pick us up.

I was feeling rather nervous as we hadn't met this guy.

'Hi, is that Stan?' I asked, swallowing hard.

'Yep,' came his answer with all the enthusiasm and scepticism of a supervisor who is being rung early in the morning.

'Umm, yeah, this is Hap, one of the Kiwis that you have working for you on this job.'

'Yeah . . .'

'We are close to the airport, but our car's a bit stuck, I was wondering if you could come by and pick us up?'

'A bit stuck? Ummm, I'll come and get ya'll. Where you at?'

'Turn off at the gas station, then drive towards the long-term car park.'

'Why don't you get the shuttle service from the car park?' he enquired.

'Umm, well, we're not technically parked in the car park.'

'OK,' he said in a wary voice, knowing it was better not to ask further questions.

Barney and I put on our gumboots and started to unpack the car, taking out all our work gear and other valuables and placing them by the roadside. We hoped we could store them at the airport or in our supervisor's car. With our car lying abandoned in the vacant lot for at least two weeks, it would be a sitting duck for would-be thieves, which wasn't a good situation considering all our remaining worldly possessions were in it. Plus the adjacent road, which had been deserted last night, was now busy with morning traffic going to work in the nearby industrial area.

Just as we had walked the last of our must-take gear from the car through the mud, a car pulled up. It was the security guard from the fenced car park next door. He got out and told us that we couldn't park there, and that if we did our car would get broken into without doubt.

Then the boss rang saying he couldn't find us and was getting a little nervous as our flight was leaving in 40 minutes. Barney took off to the main road to try to wave Stan down as we couldn't give him detailed enough directions.

Soon another car pulled up. Not just any car, but a cop car! Who was in the front seat? Barney. The cop got out with Barney and walked towards me. I looked to Barney for some kind of explanation of what had happened and only got a look that said, *Bro, this couldn't be any worse.*

The cop announced to me with a hint of suspicion in his voice, 'We have had complaints from passing motorists that there are two guys breaking into a car. I picked up your friend running down the street.'

Just as we finished showing the cop our licences and ownership papers and explaining how we ended up in a muddy paddock emptying our car of its contents, our supervisor pulled up. Talk about making a lasting first impression: a car stuck in mud with all our belongings lying on a tarp on the roadside, a security guard and a cop questioning us, and our plane leaving in 30 minutes.

Between the cop, Barney and I, we explained to Stan what had happened. Stan, a six foot four guy nearing 40, who had probably worked the oil field since he was sixteen, looked at us as though we were a couple of special needs kids he had been given the duty of caring for—and with good reason.

Luckily for us, he was a down-to-earth guy and one of the most relaxed oil field workers we were to come across.

## Homeless Pig

Everything about him, from his calm demeanour, size and mannerisms, reminded me of a big sleepy grizzly bear. After our long, convoluted explanation, the first words out of his mouth were, 'Don't they have mud in New Zealand?'

The cop and security guard were insistent that if we left the car there it would get done over. With our charter plane leaving in 25 minutes, we were in a situation. Surprisingly, Stan, a guy with a high-paying supervisor's role, drove an old, dented Ford pickup truck last seen in a Chuck Norris movie.

Barney and I were stressing. Stan strolled like a cowboy over to the tray of his truck and got out a short tattered piece of rope. He attached it to his tow ball and then to our tow ball. Then he started the truck and drove it forward. Slowly the rope took the strain then his wheels started spinning, sending Alberta mud flying all over our car and the maroon interior of the driver's side door that I had left open. Next the rope snapped and our car lay there like an Indian cow, unwilling to budge for anything.

Stan, unperturbed, suggested that he just go bumper to bumper and push us out if we didn't mind denting our bumper. Sounded good to us. As he slid his pickup truck deeper into the paddock, his wheels spinning, it looked like we were going to be responsible for getting our supervisor stuck and missing the plane as well.

Maybe it was an act of God, who knows, but he gained traction, his front bumper pressing against our fat lazy maroon cow of a car, and nudged it to the safety of the bitumen.

Stan pulled up beside us and I wound down the mud-caked window, leaving a pile of mud on the windowsill where you would usually rest your arm during a summer's drive.

Now Stan had a bit more urgency about him. 'Follow me, we can still make the plane. It leaves in fifteen.'

We waved goodbye to the cop as we sped off in pursuit of Stan, mud flicking everywhere.

Barney looked over at me and started laughing. 'Pretty good first impression, eh?'

## Hitting the rig time

We managed to make the flight. Just. We touched down in Fort Nelson, a small shithole town in the north of British Columbia that exists to service the oil industry and people on their way to Alaska. After the rest of the crew had cleaned out the gas station of its porn collection, we drove in a three-car convoy for two hours into the middle of nowhere. The muddy rig road snaked through the flat swampy scrub landscape. Every now and then Stan's voice came over the two-way radio from one of the other 4WDs: 'Oi Kiwis, you know what this is? Mud.'

Turned out, the mud escapade was the best first impression we could have made. On our first day everyone knew about the long-haired Kiwis who slept in their car and got stuck in the mud. The movie *Brokeback Mountain* about the two gay cowboys had just come out and we were nicknamed the 'Brokeback boys'.

The work was hard. The rig operated around the clock with a twelve-hour day shift followed by a twelve-hour night shift, seven till seven. We worked for an underbalanced drilling company which, without getting technical, is a drilling company that uses surface control equipment to flow the well, and is generally called in when the rig is losing fluid to the formation with traditional overbalance drilling. Umm, maybe a bit technical . . .

My nightshift crew consisted of Mac my senior, and Tyron my operator. Mac was a likable team player who chewed tobacco and even had black rotted stumps where his front teeth used to be. Mac, who was in his late forties, was a typical male in the sense that he could only do one thing at a time. Whenever I asked him a question while he was doing something, he would say, 'I can't fucking chew gum and walk, OK?'

Tyron, a guy in his early thirties, was a squeaky-voiced

steroid-taking oil field worker, and had been since he was sixteen. I liked him; he was patient with me and answered all my questions while Mac was focused on doing up his shoelaces.

Little did I know at this point that Mac was the most paranoid guy I was ever going to meet on my working-the-world quest. He was so highly strung that Stan, our sleepy grizzly bear, was the only supervisor out of seventeen in the company who could work with him. Mac was so paranoid he told me that it took him three years before he could sit in front of the computer screen without wearing safety glasses.

Looking back, Mac wasn't the best the guy to have as my first shift boss. Especially as my junior position meant I was in charge of the 'bomb'. After spending the first three days setting up and hauling pipe through the mud and heat, which come winter would be snow and -40 degrees Celsius, Mac ran me through my job as bomb man.

His introduction to my lesson went like this: 'Hap, you're in charge of the bomb, and I'm not fucking kidding when I call it a bomb.' This was followed by a lot of 'Don't fucking touch that', 'If that goes beep you're fucked', 'If you open that lever, then first make sure that one is closed, if not you're fucked'. From what Mac told me, I could tell I was going to be pretty fucked.

The idea behind the bomb was to separate out the gas from all the stuff that came roaring to the surface when the rig drilled down. At the surface this mixture made its way through pipes to the bomb, which was a massive capsule-shaped vessel housed in a 12-metre sea container. Once in the bomb, the fluid and sediment were separated from the gas and the gas was then piped through to an 18-metre-high pipe called the flare stack which erupted into a constant massive flame, resembling a gigantic candle.

I was in charge of the labyrinth of pipes and levers that came out of the bomb. I had to keep an eye on the level of fluid in the bomb and drain it when it reached a certain volume. I was also in charge of the bomb's gas output which fuelled the flame coming out of the flare stack. By leaning my entire body weight into a 1.5-metre-long lever, I could vary the gas output and therefore the size of the flame. If I shut all the levers off, then the high-pressure gas coming from deep within Mother Earth would pressurise the 12-metre bomb, making it very hard for you to take it through airport security. Mac forgot to mention to me that there was a plethora of alarms at his control panel to give prior warning of this happening.

You can imagine my first 'swing', which is what a continuous series of mining shifts were called, looking after the bomb; I felt like a priest in a whorehouse. I was excited and nervous. I had absolutely no clue what I was doing but loving every moment of it as the flame from the flare stack lit up Canada's northern skies.

My thoughts were cut short by the static of the radio. 'Oi sheep shagger, you figured out what mud is yet?'

I knew I was going to love this job.

## To run or die?

It was during this first swing that I thought I was going to die. It was about 5 a.m., and I was cleaning the bomb for Barney, who was coming in at 6.45 to take over from me. Mac was up in the control room looking over the gauges that monitored the surface control equipment. The control room was located on top of the container in which the bomb was housed.

As I was hosing out the floor, the deafening roar of gas rumbled down the tree-trunk-sized pipes, on its way to the flare stack. This rumbling was a constant reminder of how much pressure I was dealing with. I was just starting to think about crawling into bed, an actual horizontal bed with white sheets that didn't have a steering wheel over it, when all of a sudden gas started hissing out from where a gasket must have burst. The alarm that Mac told me signified hydrogen sulphide ($H_2S$) gas started wailing. From the compulsory $H_2S$ course Barney and I had completed, I knew the dangers. Hydrogen sulphide is a deadly odourless gas that will drop you without you knowing it. The classic scenario is that a person inhales the gas and hits the ground. Then someone will run to their aid and they too will drop dead, and this continues until the next person realises there's a deadly gas that needs to be contained.

So with my training and the tell-tale signs of gas hissing out like water from a burst fire hydrant coupled with the $H_2S$ alarm wailing, I should have clicked and taken flight. But instead I just stood there like a possum in the headlights wondering which side of the road to run for.

Mac snapped me out of it as he charged into the bomb. 'Hap, get me some fucking wrenches.'

All of a sudden I leapt into action like I had just been jabbed with a cattle prod. I took off slipping and sliding across the mud as though my life depended on it, which I thought it did. If the $H_2S$ didn't get us then I thought for some reason it was going to blow.

Like a frantic burglar, I threw tools everywhere trying to find the wrenches. I got an assortment and sprinted back across the mud and into the bomb with the piercing sound of the alarm still wailing. I thrust the wrenches into Mac's outstretched hand where he was precariously perched 2 metres in the air, wrapped around the pipe like a monkey. I breathed a sigh of relief as he tightened the join and the gas stopped leaking.

I was alive. Then I started to think. There had been gas in the confined area, the $H_2S$ alarm had gone off, so why was I still alive?

I put my question to Mac: 'Mac, why did you come running in here like that when the $H_2S$ alarm was going off? Aren't you meant to put on the breathing apparatus and assess the scene?'

Mac replied, 'Hap, I'm fucking trying to get down from here. I can't chew gum and walk.'

Tyron's steroid-ridden bulk appeared at my side and he answered my question while Mac focused all his attention on getting down from the pipe. 'Oh no, Hap, this well ain't sour, which means it doesn't contain $H_2S$. That alarm picks up other gases as well, we just call it the $H_2S$ alarm.'

'Shit, thanks for telling me.'

With Mac firmly on the ground and able to concentrate on something else, he now reprimanded me. 'Hap, I'm going to have to report you to the safety officer for running. You shouldn't have run to get those wrenches. Running on site is a safety hazard!'

## Life as a rig pig

Straight away I fell in love with work on the rigs. There was nothing PC about working there; a spade was a *fucking* spade. If you didn't work hard your crew would make your life a misery until you quit, although that has probably changed these days with stricter workplace laws. Probably.

The work was physical, with crap conditions—mud and flies in summer, snow and freezing temperatures of below -40 degrees Celsius in winter. It was just you and your crew out in the middle of nowhere. I loved the camaraderie.

As well as the work I also loved the lifestyle. Considering I was used to living in a car with Barney, it was like a holiday camp. Barney and I shared a room at the camp, but were never there together as he did the day shift and I did the night shift. We had a horizontal bed each, clean sheets, a shower, three meals of as much food as we could eat a day, house cleaning, TV, and I was paid the most I had ever been paid. To me it was like Club Med in the mud. A mobile camp that housed about 40 workers, located in a muddy clearing among pine forest and surrounded by an electric fence to keep the bears out.

Before taking on the job I was constantly warned about the

rig pigs, the name for guys who work the rigs and behave like stereotypical mongrels. But I found the majority to be great guys, and the actual rig pigs were rather entertaining, although a few characters worked hard at keeping the reputation of the rig pig alive, and still are if they haven't yet been fired.

To give you an idea of what a rig pig is like I'll tell you about the crew on my second swing, a swing I won't forget in a hurry. The crew was completely different from my first swing. Named in order of hierarchy, the supervisor was the polar opposite of Stan; he was a sex-obsessed loose cannon. My senior was a pothead from Newfoundland (the east coast island province where the men are true working-class men), and my operator was another tattooed steroid monkey who wore his hard hat backwards.

Long before meeting my supervisor, I had heard of his reputation. The first time I met him was when he called a meeting. I was waiting with the rest of crew for him to arrive when all of a sudden an arm went around my shoulders and the supervisor I hadn't met purred into my ear, 'I won't tell anyone you have splinters up your arse, just as long as you don't tell them I have a wooden cock.' He slapped me on the back, roared with laughter and then opened the meeting by recounting every sordid detail of his sexual escapades whilst on his R&R. But I will spare you the details.

My senior on this swing, the young Newfoundland guy, or 'Newfie' as they are called, came to work the rigs after the fishing industry in Newfoundland had hit tough times. He loved his pot, which he talked about with much affection. But it was with great disappointment that he would refrain from smoking at work, probably due to the sniffer dogs smelling our luggage before boarding the private charter planes, as the rig camps were mandated drug and alcohol free. So with no pot at work he poured his energy into his other passion, which was rally driving. As you can imagine, with a bunch of males stuck out in the middle of nowhere there was a lot of testosterone floating around, so we harnessed this into creating competitions to pass the time.

One competition we had was to see which crew could get the fastest drive time from the rig back to the camp that was located 20 kilometres away down rough, muddy rig roads. My Newfie supervisor was in his element and we ended up keeping our hardhats on for the drive home. We were glad of those hardhats when he managed to get us airborne over the numerous bumps of the road. I'm happy to say I survived, and my supervisor would be happy to say that he had the record for the fastest time. Now I could understand why there were three written-off pickup trucks in our work yard back in Red Deer.

I had been there in the workshop when the third write-off for the year arrived. The company's safety officer came storming into the smoko room, where ten of us were having yet another long lunch, and shouted at us in frustration, 'I've been up to the rigs a bunch of times and never seen a fucking moose, but every FUCKING incident form for these three write-offs says the cause of the accident was swerving for a FUCKING moose.'

As I mentioned, the rig camps were mandated drug and alcohol free, but on this swing my supervisor had somehow managed to get a little stash of pot past the sniffer dogs and airport bag check. After one particular hard shift, where we had been worked to the bone, my Newfie senior wanted to show his gratitude to the operator and me. His appreciation was so great that he offered us a smoke of his limited pot. Trust me, this was the highest form of appreciation for this guy, that pot he smuggled up was more valuable to him than gold. In the name of team bonding and good will, I joined him and my operator against my better judgement, knowing full well that random drug tests took place. When in Rome, right?

After a good night's sleep the following day started well. But it didn't last long. Our tattooed operator had rigged up a hose to

## Homeless Pig

transfer diesel from one tank to another. The rig's motorhand, the guy who drives the machinery, ran over the hose in a front-end loader, causing it to break at a join. The break was not spotted until 800 litres of diesel had leaked!

The shit hit the fan, everyone ducking the blame. Our operator and the motorhand were pointing fingers at each other. The first golden rule you learn when filling something up is that you stay and watch it until it's full, no excuses.

A spill of this magnitude would mean an excavator would have to be called in to dig up the contaminated dirt and then transport it away to be disposed of. Considering our location, the cost would be huge. The other thing this meant was a visit from the safety officer who would have to fly out to drug test us all. As you can imagine, this put my whole crew in a tailspin, including me. I was now cursing my mid-twenties-male short-sightedness, the attitude of *she'll be right*. My Newfie senior called me up to the control room and told me to bring some Spray Nine in a cup. Spray Nine was legendary stuff that could clean anything; it even said on the bottle that it got rid of herpes and HIV.

My senior told me of a previous occasion when he had to be drug tested. He had gargled Spray Nine and passed the test which was done by a mouth swab. This was great news to me as I loved this job and had great opportunities ahead of me. Plus when I wasn't working on the rigs I was still sleeping in the car; I needed this job.

Straight away I went to the Spray Nine bottle and poured myself a glass and started to gargle the afternoon away. After gargling half the bottle over the afternoon, I started to feel a little sick and got super paranoid that I had ingested this killer-strength cleaning liquid and that it was eroding my stomach. Then I threw up, and started stressing that my drug test would show that I had a Spray Nine addiction!

After throwing up, I walked back into the bomb room and

was met by my senior who asked if I was feeling okay. I told him how I had been gargling Spray Nine all afternoon.

He just laughed that hearty Newfie laugh and said, 'Oh Haaap, you dumb fook, you only gargle it just before the test. And that shit you're gargling is concentrate—you're meant to dilute that with water! Oh and by the way I came to tell you that the safety officer can't get a flight so he won't be coming up.'

The other tool to complete my crew toolbox was the operator. He was a guy who was all about the image. He did steroids and openly talked about them as being the best thing since sliced bread. It was the first time I had ever come across the use of steroids, and I was quite surprised how many of the young guys used them on the rigs.

After our swing, I went out and partied with him back in Red Deer. As usual we went to the local strip club. It didn't matter who I went out with during my time in Red Deer, whether it was girls or guys, we always started drinking at the strip club because it had the cheapest drinks. The gyrating ladies were an added bonus.

My operator was talking to the skimpily clad waitress about hooking him up with her eighteen-year-old friend who worked at the bar, but was not on this shift. The waitress rang her friend and told her that my operator was keen on her. What surprised me was that she didn't even mention anything about him, she simply said that he earned good money on the rigs and had just bought a sweet new truck. I wondered how I was going to go with the ladies in Red Deer. 'Oh yeah, Hap's real cool, he sleeps in his car with his long-haired friend. He'll probably take you out to dinner at the local soup kitchen . . . they have chocolate cake on Sunday.'

The operator was always talking about fighting and couldn't believe I had never been in a fight. One day in the showers I nearly saw him in action; fighting, that is. I tell people the following yarn if they want to know about rig-pig culture.

I was back at camp after a shift, washing my hands in the basin opposite the showers that were all currently being used. As my operator walked in, one of the showers became available. The rig worker who was vacating the shower looked a bit flustered that the operator was going to enter his shower cubicle.

He stopped him, and said, 'Sorry, I didn't realise someone was going to come in straight away. Ahhhhhh, don't touch the tap.' Then he hurriedly exited the bathroom.

My operator gingerly opened the shower door. He then went red with rage and let out a barrage of obscenities. I poked my head in for a look and there, dripping from the shower tap, was a disgusting load of what looked like white creamy shower gel, but was obviously not!

## Viva Las Vegas

Life was great on the rigs. I remember Barney and I eating out one night—in an actual restaurant—and doing a cheers to never working a $10-an-hour job again. After our two months of sleeping in the car, a fellow workmate let me and Barney rent out their basement room where we slept on a couple of inflatable mattresses.

About a month later, Barney and I had reached snapping point with each other. We were like a married couple, but without the benefit of sex. For nearly two years we had slept in the same room or car together, worked together, eaten together, drank together and travelled together. We were best mates and always will be. But even best mates need their personal space. We decided that Barney would stay in the basement room and I would rent a mate's room in Sylvan Lake, about 40 minutes out of Red Deer. It was the first time in two years that Barney and I had had our own rooms, a space to call our own.

On our time off, Barney and I continued to roadtrip through British Columbia and Alberta, and made one massive journey from the easternmost point of Canada in Newfoundland to the westernmost point of Vancouver Island. We loved it!

Our company had decided to sponsor our work visas to keep us on. We had also come to an agreement where we would work the busy four to five winter months and then take the rest of the year off. This would allow me to travel and do volunteer work in other continents—perfect.

Well, not quite perfect. After nearly six months of working the rigs, I arrived at the Red Deer workshop on a Monday morning and opened up a letter from Canadian immigration. The opening lines read, *This refers to your application for a work permit. Your application as requested is refused.* I stood dumbfounded in the concrete changing room surrounded by grey metal lockers and the smell of stale urine. I couldn't believe it. I had to cease work immediately and leave Canada within two weeks. Boom! How things change.

The frustrating part was the reason for the refusal. My visa application, which I had completed and sent away, lacked a work confirmation number from my employer, which they were in charge of applying for. Since Barney and I were in the same situation, the company's HR manager had sent away our applications for a work confirmation number together. But as the cover form only had room for one name, she had written Barney's. So even though mine was attached, immigration missed it and therefore my work visa was denied. And yep, Barney was sweet; his visa application was now in the queue to be processed.

When I rang up immigration and found out what had happened, I thought it could be easily fixed. They would just put my work confirmation number with my visa application which would be put in the queue with Barney's. But no, every single customer service person I talked to just told me, 'That's a very unfortunate situation, sir.' I was in the system as having my work visa refused, and would have to start the process all over again, which to this point had taken three months. In the words of my sex-obsessed supervisor, 'Your cock-up, my arse!'

I felt angry and helpless. I had done everything right; I had crossed my t's and dotted my i's, and had friends double check that I had crossed my t's and dotted my i's. But here I was being punished for someone else's cock-up.

Since I couldn't work, and the thought of staying in a -40 degree Alberta winter waiting for my work visa to come through sounded as appealing as locking myself in a freezer, I decided to get the cheapest flight out of Canada before my couple of weeks was up and I was put into the immigration system as an overstayer.

A week later I was heading down the highway for the Calgary car auction yard with trucks and cars buzzing past me. The reason why everyone was overtaking me was because our car was only running on four out of its six cylinders and would cut out if I went over 50 kilometres an hour. As well as only running on four cylinders, three of the tyres had slow leaks and the engine leaked more oil than the MV *Exxon Valdez*. I dropped it off at the yard, where it had to sit for a month until the next auction, after which time it would have three flat tyres, be unable to start and be surrounded by a lake of oil. We were stoked when we got $125 for it. My share was $62.50. This marked the death of our third Canadian car in fifteen months.

With the car buried, my new visa application sent away, three months' advance rent on my room paid and my flag-covered backpack full of boardies and singlets over my shoulder, I caught a bus to the airport. I was off to where the weather would be warmer.

## Chapter 7
# THE WAITING GAME
**NORTH AMERICA: Mexico, 21 November 2006–13 April 2007**

It was in Tulum, a small, laid-back town with golden-sand beaches known for its Mayan ruins set in idyllic surrounds on the Mexican coast, that I met Sam. Sam was a 27-year-old Englishman with high standards, specifically high bathroom standards. He was appalled at the Mexican style of toilet which had no seat, and the thought of not wearing jandals in the communal showers sent him into panic attacks. Sam's hands wouldn't stop shaking until he had his morning cigarette and pint. In the real world back in London, England, he was a BMW salesman by day and a house DJ and party boy by night. He was backpacking with his soon-to-be-married best mates from Australia.

I joined the good-times-focused threesome and we made our way through southern Mexico's backpacking haunts, including

## The Waiting Game

five hazy and amazing monsoon-drenched days in a little tin-shed bar in the middle of the Palenque jungle. I was meant to be leaving the jungle party community to go on my own independent travels, catching the 5 a.m. bus the next morning. Unfortunately I decided to stay up all night with the threesome and drink myself awake. However, I fell asleep only to wake at 6 a.m., my alarm clock lying in a smashed heap at the bottom of the wall.

So I carried on with the good-time gang and we made our way by boat to Guatemala. This is where Sam and I became a duo as the soon-to-be-married couple left to start married life in Australia. We went onwards through Guatemala and then up through Mexico, arriving a month later in Sayulita, located halfway up the Pacific coast of Mexico close to Puerto Vallarta, just before Christmas.

Sayulita was a small over-priced surf town, where there seemed to be more foreigners than Mexicans. Half the population was North American families escaping winter, and the other half a mix of surfies and hippies. The waitresses would ask for your order in perfect English and the local Mexican surfers wore backwards gangster caps and scowled at the gringos and sleazed on the gringas.

Luckily Sam and I were saved. We found love. Sam met Penny, a free-spirited Canadian living in Sayulita and I met Mandy at the local bar. She was a lively American beauty with a Colgate smile who was in Sayulita for the Christmas break with her friend, sister, brother-in-law and nephews. Sam and I spent the majority of our time with Mandy's family. After a week, Mandy left with her friend to spend a prearranged New Year's in Guadalajara. With Mandy gone, Sam and I celebrated New Year's in Puerto Vallarta.

The end of my Mexican trip was fast approaching; with a flight out of LA back to Canada booked for 7 January, I had to get a move on. The next morning I left Sam after six weeks of memorable backpacking good times. He was going to stay in Sayulita with Penny; they were talking of buying property there. As destiny would have it I ended up in Guadalajara where I spent one last night with Mandy before she flew back to Denver, Colorado, the next day.

I had got an email that my Kiwi friend Lucy was coming to Guadalajara. So Mandy had left that morning and Lucy arrived that evening. Even though Lucy was like a sister to me, the hostel staff must have thought I was some kind of nomadic playboy.

One day while sitting in the sun at a park with Lucy, I reconsidered my plans. The thought of spending 50 hours on a cheap, second-class bus with no air-conditioning all the way to LA to catch a flight back to well-below-freezing temperatures in Alberta seemed pointless. I still hadn't heard if my Canadian work visa had been approved. I thought, Stuff it. It made more sense to be broke and warm in Mexico, living off $10 a day in a tent on the beach and learning to surf. Lucy had no plans and was up for a mission, so we headed to the coast with my inherited tent which I'd got from some guys I had met in Sayulita.

After changing buses four times through the night, we finally got on a small local bus that dropped us on the side of the road, 20 minutes from our destination. The friendly bus driver pointed to an inconspicuous cobblestone road and said, 'Nextpa.' As we hauled on our packs the sun had just started to rise over the crashing waves of the Pacific. We walked down into the village of 50 people, renowned for its left-hand point break.

It was love at first sight with our new home: we had an isolated camp spot at the end of the beach consisting of a palapa (a stick structure with a palm roof), two hammocks and a plastic table and chairs. All for $1.50 each a night. It was just what the doctor ordered. After six weeks of bodily and credit card abuse with Sam, I couldn't think of a better place in the world to wait for my Canadian visa to be processed.

A couple of days later, I hitchhiked 20 minutes up the road through army checkpoints—there had been shootings between the army and the drug cartels the previous month. I wanted to check my emails because I had been keeping in contact with Mandy the American beauty. Barney was on Messenger at the time and we started chatting. I asked him about the work visa and there was a pause. He typed something along the lines of:

> *Bro, not good news. It's really slow at work this season, big down turn. It's too much hassle for them to sponsor us now, especially when there are so many local long-term guys needing work. They aren't going to sponsor our visas. I'm heading back to New Zealand. Sorry to tell you like this, bro. Been awesome travelling with ya, I suppose this is goodbye.*

## So that was that

It was a funny feeling. Working the rigs had been the perfect job: a job I loved to do, which paid great money and would allow me to work part of the year and travel the remainder. I had all my belongings and a room waiting for my return. And now with one Messenger conversation with my two-year working-the-world best mate, I found out that I had no job, no money, and was stuck in Mexico.

However, it felt bloody fantastic! Once again I felt free: no plans, nothing holding me down, anything was possible. I would see sailing boats in the bay and think, *If they need an extra crew member to sail down to Argentina, I can do it. I'm free.*

The wonderful feeling of an uncertain future and endless possibilities filled the short-lived void of my visa disappointment.

Lucy and I hired surfboards and Nextpa became our home for a couple of weeks. As it wasn't the surf season only a few chilled-out surfers were staying along the beach in rustic cabanas. We had no electricity, no fridge, no shower, no flush toilet, no bed, just great people in this little paradise.

During our weeks in Nextpa I learnt to surf, the friendly

surfers giving me pointers as I sat out back waiting for sets to come. On my last night there, I rode my last wave in to shore with the sun setting over the Pacific behind me. I couldn't think of a better send-off.

Lucy and I hitched and bussed our way further down the Pacific coast, stopping off in Zihuatenejo and Puerto Escondido. In Puerto, I forked out $70 from my last $150 and bought a surfboard. Well, actually it was two surfboards. It was the nose of one and a tail from another that had been put together after being smashed by the notorious Puerto Escondido waves.

Then it was time for Lucy and me to take different paths. Lucy was headed back north and I had a new chapter waiting for me in the south of Mexico.

After leaving Lucy, I spent a further couple of weeks stopping off in small surf spots along the coast. Life was just one big adventure.

At this point I was looking like a bedraggled hippy. I hadn't shaved for five weeks, hadn't showered for seven, as I had been in the ocean most days. I hadn't washed any clothes for five weeks, and my once-Italian-porn-star curly locks were a matted mess. I now just slept on the beach in the dirt-smeared duvet that I used to wrap my surfboard in for transporting. Setting up the tent seemed unnecessary. Somewhere along the way someone had taken my jandals while I slept, so I had no shoes. I must have been a sight standing barefoot on the side of the road with my duvet-wrapped surfboard and my thumb out.

The hippy was really starting to come out in me. I had taken to wandering naked on isolated beaches. Before I started hugging trees, becoming attracted to woman with hairy armpits, and taking part in free-love group orgies, I was rescued. Andy, an Australian guy who I had met through my Aussie mates from Banff, picked me up in a van and drove me eight hours south to the Guatemalan border where I would start my next chapter of working the world.

## Chapter 8
# HOPE AND HUGS

**NORTH AMERICA: Tapachula, Chiapas, Mexico,
10 February–13 April 2007**

Aussie Andy drove a dark green van, which reminded me of the first vehicle Barney and I had bought back in Vancouver. We flew down the plastic-bag-littered highway, hitting the brakes every now and then to avoid bellying out on unmarked speed bumps at 100 kilometres an hour.

Our destination was Tapachula, a border town of 200,000 people, the gateway to Guatemala. A place my guidebook described thus: *If you don't have to change bus here on your way to Guatemala, don't bother getting off. It's hot, humid, dirty and there's nothing to see.* Well, as sad as that sounds, it sums up Tapachula perfectly, and it was just what I was looking for. After two and half fun-filled months of backpacking, sleeping on the beach and surfing the gringo trail I was ready to get myself a real bed.

A month earlier, the Aussie mates from Banff had told me

about an orphanage run by an Australian couple. They were always looking for volunteers so I had got in touch with them. They told me that Andy would be in Puerto Escondido getting some surfboards fixed and could pick me up on his way back down the coast.

Tapachula was like any Mexican border town. It was rough, poverty was everywhere, and it seemed that everyone was trying to scrape by to survive. It was a festering settling pond for all the Central American immigrants making the pilgrimage north to get their share of the American dream, which in reality was working illegally at a backbreaking below-minimum-wage job. The town oozed with sleazy seediness and lawlessness. You could feel the criminal underbelly rumble as you walked the streets at night. In fact you didn't even have to be walking at night to feel it.

The orphanage had had a visit from an American expert investigating the child sex industry, who had come down from the northern border towns between Mexico and the US to see how bad it really was in the surrounding areas of Tapachula, namely Ciudad Hidalgo, Mexico and Tecún-Umán, a short drive from the city, just across the border in Guatamala. The expert said that this location made Tijuana look like Disneyland.

Tapachula is a rough place, and even rougher if you were born into life on the streets. I can only imagine it being near impossible to find hope in the cardboard box that you call home after a day of shining shoes and eating from rubbish bins.

But the orphanage provided hope for the 30 kids who called it home when I was there, with this number rising to over 50 with the ebb and flow of the homeless. These were kids who had been found wandering the streets, all mixed bags of abuse, physical, mental and sexual. Kids whose reality was most people's idea of a nightmare.

At the orphanage, the kids were given this little thing called hope to hold onto and these other things called opportunities. Things that as a kid I had taken for granted.

## Hope and Hugs

### 'Skuse me please

There are so many stories I could share with you about the amazing people I met at the orphanage, people who were just interested in playing soccer, dancing to music, dressing up in a pretty donated dress, playing with insects found crawling in the drain and eating unripe mangoes from the tree. These were the stories of the little souls that called the concrete structure, the orphanage, home.

But first I want to tell the story of Pam and Alan Skuse, Mum and Dad as the orphans called them. Pam and Alan were a couple in their late forties or early fifties from Queensland, Australia, who had gone to Tapachula in 2000 with their daughter to volunteer for twelve months. Halfway through their intended stay, the organisation they were working for shut down. The seven kids that Pam and Alan had in their care would have been given back to the welfare department, and they would probably have just run away and ended up back on the streets.

Pam and Alan made a decision that would change their lives forever, and not just change it but send it into an out-of-control tailspin. They decided to stay, and give these kids a real family life, to give them a chance.

I can't even comprehend the sacrifice they made. They had five grown children back in Australia who would be starting families of their own in the near future. They had retirement to look forward to as a reward for working hard all their lives. Now they were going to start a family with seven abandoned, neglected street kids in a sweltering dirty city in southern Mexico where they didn't speak the language.

It didn't stay a family of seven kids for long. Welfare would turn up with another child and Pam and Alan couldn't say no. Numbers swelled, and if they were lucky they would get some basic food supplies every now and then from the government. They had to survive off their savings and donations from Australia.

## HAP WORKING THE WORLD

If you have visions of a utopian setting with little kids in freshly ironed clothes, singing songs and picking daisies, holding hands and laughing, then think again. Yes, there were times like this, but you have to remember that these kids came from the streets. They had no discipline; they didn't know what love was. The orphanage was not a grassy oasis at the end of the rainbow, but a concrete building with bars on the windows, no running water or flush toilets or air-conditioning, and no grass to play on, just a small concrete courtyard that had tattered rope stretched across it to hang the piles of washing.

The thing that blew me away was that Pam and Alan lived this life 24/7. Their room, if you could call it that, was a windowless concrete space that barely fitted a double bed. It was sectioned off by a stained curtain from the 30 kids who woke all through the night from nightmares about their pasts, and from wetting their beds. I would presume that a good night's sleep was a thing of the past for Pam and Alan as they always had kids crawling into their bed. I do not know how they did it, though I'm sure they cried a lot, and doubted what they were doing at times. I can say to you that I could not do what they were doing. What was the future for them? They had 30 kids who called them Mum and Dad, the youngest being three years old, plus they constantly had new kids coming in. Theirs was the most inspiring act of selflessness I have ever come across.

People tell me how amazing it was of me to volunteer at the orphanage. If you want to know what amazing is, it is Pam and Alan.

For me the orphanage was also a saviour. As well as getting a satisfying feeling from helping the kids, I could get fed and have a bed to sleep in. These kids put my situation into perspective. Yes, I did turn up in Tapachula barefoot, unwashed, in debt, with all my belongings still in Canada, but at the end of the day, I had a choice; they didn't.

One day while melting in the oppressive caged-in heat of

the orphanage, with a kid asleep on my lap, I saw a little ripped piece of paper stuck to the cracked wall. In the scrawled message lay a quote that summed all this up for me:

> *There is more to be learned in one day of discomfort, poverty, and anxiety than in a lifetime of apparent happiness, security, riches and power.*

## Orphanage life

From the first moment I walked barefoot into the orphanage, it was chaos. Visions of smiling, obedient kids were lost in the whirlwind of dirty toilets and dishes, shouting, hugs, punches, piles of laundry, smiles, crying and 30 kids vying for your love and attention.

To give you an idea of the chaos, I will introduce you to Mother Teresa. I called her Mother Teresa as she wore a postcard-sized crucifix around her neck and had straight shoulder-length grey hair. After I had been there a while she arrived for a six-month stint which she had organised with Pam, but neither of them had realised that Pam was going to be in Australia.

When she arrived she was full of enthusiasm and had had a lot of experience with troubled kids, having brought up foster children her whole life. She was softly spoken with the calm aura that highly religious people seem to have. She lasted not even two weeks.

The main reason she left was the chaos. Any family is a challenge, but a family that consists of 30 kids from abusive, dysfunctional backgrounds and who had lived on the streets was a particular kind of challenge. That type of set-up is going to be hectic at the best of times. But while I was there, it was chaos on steroids. Pam had left several days prior to my arrival, taking three of the older kids to Australia for a three-month scholarship. Pam ran the house and enforced rules and the three older kids with her also played an integral role in the day-to-day running of the orphanage, as the younger kids looked up to and respected them. The older kids organised the younger ones to do dishes, put away clothes, get to bed, sort out fights, sweep, wash, change nappies, do homework and so on. Without those four there to keep the discipline and order, there was mayhem even as some of the younger kids tried to fill the roles left behind.

You can imagine an eight-year-old girl trying to pull a full bucket of water up from the well using a rope, then trying to carry it 20 metres through the orphanage to the girl's shower area. Then try to imagine a dirty teenager's room and multiply that by fifteen. Add to that little three-year-old Ali throwing tantrums and screaming, keeping all the other girls awake. Factor in the heat and the humidity, and you start to get the picture.

I tried to get the older kids to step up and set examples, writing up rosters, giving them incentives to try to gain some structure. Some days I would leave feeling as though I had made a difference, only to come in the next morning to find that a Mexican version of the Tasmanian Devil had been let loose during the night.

The orphanage was going to be one of my most challenging and hardest jobs, but my most humbling and rewarding. Although I didn't get a pay cheque, I was compensated in the best currency: innocent smiles and warm hugs.

## Subsidising orphanage life

I would have lived and breathed orphanage life seven days a week. But I had to subsidise my volunteering, as I needed some pocket money for everyday necessities. Like an ex-convict getting out of jail, you fall back into what you know. But instead of dealing drugs, I dealt grammar and punctuation. I turned to the standard for an English-speaking foreigner in a foreign

## Hope and Hugs

country—teaching English. Even though I don't really enjoy teaching English, it pays a decent wage compared to local wages no matter where you are in the world.

I hung up posters at the local university and put the word out that an experienced English teacher was in town. To think only the year before I was a rig pig in the northern British Columbia gas fields, hauling pipe in the mud! What was more comical was the toast Barney and I had made to never having to work a minimum wage job again. At this point the Canadian minimum wage seemed like a fairytale of riches and treasures.

I ended up teaching an air traffic controller for her upcoming exam. On Wednesday and Saturday mornings she would pick me up at 6 a.m. and I would Alpha, Bravo, Charlie it up as we sat in the control tower watching the sun rise against the backdrop of the towering volcano Tacaná, on the Guatemalan border. This was always a time that made me stop and think where I was and really take in what I was doing. I was volunteering at an orphanage and teaching English to a Mexican mother of four in an air traffic control tower near the Guatemalan border.

### $100 Guatemalan escape

With all this work I required a little getaway to recharge the batteries, and to make the most of my time in the area. When I had travelled through Mexico with Sam we had ducked down into Guatemala for a couple of weeks. The one place that we kept hearing about from other backpackers but hadn't got to was called Semuc Champey. It was a little highland town, out of the way, in a lush Guatemalan valley. The attraction for me was not only the crystal clear rock pools and caving, but also a hostel that at the time had gained legendary status from fellow backpackers.

The most I could afford for the trip was US$100, therefore my main focus was to do everything as cheaply as possible and make the money go as far as I could while having a little adventure.

It started off well. I was able to sneak across the border into Guatemala, dodging immigration and therefore avoiding handing over my Mexican tourist card, US$24, and paying the Guatemalan entry fee of US$12.

Once in Guatemala, my plan was to catch all local buses. These consisted of the usual developing-world classics such as overloaded mini-vans, known as *collectivos* or 'chicken buses', and dilapidated American school buses which had been given a paint job and usually had across the top of the windscreen a quirky message saying something about God or an English football team. I could have got the air-conditioned first-class bus for double the price, but the name of this little adventure was thrifty. The other reason I took the local transport was for all those experiences and interactions that I could have. Experiences of being crammed into a fourteen-seater van which has 30 people in it; hitching a ride on the back of a pickup with the smiling locals, breathing in exhaust fumes and seeing the road below through a rusted hole in the floor; answering in Spanish the questions from the elderly man sitting beside me about the faraway world that I came from; sharing food with the large colourful motherly lady squashed in on my other side; having the other *collectivo* passengers looking out for me and guiding me as to when and where to get off and wait for the next bus.

The downside to doing it the cheap local way is the time-consuming part of waiting around and changing buses. That day I spent a total of sixteen hours in transit and still hadn't arrived at my destination, which I would have had I taken the other bus. I arrived at Cobán, a busy little market town of around 20,000 that was the interchange to get to Semuc Champey, still a couple of hours away. When I arrived it wasn't bustling; it was 11 p.m. and raining. Wearing my $1.70 jandals, shorts and singlet, feeling tired, and shivering due to the crisp mountain air, I walked the streets feeling a little apprehensive as you do on dark, wet, deserted streets late at night in a foreign place.

## Hope and Hugs

The first hotel I came across, with peeling paint and a general feel of neglect, looked like it was in my budget. I went and booked a room without even inspecting it. I had my mind on a hot shower, not only because I was cold but also because I hadn't had one for over four months, just ocean bathing while surfing and buckets of cold water at the orphanage. I should have known, of course, that there was no hot water. The room I walked into was the worst I had stayed in during my working-the-world quest—at least the car had been warm.

The shower was tucked into the corner with only a tattered shower curtain separating it from the room, but not helping to isolate the foul stench of mouldy body hair filling the room, emanating from the plughole. The flaking pale green paint gave off an atmosphere of a civil war hospital in the developing world. Chewing gum was stuck to the wall and tissues were stuck in the door to plug up peepholes. The bed was made but the sheets clearly hadn't been changed as I spotted hair and miscellaneous dried-up crumbs of dead skin. A drab sheet was nailed into the wall, covering the window that looked onto a concrete storage space. Of course there were cockroaches as well, but I was used to these from life in Tapachula. On the bright side, at least the cold mountain air kept away the mosquitoes.

As I opened up my small daypack I cursed myself for being so foolish and bringing only one T-shirt and two pairs of boxers. While packing back in the sweltering heat and humidity of Tapachula I had overlooked that I was going into the mountains. I couldn't face a cold shower. I put on the T-shirt and wrapped a pair of boxers around each foot to try to get warm. I then walked into the hallway and turned off the light as there was no light switch in the room. I climbed under the paper-thin top sheet, hugging it for all it was worth. I thought back to a statistic that I had heard on the radio while working in Ohio. Tests had shown that hotel bed covers are the dirtiest items in hotel rooms, even dirtier than the toilet seat. Not worrying about this,

I curled up tighter into the foetal position and rested my head on the mattress as there was no pillow. The room next door was filled with giggling girls and when they finally called it a night, on cue a baby started crying.

The following morning I caught the first bus to Semuc Champey. The rain from the night before had given way to glorious sunshine as we wound our way through the hill roads, looking down into the lush green valleys below. Because of the effort of getting there, Semuc Champey exceeded my expectations, which was a relief as high expectations can easily ruin a destination.

As fate would have it the first person I bumped into was the very person who had told me about Semuc Champey while I was with Sam and his friends at the tin shack in the jungle of Palenque all those months ago. He was now living at the hostel and managing the restaurant.

The following day I did a caving trip, which had a very Guatemalan feel about it. Safety gear consisted of a candle for each person, which was fine but made it a tad more difficult while swimming through areas of the underground river that were too deep for walking. There was no abseiling equipment for climbing up the waterfalls and mini-cliffs, just a knotted rope and rickety old ladders made from tree branches, and the friendly guide telling you 'No problem.' The other part I loved was jumping from the cave wall to the rock pool 3 metres below. The guide would flick the beam of his torch on the dark water of the narrow rock pool and say to aim to miss the rocks—'No problem.'

Unfortunately the three nights spent eating at the communal hostel buffet and drinking beers with all the other like-minded travellers had eaten away at my $100. At 5.45 on a Sunday morning and I had to make it back to Tapachula as I had no more money to pay for accommodation. I hurriedly packed my small daypack and took off up the hill to catch the 6 a.m. *collectivo* back to Cobán.

## Hope and Hugs

Things did not start well. I asked a local lady where I should wait to catch the mini-van. She informed me that I had missed it and would have to wait for the 7 a.m. *collectivo*. As I headed back to the hostel to get another 30 minutes' sleep, I stopped to take a photo of the sunrise hitting the mist draped over the green mountains.

Just as I snapped the photo I heard a mini-van approaching the crest of the hill. I waved it down and it so happened to be the 6 a.m. *collectivo* that had supposedly left. I quickly put my camera in my pants pocket and jumped in. As we wound our way through the quiet gravel mountain roads I thought about how much I was loving life and looking forward to the challenge of getting back to Tapachula.

My content mood only lasted as far as Cobán. The driver pulled off to the side of the road, signalling the end of the line and everybody piled out. Then I had a sinking feeling as I got up and realised something was missing. There was no weight in my pocket. Where was my camera?

I remembered when I had got on the mini-van that I was going to tie it onto my loose-fitting cotton pants. I always did that to avoid this exact situation, of having my camera fall out while sitting. But in my rush to catch the *collectivo*, I had not done it. Once I was in there was no wriggle room for me to tie it on and I had eventually forgotten about it.

A passenger helped me scan the floor of the van but it was nowhere to be seen. The only thing that I could think had happened was that it had fallen out of my shallow pocket when I clambered into the *collectivo*. The driver then came over and pointed to one of the other passengers, a Guatemalan man in a worn grey suit but with an air of hill town class about him, and told me to follow him.

As I quickened my stride to catch him up I was cursing myself for being so careless. The man didn't say much and I got the feeling that he was in a rush to do whatever he had

131

come to Cobán to do. Up ahead I could see the entrance to a local bus station where *collectivos* and slightly bigger vans were congregating. I thought the man was taking me here so that I could get a bus back to Semuc Champey to retrieve my camera from the side of the road. I was tossing up whether to do the four-hour round trip in the hope that my camera was still on the roadside or to get on with my marathon mission back to Tapachula. As I was pondering this, we entered the double-gated entrance of the concrete and corrugated-iron bus station. The grey-suited man stopped, and pointed to one of the young guys in the crowd about 5 metres away and said, 'Camera.' Then he walked off.

I recognised the young guy as the one who had been squashed next to me on the van. As I walked towards him I felt awkward; I was adamant that the camera had fallen out of my pocket, but because the man had pointed to him I had to ask him about my camera. My Spanish wasn't quite up to the task.

The young guy was dressed in jeans and T-shirt and he wore a gold necklace. He recognised but didn't acknowledge me when I arrived by his side. Because I couldn't explain myself, I just asked in Spanish, 'Do you have my camera?' hoping that he would then show me to the bus going back to Semuc Champey. I felt like I was accusing him of stealing the camera, but that was all I could say. He looked offended and pissed off. He emptied one pocket, opened his hands then spat at me that he didn't have it. Even though I had basically just asked him if he had stolen my camera, I didn't like his attitude, which included trying to ignore me. At this stage I still thought the camera had fallen out of my pocket, but I had to ask one last question to ease my mind. I pointed to the sweatshirt that he had wrapped in a ball around his hand, which had come to my attention when he had spreadeagled his hands in the universal gesture of *I don't have it*. He just turned his back and walked away from the crowd who was paying us no attention. I followed him as he headed towards

## Hope and Hugs

the exit gate. I trailed a couple of metres behind, thinking of how to delicately rephrase my question when he started to walk faster. It was about now I started to have doubts about dropping the camera when he got outside the bus station and sprinted off down the street.

I thought, *Oh no, here we go.* Luckily I was only carrying a small, light daypack and took off after him in my $1.70 jandals. He turned onto a busy market street that was just coming alive as the day began. I felt like I was Jean-Claude Van Damme with my curly mess of shoulder-length hair bouncing behind me as we weaved between the obstacles of people and wooden crates. I wasn't gaining on him but he also wasn't getting away. He then darted down another street that had no traffic on it and bolted along the middle of the cobblestone road with houses and shops lining the raised footpath. Now I was able to make up some ground without having to dodge people.

I started shouting out 'Stop, Stop!' to gain the attention of the people on the footpaths as I caught up to the young guy. When I was 5 metres away from him he spun around and in one fluid movement unravelled his sweatshirt and threw me my camera. As I caught it he took off back up the street while I exhausted my Spanish expletives.

He did not get very far though. A bunch of locals looking like cowboys blocked his getaway and violently tackled him to the ground. They proceeded to kick him with their pointed boots. When I arrived at the scene the bandit's face was a bloody mess. I tried to stop the cowboys who now had the bandit cowering against the wall of a house. I had my camera, that was all that mattered to me. Plus I didn't want to get involved with the police. First, because in countries like Guatemala they are usually more hassle than help; second, I had entered illegally; and third, I still had ten to twelve hours of bus hopping to get back to Tapachula.

With all the commotion it didn't take long for a crowd to

form. As every local man found out what had happened he would go up and kick the bandit. I could tell they were ashamed of him giving them a bad name. For the record I had found the Guatemalans to be nothing but friendly and helpful. One man even ripped the gold chain from the bandit's bloodied neck and handed it to me, but I didn't want it. As I tried to leave a transit police car arrived and the officers said I had to wait for the normal police to arrive.

The bandit kept wearing kicks under the watchful eye of the transit police until the normal police finally arrived. They took the bloodied bandit, roughly pushed him into the twin-cab pickup truck and gestured for me to jump in the tray. As we took off down the street I looked back at the crowd, which was starting to dissipate back to their Sunday activities. I couldn't really comprehend what had just happened. A couple of hours ago I had been marvelling at mist surrounded mountains, now I was in the back of pickup headed for the police station.

We arrived at the small nondescript concrete police station which looked like all the other no-frills buildings on the street. The bandit was taken through to the back of the station while I was shown to a wooden chair in front of a bare desk at the entrance of the small front room. The officer right away asked for my passport. I tried to play dumb foreigner and pretend not to understand but you can only play dumb foreigner for so long when the Spanish for passport is *pasaporte*. Reluctantly I handed it over, thinking that I would be joining the bandit in the cell as I had no money to pay a spot fine for my illegal entry.

The officer turned to the front of my passport. He pulled out a scrap bit of blank A4 paper and started to write down my details. After writing this all down he asked me my mother's name. After I answered, he handed me back my passport without checking for my Guatemalan visa. Then he focused his detective work on my camera. He started to play with it like a baby does when holding an iPhone for the first time. Looking at the viewfinder,

Sanding wooden shutters in a factory on the Gold Coast, Australia, where the seed of my working-the-world idea was planted.

Getting to grips with the local cuisine in Korea.

Bucheon, South Korea. I could never understand why they put advertising signs over the windows.

The classroom in my house at the Malikov estate in Alicante, Spain. I could possibly be the world's skinniest teacher.

Backpacking through Brazil before entering the corporate world.

Assistant marketing manager, Columbus, Ohio. In my new office with windows!

The finished result of the tent village in North Carolina. An erection never felt so good!

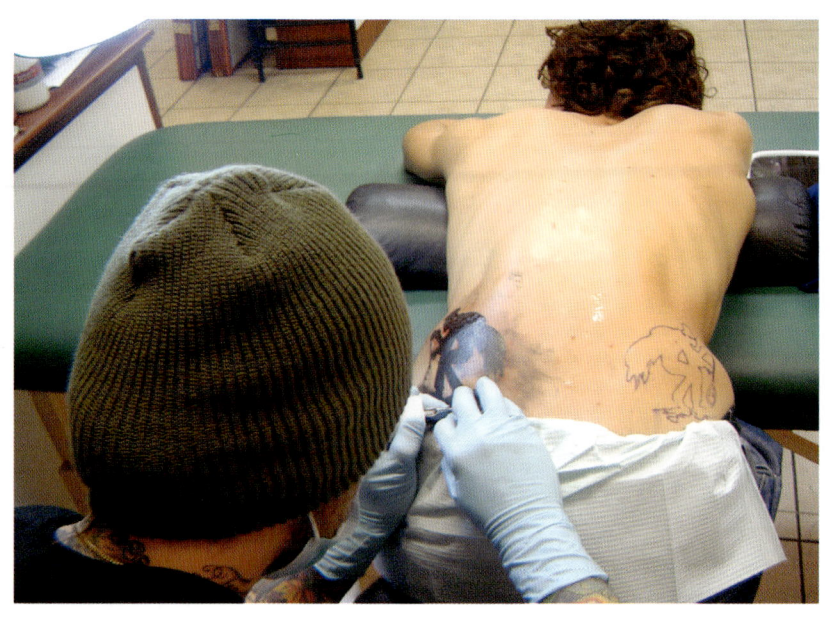

My 24th birthday in Vancouver, getting my twin thieves tattoo.

Doing the hokey-pokey in Banff, Canada.

Barney and me with our portable house in Red Deer, Canada.

Arriving at the rig camp in Alberta, Canada. Notice the electric fence surrounding the camp to keep bears out.

Hitchhiking with my new surfboard wrapped in my duvet at Puerto Escondido, Mexico. I still have my jandals at this point.

Sunday funday with the kids in Tapachula, Mexico.

'Bumming' around in Colombia. Photo by Mandy!

Mandy and I having the time of our lives in Colombia.

Mum looking on as her daughter lies beside her in pain and her son is treated for spinal injuries in Marlborough Sounds, New Zealand.

My favourite job, working as an exploration field assistant in the Australian outback.

Mandy and I united in Bali after ten months apart.

Downtown Asunción, Paraguay, with carts and cars.

Make me look like a 'six-star waiter'. At the hairdresser's in Ushuaia, Argentina.

Acting the dream. I did say I would do ANYTHING to work in Antarctica.

Antarctica, my Everest. My first time on the elusive white continent. Photo: Richard Sidey

The 'penguin refugee camp' at St Andrews Bay, South Georgia Island, Antarctica. Photo: Richard Sidey

Sich camping on the pull-out couch in our shoebox apartment in Melbourne. He'd been filming for our documentary *Bikes for Africa*.

A unique bike workshop, Namibia. TIA: This Is Africa.

Our best days in Africa. With Mandy, celebrating our achievements with a bottle of champagne on top of Victoria Falls, Zimbabwe.

Moses in the Namibian bike shop wearing the new blue uniforms he bought with the profit from the shop.

Relaxing on the Kwando River, Namibia, with Simon on his boat. I'm feeling a lot safer on that than in a hollowed-out log.

Camping on the shores of Lake Kariba, Zimbabwe, I was visited by an inquisitive elephant.

On the side of the road in Zambia. I often got called Jesus or Osama bin Laden.

Uhuru Peak, Mount Kilimanjaro, Tanzania. We got the photo, now let's get off this mountain!

# Hope and Hugs

he asked me, 'Digital?' Once I confirmed that yes it was digital, he wrote that on the scrap bit of paper and gave the camera back to me. I sat there waiting for him to take a statement or quiz me further. Then he gave me a look that said, *What are you still doing here?* I took my camera and passport and put as much space as I could between me and the police station.

I arrived at the bus station just as the bus I was wanting was pulling away but I managed to flag it down. To my relief it wasn't jam-packed and I flopped down into a seat with my mind still racing from the morning's events. Due to my adrenaline-frenzied state I hadn't even acknowledged the well-dressed young college kid beside me until he asked me, 'English?'

I absentmindedly replied, 'Yes.'

To which he responded with, 'Do you like chicken?' followed by 'Do you like tortillas?' and 'Do you like football?' From here you can imagine how the rest of the trip went.

After an uneventful chain of chicken bus and *collectivo* changes I walked back across the border in torrential rain. I avoided the immigration guards and re-entered Mexico without getting stamped or having to explain my absence of visas.

With my newly appreciated camera and $2 to spare from the $100, I arrived back at the orphanage. Not so much rested, but glad to be home with my family.

## Stories of hope

As my time passed at the orphanage, I slowly found out the stories behind the faces. Hearing some of the experiences of the kids made me wonder about the world. Why are there people who feel the need to screw with others' lives? The stories of emotional, physical and sexual abuse, torture and neglect haunted me. I suppose it's the old cyclic thing, isn't it: their parents did it to them. I could see it in some of the kids. They carried a lot of emotional baggage, and had been exposed to things that nobody should have to see or experience and this in turn had an adverse effect on their behaviour. It's sad, and when I heard the history of one of the boys, it was even sadder. His uncle, who he had shared a one-room shack with, used to get drunk and bring men home to service them. So what effect does that have on a wide-eyed little boy trying to sleep in the corner of that shack?

There were stories that left me thinking it was a cruel world, but also stories that left me appreciating how precious the children's little mischievous smiles were. To me, these smiles represented hope. The kid with the biggest smile was Bruno. Behind Bruno's smile was a tortured past. He had been hung upside down and beaten by his father.

I loved Bruno. If he had been born into the middle class of an industrialised country he would have been a tradesperson, making a good living. He loved physical work and was a hard worker. In my first week at the orphanage there was a drain that had been blocked for ages so I set about cleaning it out. Four rubbish bags of foul-smelling black sludge and toys later, it was clear. And who was there helping me all the way as I dry-retched, and who was pleading to stay and help instead of going to school? Bruno!

Even though he was a teenage boy, he loved a hug. He wasn't the most co-ordinated of kids, although he was very muscular and athletic. I would take him to basketball on Saturdays and watch him play, like a father does with a son. It was rather hard at times watching him as he didn't know how to position himself. His ability was far below that of his team mates, so this meant he didn't get much court time. But when he did he ran around like a hunting dog that had picked up the scent of a pig. His finest moment was when he scored a basket; he turned around and you couldn't wipe the smile off his face. I was proud. The fact that he had scored an own goal didn't matter; in my eyes, a basket was a basket, and I bought him an ice-cream on the walk home.

**Hope and Hugs**

## Simple Sammy

The greatest story of hope came in the form of a pot-bellied, cross-eyed four-year-old boy with a disproportionately sized head that looked like a watermelon on a stick. He regularly shat his pants and couldn't talk properly. His name was Sammy and he called me 'Appa' because he couldn't pronounce the letter *h*, which is not unusual in Mexico as the Spanish *h* is silent. But then he couldn't pronounce a lot of letters, including *b*.

Sammy was brought to the orphanage one evening by welfare, wrapped up in a blanket like an orphan taco. He was about one year old, but with many of the kids you never really knew their age as they were parentless and had no birth certificates. Pam and Alan took Sammy, unsure if they could handle a baby in the orphanage. When they unwrapped him, they were saddened by the sight. Sammy was a little malnourished bag of bones who made breathing look like a struggle. They didn't know if he would make it through the first night, but our little Sammy did.

Three years on, when I saw him racing around in his unsteady duck-footed way, I laughed. He had so much energy and an aura that made people love him. He was like a baby in a four-year-old's body. Everyone loves babies and thinks they are cute, but Sammy was as boisterous as any boy, running, hitting and playing with insects.

I had many a fond moment with Sammy, and a lot of them involved the toilet because he needed toilet training. I took it on myself to help train Sammy, mainly because of my aforementioned weak stomach. Having to clean up Sammy's mess off the floor sent me into convulsions. It just seemed more productive for me to put my time and dry-heaving into getting him to go in the toilet than to clean it up. Every time I saw Sammy, I would ask him, 'Sammy, poo poo *baño*?' (*Baño*, pronounced ban-yo, means toilet.) He usually shook his head, but I used to stick him on the toilet anyway, especially if he hadn't been for a while.

The first time I did this it didn't go too well. I got Sammy sitting on the toilet, then without warning he started peeing. Unfortunately, his water pistol was facing up and I was in the line of fire! I tried to mime and tell Sammy that he needed to point his pistol down between his legs, but little Sammy just sat there looking back at me with his goofy cross eyes, smiling as though nothing was the matter. In the end I was the one left looking as though I needed toilet training.

Then the triumphant day came; Sammy came to me and held my hand, looking at me with a four-year-old's concerned face and said, 'Appa, poo poo *baño*.' I took him to the toilet, got him set up on his little throne and left the king to his business.

I came back and popped my head in the door. 'Sammy, poo poo?' I asked.

He nodded with a victorious smile, and when I looked in the toilet there were two little nuggets. I felt like a miner striking gold. I gave little Sammy a high-five then went straight to announce the news to the Honduran ladies who slept at the orphanage during the week and did the washing. The fact that Sammy shat his pants the following day didn't matter—it was one duck-footed baby step at a time!

## Sunday funday

On my first Sunday at the orphanage all the kids piled into the van, the music pumping, playing some Mexican pop music that they sang along to in harmony. The energy of their anticipation was consuming, like a shaken champagne bottle.

Once at our destination, the door was opened and the excited kids popped out. We had arrived at a magnificent beach house, complete with pool, palm trees and huge barbecue area and lawn. It was owned by a friendly retired American who let the kids overrun his house every Sunday.

The older boys went straight to the storage room where they pulled out their surfboards and began waxing them. Alan and Pam were from the coast of Queensland, Australia, so the beach had been a big part of their family life and they wanted to give these kids the same experience. Previous Australian volunteers had organised surfboards and a sponsor to keep the orphanage supplied with them. The effect was amazing; these kids ripped. When I said that I surfed, I meant I stood up. These kids were worthy of the term surf. They were dropping into the murky brown waves that had me wanting to join Sammy shitting my pants on the beach. They had the fearlessness of youth mixed with natural ability.

This was no golden-sand beach with clear water. No, it had grey sand littered with driftwood and plastic bottles, thundering waves and a nasty rip. To go surfing, you would walk a hundred metres up the beach from where the house was, and then ten minutes later you would be back in front of the house because of the strong rip. We would always have the beach to ourselves, and there were no such things as lifeguards or swimming between the flags, so it was paramount that all the kids were supervised. The kids knew the rules: no young ones left the fenced-in house without an adult.

On that first Sunday I walked back in from the beach past the swimming pool where a few of the kids were in the shallow end. But as I passed the deep end I saw a body in the depths. I waited for a moment to see if it would surface as its arms were moving. Then it got to that uncomfortable stage. I knew that all the kids could swim except the young ones, but this kid wasn't small.

I jumped in and grabbed the body with my arm and brought it to the surface. It was Angela, the new girl who had arrived the day after I had. She had never swum before, and had been told not to go into the pool. But just as the person watching the pool was helping another kid get into their bathing suit, she had decided to take the plunge. I can understand Angela's desire to explore the water as I had done the exact same thing as a six-year-old wearing my Bambi Speedos at the local river, requiring Dad to come running into the water fully clothed to save me.

Straight away I grabbed a kickboard, took her to the shallow end and promised myself that every Sunday I would give her lessons and she would be swimming before I left. From then on, Angela and I had a bond. Angela was eleven and her passion was dancing, and she would always be the instigator of the blasting music in the dining room once all the tables had been put away and the floor swept.

The Sundays were an escape, an escape for the kids, for Pam and Alan, and for the volunteers; an escape from the mayhem of everyday orphanage life, an escape from the concrete and metal confines, and an escape from the kids' pasts. When the older kids were out surfing they were free. They weren't orphans, they were surfers. No one surfed in Tapachula even though there were some amazing waves. Tourists had stayed away because there was nothing there, and the locals weren't interested, or just didn't know how.

For the younger kids, it was a time to be a real kid, to play in the pool, chase the dogs, kick the soccer ball and make sand castles.

Everybody looked forward to Sunday.

## Hasta luego, amigos

As my time at the orphanage was coming to an end, I reminisced over some of my favourite memories:

Around every corner there was a kid waiting to hug you, to be tickled, to be loved.

Driving to the park with 30 kids packed into the twelve-seater van, singing along to a pop song on the radio.

The kids dancing in the dining room without a worry in the world.

### Hope and Hugs

Coming back from a Sunday at the beach with a wet little kid snuggled up in my arms asleep.

Taking the older boys on an overnight hike up a 4000-metre volcano, where they experienced cold for the first time, seeing their breath in the air, and sharing with them the joy of hiking and the camaraderie it involved. They made me proud, working together as a team and not complaining when I decided it was too dangerous to reach the summit due to the poor visibility and lack of track. (There are no such things as signposted tracks in Mexico.)

Dozing off on one of the little boys' beds with a glass of water in my hand. One of the five-year-olds came in and, thinking I was asleep, took the cup out of my hand like a father, put it safely on the floor and then lay down on the bed using my chest as a pillow. We were joined shortly by the two other five-year-old boys who quietly crawled in to also use me as a pillow. I pretended I was asleep and enjoyed the moment.

On my final Sunday, I watched Angela swim the width of the pool unassisted. Although her swimming style may have resembled a poodle on horse tranquilisers, she did it, and I was so proud. I gave her the biggest hug ever.

It was with these special memories floating around in my head that I said an emotional goodbye to the kids who had been my family for every day of the two months I had ended up staying.

With tears in my eyes, I walked out of the orphanage with my pack and some new $2 jandals, boarded a bus and headed north to catch a flight, off to my next chapter, chasing love.

# Chapter 9
# AMERICAN BEAUTY
### NORTH AMERICA: Denver, Colorado, USA, 17 April–27 June 2007

After knowing the American beauty named Mandy for only six days in Mexico, I was now going to live with her in her one-bedroom apartment in Denver, Colorado.

After Mandy left Mexico, we harmlessly emailed each other. But it was through those emails that our love grew. We found out we had so much in common, a love for travel being at the top of the list. Mandy would send me snippets from the Paulo Coelho book she was reading, and we would write about our views and thoughts on life. I started to live for Mandy's emails.

Mandy was the most amazing person I had met on my working-the-world journey. Behind that smile was a determined, caring, loving and adventurous soul.

I was lucky enough to have grown up in a stable, supportive

family. My dad coached my soccer team, umpired my cricket games, and my mum would have dinner ready at six o'clock. Every Christmas we would go camping at the stunning beaches near where I grew up.

So when I met Mandy, a beautiful, bubbly, outgoing girl who had studied in Spain, graduated with a degree in Spanish and education, travelled extensively, had worked in Paraguay, and was now working her fourth year as a high-school Spanish teacher while studying for her masters at night school and working in a restaurant on the weekend, I assumed she had had an upbringing like mine. One evening as the sun was setting on the beach in Mexico we were having a deep and meaningful conversation about our dreams and lives, as you do when you're travelling. When she told me her story I thought she must have been talking about someone else.

Mandy had grown up in the suburbs of Phoenix, Arizona, a sweltering desert metropolis. She lived with her mother and father, her pregnant sixteen-year-old sister having moved out when Mandy was ten. Her father was a local character who everyone knew and loved. He wore red suspenders with his jeans and snakeskin boots, and had curly red hair and a ZZ Top beard to match. He had grown up travelling in the circus, performing with his family: acrobatics with his brothers and later playing in a three-brother band. He tried his hand at the military (working as a cook and playing in the band) before meeting his wife and having some rug monkeys. He worked at the local bar pouring beers and many of Mandy's memories were of playing pool at the bar with the other kids on Sundays, cleaning ashtrays for quarters. Although you would usually see a smile on his face, he suffered from what we would now recognise as depression. He was an alcoholic—not a violent alcoholic, but a happy, yet melancholic alcoholic who everyone loved. Mandy remembers he would always invite people to sleep on their couch if they were too drunk to drive home as their house was only a few blocks from the bar. Like Mandy, he was a caring soul.

Then one night, eleven-year-old Mandy woke in the middle of the night to the sounds of an argument, and she wandered out to see what was wrong.

Her dad told her to go back into her room, followed her in and said, 'I'm sorry, baby, I love you. All my guitars, they're yours, I'm sorry.'

He closed the door behind him and moments later Mandy heard a gunshot in the room next door, followed by her mum hysterically screaming 'Stay in your room, stay in your room!' Apparently it had all got to be too much for him, and he took his own life.

Mandy's mother, trying to come to grips with a husband who had committed suicide and raising a family on a blue-collar income, found comfort in drugs. Meth was her drug of choice. Although she was still a loving mother, when you are addicted nothing beats the love the drugs give you. So now instead of friends from the bar waking up on the couch on Sunday morning, her mum started hanging out with new friends behind closed doors.

Nowadays Mandy's mother has been clean for years and attends AA meetings. She is a lovely lady who has been dealt a tough hand and now has to live with the decisions she has made.

So, at age eleven, Mandy had to learn to look after herself. At that young age she told herself that she was going to get out of her situation—she wasn't going to live on the unemployment benefit that was the norm in her neighbourhood. At fifteen she lied about her age and got a job at the local supermarket and had a friend across the alley teach her to drive. She had to save herself, give herself the best opportunity in life; her house became just a place she would sleep.

Luckily for Mandy she was an intelligent student and her teachers saw this. In her last year of high school one teacher wanted her to go on the school trip to Europe, so he paid half the cost (which she later repaid), and the other half she paid with a loan from a generous friend and savings from her supermarket job. From that point on, Mandy knew what she wanted to do: travel.

She came back from Europe, left home and drove to Flagstaff, Arizona, a university town, where she lived, worked in a restaurant and studied on academic scholarship to be a Spanish teacher. In her third year she used her student loans and maxed out her credit card to study in Spain.

After Spain, she came back to the States and met a lady who ran an English language school in Paraguay. Again, not in a financial situation to be able to live abroad, she was blessed by the generosity of a family friend who deposited enough money in her bank account to make her minimum payment on her maxed-out credit card while she was away. Mandy went to Paraguay and taught for half a year, making only enough money to live on, and fell in love with the small landlocked country in the heart of South America.

She came back to the States with a five-year plan: she was going to get some teaching experience under her belt, pay off her debt, gain her masters degree and spend some much-desired time living near her sister, brother-in-law and nephews. Then, after the five years was up, she would be ready and able to travel and once again live abroad.

All was going well two years into her plan. She was holidaying in Sayulita, Mexico, with her sister, brother-in-law, and two teenage nephews who were a big part of her life. Outside the toilet of the small town bar, she met me, a scruffy long-haired Kiwi. I remember her asking me 'Are you partying?' to which I replied 'Yup,' and the party started.

During our time in Sayulita, my English backpacking buddy Sam and I were welcomed into her fun-loving family. Sam would even go and use the shower at the holiday house the family were renting, as he couldn't face the grimy concrete shower of the hippy camping ground we were staying at.

## HAP WORKING THE WORLD

Days were spent relaxing and nights were spent eating and drinking with the family, bonfires on the beach, and dancing to the local bands. With Mandy's thirteen- and sixteen-year-old nephews around, we kept our feelings suppressed, but when everyone else was dancing at a beach bar or had called it a night, we would walk the beach, and skinny dip in the moonlit ocean, with sparkling phosphorescence lighting up the water. We would retire to my tent under the palm trees where the fairytale would continue until we woke in the quiet hours of the morning, a slight chill still in the air before the morning sun started to heat up the tent, marking the time for Mandy to pull on her clothes and go home.

Six days later, Mandy and her friend hopped on the bus to the city of Guadalajara for New Year's, where they had a pre-booked hostel and where they would be flying back to the US. As I waved her off, Mandy had tears in her eyes; she was torn between staying with me and celebrating New Year's with her family in Sayulita or sticking to her travel plans. *Another travel romance over*, I had thought.

Two days later, Mandy emailed me because she knew I was going to start my journey north to catch a flight from LA back to Canada. In her email she wrote that she had had a great time with me and if I wanted to I should come to see her in Guadalajara and gave me the address of the hostel.

The next day when I packed up my tent, said goodbye to Sam and started hitchhiking, I was going to leave it to fate as to whether I would go to meet Mandy. Guadalajara was south, and I was heading north. My first ride was easy. As I watched a cow being slaughtered in a nearby paddock, a farmer pulled over and I jumped on the back of the pickup truck, perching on a pile of coconuts under the blue Mexican skies and basking in the sun. The farmer dropped me off at a crossroads: one road led to LA and the other to Guadalajara.

After a couple of hours of standing on the dusty verge with

my thumb out, I wasn't enjoying basking in the Mexican sun without lying on a pile of coconuts and without the wind in my hair. I walked to the bus station. On the schedule board, there was one bus leaving that night to Tijuana on the US–Mexican border which was going to take 60 hours, or another leaving in two hours to Guadalajara where I could be by the evening. At the end of the day, a five-hour trip to Guadalajara where I could spend the night wrapped in the warm embrace of the American beauty won.

I arrived at the hostel reception where Mandy beamed with a surprised smile as she just happened to be talking to the receptionist. One last night was spent together and in the morning I waved Mandy goodbye as she hopped in a taxi and headed for the airport, back to the reality of being a high school Spanish teacher in Denver, Colorado.

After Sayulita we emailed religiously. Most days I hitchhiked from whatever little town I was in to find an internet café, and Mandy, back in America, sat at her teacher's desk, constantly checking her inbox on the classroom computer.

In the emails we shared thoughts with each other, opinions on life and dreams, and from those emails we created a bond. We had a similar outlook on life; we both didn't like TV, preferring to be around people, being active and living life. Four months later, my backpack was resting in Mandy's closet with its contents on the shelves above the vacuum cleaner in her one-bedroom Denver apartment.

From then on our lives fell into a natural routine. After a couple of months' living in Denver I did two weeks' work for Jimmy in Pennsylvania at the US Golf Open. Mandy's school holidays were coming up, so we decided to fulfil our shared desire to travel together. We booked flights to Colombia for six weeks of backpacking.

## Chapter 10
# A MEMORABLE STOPOVER
**NORTH AMERICA: Atlanta, Georgia, USA, and Vancouver, British Columbia, Canada, 27 June–19 September 2007**

When travelling you are constantly having to make decisions, like one of those pick-a-path books you read as a youngster: which bus to catch, where to have lunch, who's paying for what, what hostel to stay at, how long to stay in one town, whether to lie on the beach or visit the Andean herbal museum, how much money to get exchanged, what direction to go. They may seem like easy decisions, but when you are travelling with someone, being with them 24/7, they are the everyday decisions that can break you. If it's uncharted territory for both parties, neither has the knowledge to make informed decisions, but each person will always have an opinion, or maybe neither of you have an opinion, making it just as hard.

One thing that came out of the six weeks in Colombia was that Mandy and I made a great team. We complemented each

## A Memorable Stopover

other socially, and enjoyed the same way of travelling. We liked relaxing in a café watching the model-like Colombian women walk past with their greasy-haired soccer-shirt-wearing boyfriends. We enjoyed camping out under the stars in picturesque Parque Tayrona, skinny dipping at Playa Blanca once all the tourist boats had left for the day, walking the romantic cobblestone streets of quaint Villa de Leyva, going to the tripped-out nightclub with other backpacker friends we had made, sleeping on the deck of a weekly overnight cargo boat to get to the out-of-the-way island of Providencia, partying until the sun came up in the old city of Cartagena, day tripping to swim in the mud volcano, having salsa lessons in Medellín, hiking through the Andean jungle to the lost city and toasting the end of each day with a cold bottle of Aguila.

After our South American fairytale, it was back to reality. We got the overnight bus from Medellín to Colombia's capital, Bogotá. We arrived at the airport after a sleepless night on the notoriously steep, winding roads where the bus driver drove like my Newfie rig supervisor. We were red-eyed, hot, sweaty and bedraggled, and played cards for four hours until our plane departed at 9.30 a.m.

We touched down in Atlanta, Georgia, and once in the airport, I went straight to the toilet, splashed water on my face to wake up and tied back the dreadlocks that Mandy had done for me before Colombia. Feeling a little refreshed, Mandy and I walked to the passport stamping area and were met by a sea of people milling around like in an African marketplace. After an hour of waiting, surrounded by the stress and frustration of people missing their flights, we became worried. We still had at least another hour's wait in the queue until we got through customs and our plane for Denver was departing in an hour. Mandy talked to the immigration official who was walking around directing traffic and answering angry questions. He told her that if I missed my flight I could be put on another because I was held up in the foreigner's queue. But if she, as a US resident who could use the much shorter queue, missed her flight she would have no excuse.

In yet one more of those tense travel moments, where we couldn't afford financially or timewise to miss the flight, we made a split-second decision. Mandy would go through the US resident queue and change our Denver-bound flights to a later departure and we would meet at the baggage claim. With a rushed kiss, Mandy was off towards the US immigration booths. In hindsight I could have gone with Mandy through the US resident queue instead of waiting in the foreigners' queue, but at the time it never crossed our minds.

An hour later I was at the front of the queue. I approached the friendly-looking official in an upbeat chirpy way. In a tired gentle manner he asked me the usual questions, 'What are you doing here? How much money do you have? Do you have onward passage? Where have you been?' He took my fingerprints and processed my passport. Then he looked at the computer screen a little longer while still holding my passport, and said to me, 'Sir, we will have to take you out back for further questioning.'

I was escorted to the questioning area, and taken through the locked security doors to be met with a packed waiting room of around 30 people. My escort put my file on top of the bulging pile and I found a space on the floor to wait.

It was clear that the immigration officials were under the pump. It was an unusually busy day. There were only three of them questioning and people were being brought in faster than they could process them.

I sat and waited for my turn, knowing it was going to be a long time. I was worried sick about Mandy. I didn't know if she had got a flight to Denver or not. Where was she? Was she OK? Would I see her? In our haste saying goodbye, we hadn't made any contingency plans for me being held up. Therefore I had all her cash and her credit card on me and we had no way of communicating as both of our cell phones were in Denver.

## A Memorable Stopover

After two hours of worried waiting in the packed room I was called up to the counter. The tired official breezed over my file and said to me, 'So you're coming here to stay with your girlfriend?' With a weary laugh he told me that I required further questioning. I tried to plead with him and told him that Mandy was waiting for me, could I please just get a message through to her to let her know what was happening. He said no. I didn't blame him; he was just doing his job and I was in the same situation as everybody else in the waiting room. My file got put into another pile and I went back to my spot on the floor and tried to get comfortable.

It had now been about five hours since we had landed in Atlanta. I knew Mandy would be feeling helpless at not knowing where I was or what had happened to me. At that moment, sitting on the floor of the waiting room, separated from Mandy, I was overwhelmed with this intense feeling of love towards her. I wanted nothing more than to wrap her in my arms, kiss the top of her head and reassure her it would all turn out fine.

After a long wait the flow of people finally stopped coming into the waiting room and it was slowly emptying out. Then, at around 11 p.m., roughly eight hours after touching down, my name was called. I was taken to another room across the airport, which now seemed like an empty stadium after a grand final, quiet and big. It was hard to believe this was the scene of the African market earlier that day.

An official that I hadn't seen before sat in front of me. Like all the other others, he looked exhausted after the hellishly busy day. He had short trimmed blond hair and sharp middle-aged features. I felt scruffy and insignificant, like a ragged stray dog in the presence of a groomed prize-winning golden Labrador. I felt as though he had taken one look at my dreadlocks and stubble and was judging me, and after all, it was his job to judge me.

From what I remember he didn't start with the usual questions: What was I doing here? What had I been doing in Colombia?

## HAP WORKING THE WORLD

How did I fund my travels? Instead he started off by asking me how much money I had on me. I answered about $80. Then he made me get out my wallet and empty it onto the counter. He counted up the notes which only came to $77. Then he asked why I had lied to him. I tried to explain that I didn't keep track of exactly how much money I had. He didn't care; he had made his point. His interrogation tactics were having their desired effect, and I was feeling vulnerable and intimidated.

Then he looked me directly in the eye and cut straight to the point, knowing he had the upper hand. 'Mr Cameron, I know you have been working illegally on the Visa Waiver Program.'

I tried to comprehend what he had said, that he knew I had been working. But I couldn't think straight, I was trying to focus on an answer but Mandy just kept popping into my mind. With my world spinning, he dealt me the killer blow.

'Mr Cameron, we're not letting you in.'

What! Was my mind playing tricks on me? Had he just told me that I wasn't being let in? Did I just hear that I wouldn't be going back to Denver with Mandy? This couldn't be happening.

I sunk my head in my hands, resting my elbows on the table. What was I going to do now?

The only thing I knew was that I wanted to see Mandy. I wanted to be back in Santa Marta where we had locked ourselves away in the plush hotel we had treated ourselves to, lying under the sheets, playing paper scissors rock to see who would put on clothes and go get freshly squeezed orange juice from the juice cart outside.

The immigration officer had fought a faultless fight. He had me against the ropes, now he set about finishing me.

He put me under oath: 'Raise your right hand and look into the camera and repeat after me: "I hereby promise to tell the truth the whole truth and nothing but the truth." What you say may be taken in evidence. You know it's an offence to lie to an officer of the United States?'

## A Memorable Stopover

I looked into the camera while he asked me all the basic questions: name, date of birth, age, country of residency. Then he hit me with the question that would put the last nail in the coffin.

'What work were you doing between this date and this date?'

I didn't fully catch the exact dates, but I knew they roughly aligned with the couple of weeks I was working at the US Golf Open in Pennsylvania. I was unsure if the immigration officer actually knew I had been working. During the job, I had been questioned by a government health and safety official who had reported me for working at heights with no safety harness. At the time I hadn't thought much of it; it seemed to me that most of the workers in minimum wage jobs in the States were illegal immigrants from Central or South America. I had thought it was just an accepted part of the US labour market. Now, standing there under oath, I felt like I had when I had been lying in bed in the Ohio hospital with the realisation that my past actions affected my future. I knew there was no point in lying, so I answered the question truthfully, something along the lines of, 'Yes, at that time I had worked for two weeks putting up tents.'

Even though they weren't going to let me in anyway, at least now it was official. I only had myself to blame.

He asked me if I had any questions.

I said, 'So I'm being deported?'

'No, you're being denied entry.'

I was unsure what the difference was but all I knew was that I wouldn't be seeing Mandy.

'When can I see my girlfriend?'

'You can't.'

'What happens to me now?'

'You get sent back to Colombia.'

As the officer was finishing up, a security officer walked into the room.

He addressed the immigration guy, 'Is this Hap Cameron? What's happening to him? We're closing up the corridor area by baggage claim and his hysterical girlfriend's refusing to leave until she knows what's happening to him.'

'He's not coming in,' he replied.

As the security officer turned to leave I asked him if he would please give Mandy her credit card. He was standoffish at first, as it could put him in an awkward situation in a world where everyone was covering their arse. I then explained to him that I had all her money and cards, and that she had nothing. He saw the genuine worry in my eyes; he had a heart, he would do it.

'And tell her I love her.'

I took a little comfort in the fact that Mandy now had her credit card and she knew what was happening to me. I focused my attention on my situation. There was no way I wanted to go back to Colombia. I would be stranded in a place where I knew no one and wouldn't be able to earn enough money to leave.

I asked the immigration officer if there was an option for me to be sent to Calgary, Canada, instead of Colombia. Since I had been so forthcoming under oath and had made the immigration officer's day, he said he would talk to his boss and see if it was possible.

The boss came back. 'There are no flights available for Calgary, but there's one leaving at 8 a.m. tomorrow to Vancouver for $520. If you want it you have to buy it now.' I handed him my credit card.

Although all my gear was in Red Deer, Vancouver was fine. The fare was ridiculously expensive, but I wasn't really in a position to bargain or wait around for a cheap flight. The good thing about Vancouver was that Lucy, who I had travelled with in Mexico, was living there.

With my credit card back in my hand and knowing that I was now heading to Canada and not Colombia, I started to relax. I was led back into the other room where I had spent the entire afternoon; it was now nearly midnight, and the airport was eerily dead.

## A Memorable Stopover

### Airport hotel

In the room were a few familiar faces from the waiting room that day. There was a chubby Jamaican guy in his early twenties who seemed polite and quiet. He wasn't being let in either, even though he had all the required paperwork. The officials didn't believe his story that he was going to visit his brother who was studying at the university where he had previously studied.

Then there was Pablo, an extroverted lawyer from Peru. He wasn't being let in as he had overstayed a tourist visa by a couple of days eight years ago.

There was a Slovakian guy who had been in Puerto Rico and was now going to New York to visit his sister, and who had onward passage to Slovakia, but they didn't believe him either.

Then there was Juan, a Mexican from Cancún who was coming to visit his girlfriend for a week as she was studying in the States. But last time Juan had been to the States he had run out of money and done a week's work. Immigration had found the pay stub in his luggage.

Then there was me, the dreadlocked Kiwi who had done a couple of weeks' work on a tourist visa and was trying to get back into the States to live with his girlfriend. I had been denied entry and had now lost my privilege to use the Visa Waiver Program, which is basically the privilege to turn up at the US border and be granted a three-month tourist visa.

After a whole day of not eating, we were given a microwave meal and informed that because Atlanta airport did not have holding cells, we would be transported downtown to spend the night at Atlanta City Prison.

Pablo, the Peruvian lawyer, started on his rant that went all night: 'Why you treat us like criminal, I do not a thing wrong and now you send me prison.'

I prodded my microwaved macaroni cheese but just wasn't hungry even though the last thing I had eaten was an airplane meal fifteen hours ago.

## HAP WORKING THE WORLD

We were then individually taken to the large, high-security, stainless-steel toilet area, complete with a viewing window in the door and a flush that was operated by the officers outside so drug dealers couldn't get rid of their stash. In the toilet I was frisked down by an officer, had my shoelaces removed, and had my travel bracelets that I had accumulated in Colombia cut off and replaced with handcuffs.

Once we were all handcuffed we were led out by an armed guard to the paddy wagon awaiting us in the Atlanta night. It was a surreal experience as we zoomed down the deserted freeway into Atlanta city. Although I was dog-tired, the craziness of the situation kept me awake. I felt like I was removed from myself, watching this other skinny, tanned, handcuffed, dreadlocked guy being escorted to prison.

We arrived at the back of the prison which reminded me of the loading bay of Mr Malikov's stockroom in Ohio, with a raised concrete platform for the trucks to reverse up to and unload their cargo. We were walked single file into the processing room that resembled my old doctor's waiting room with black vinyl benches against the wall. We were handed over to the upbeat nightshift prison guard who would induct us into the prison system.

He was a jovial black man who seemed like he had worked the job for some time. He first got us to fill out paperwork, and read to us from pieces of paper, one of which explained how to brush your teeth. He took our mug shots and led us through to get our medical checks. Then we were taken to get our prison uniforms, though only the quiet chubby Jamaican was issued one as he had to wait two days for the next flight to Jamaica and the rest of us were leaving that morning. When Jamaica walked out of the room in the faded orange overalls with 'Atlanta City Prison' stamped on his back, I felt so sorry for him. The poor bastard.

We then picked up our crisp bed sheets and were led through

# A Memorable Stopover

a further maze of daunting security doors leading to the cell wing that would be our home for the night. We entered a wide open area that felt like a highway motel car park, but instead of wooden hand rails and red doors surrounding the perimeter there was a metal gangway with grey steel doors. There were no cars in the car park, just one control desk right in the very middle that had a view of all the cell doors in front of it.

Peruvian Pablo was led to the control desk first, and was told his cell number. Complaining the whole way and saying he had rights, he walked to his allocated cell where the control desk buzzed him in. No sooner had he set foot in the cell than he stormed out again.

'There someone in my cell. I no share.'

In a non-emotional tone the control-desk guy said, 'Sorry, we're full up. You're all going to have to share.'

I was at the end of the line and stepped up to the desk.

'Name?'

'Cameron.'

'Cameron, cell 210. Up the stairs and halfway along.'

I looked over to where my room for the night was, and started the walk towards the metal stairway, holding my sheets, in no rush to get there. As I made my way up the metal stairs that reminded me of a fire escape, my mind raced. *Who was I going to be sharing my cell with? Was I going to be beaten up because it was now about two in the morning and I would probably wake up my cellmate. Was I going to be raped?* Surely the guards can't hear your screams from behind those solid steel doors.

I arrived at my 2-metre-high door, which was surrounded by smooth, thick concrete, my fists and bum cheeks clenched. I was scared shitless. I had no idea what to expect. Then my heart skipped a beat as the guard hit the button and the door clicked open.

I entered the dark cell with no light switch as all a prisoner's freedom is taken away, even the freedom of turning on a light. The smell of body odour and stale cigarette smoke hit me. I nearly tripped over the stainless-steel toilet located in the middle of the floor, unable to see in the dark. In the far corner I made out two bunks, in the light from the barred window a silhouetted body sat up on the top bunk. The body jumped down and moved groggily towards me, and as he moved further into the dim light from the barred window I could see he was Asian in appearance, shorter than me but stocky. He made no eye contact. I stopped by the toilet, unsure of what to expect as my eyes slowly adjusted.

He stopped in front of me, looked up and put his hand out. 'Phillip.'

I shook his hand. 'Hap.'

'What you in for?' he asked me in quick-fire street gangster English.

Feeling a bit like a criminal, I replied, 'Working illegally, and you?'

'Drug charges. Where you from?'

'New Zealand.'

'Okay, Mr New Zealand, you top bunk, me bottom bunk. I just on top bunk get breeze from window. Light on 5 a.m.'

Phillip took his sheet from the top bunk and put it on the bottom bunk. I put mine on top of the plastic mattress. Although my body was in a comatose state, my mind was spinning like a roulette wheel with all that had happened and what I was going to do, what Mandy was doing. Would I see her? And all the while, I was wondering if Phillip was going to snuggle me on the top bunk whenever I heard the rustle of his plastic mattress below.

After I spent the night tossing and turning in a fitful sleep, the lights automatically came on at 5 a.m. in all the cells.

Phillip welcomed me with, 'Oi, New Zealand, make bed and clean for inspection, downstairs breakfast, me go duty now.'

After tucking my sheet in, I pulled on my two-day-old

## A Memorable Stopover

clothes that were starting to smell like the cell. I went down the stairs, where at the bottom of which the other inmates were making their way into a high brick-walled and concrete exercise yard that was home to a basketball court.

In front of me was a line of Mike Tyson lookalikes all wearing prison-issue orange overalls. I felt like a boy scout selling fundraising cookies walking into a gang headquarters.

An orange line snaked its way into the breakfast area where a pellet of stacked trays lay. I followed the queue and picked up a grey tray that was sectioned off like a bento box. Instead of rice and seaweed I was faced with rubbery scrambled eggs, grey porridge sludge the consistency of spew, and dry toast.

I then made my way to the eating area where I panned the room for a table by myself, but because I was at the end of the line, all the tables were either full or only had one seat free. I walked through the eating area, not knowing what to do.

An orange giant looked up and gestured his behemoth of a hand at the spare seat at his table. With a smile he said, 'Sit down.' The three other hulks all flashed me a friendly smile and a, 'Hey dude.' These guys looked so damn intimidating but they had all been in this situation too.

I couldn't eat my breakfast. I have a touchy gag reflex at the best of times and don't particularly like porridge. As I played with my food in the warm silence of our table the guard made an announcement, 'All prisoners leaving today assemble here.'

I gave my tray of food to the friendly behemoth and said goodbye. As I walked through the canteen I heard someone shout from above, 'Oi, New Zealand.'

I looked up and saw Phillip sweeping the second-floor gangway. He waved. 'Good luck, New Zealand.'

I felt like calling out, 'Good luck small Asian guy from miscellaneous Asian country,' but instead said, 'Same to you, Phillip.'

We all filed into another room, where I was handcuffed

to Juan the Mexican. We were led through the maze of high security doors and drab corridors to our awaiting barred chariot.

In the prison wagon there were the guys from last night, minus Jamaica, and two new prisoners. The new team members were a young Cambodian guy covered in tattoos from head to toe, and the other prisoner, in his forties, was from Trinidad and said he'd been in the prison system since 1993, having moved around, in and out, but had been at Atlanta City Prison since 2003. Now he was going back home to his family in Trinidad. He seemed like a very calm guy, and I wondered how he had ended up in prison for fifteen years as I watched him look out between the bars of the paddy wagon into the free world that we sped past on the highway.

Back at the airport, we were marched along a side wall, as the airport was buzzing with incoming passengers. I felt like a criminal: unwashed, my dreadlocks itching my face and the handcuffs dragging my hands down and the stares of queuing passengers weighing on me; but in a way I found it all rather comical as the airport crowd probably thought I was a hardened criminal.

I was taken back into the room that I had spent the afternoon waiting in the day before. The handcuffs were taken off, and I was reunited with my worn backpack patched with the flags of the countries my working-the-world quest had taken me to thus far. I signed a form for the envelope that contained my shoelaces, fishhook bone-carving necklace, Wheels' Scorpio ring and my wallet with $77 in it.

I was allowed one phone call as I waited for my escort. Because I didn't have my cell phone the only number I knew off by heart was my parents' back in New Zealand. I got Mum and Dad's bubbly answer-machine message and fought back a tear as I heard their voices. Oh what I would do to be in the warmth of my home right now.

## A Memorable Stopover

'Hey Mum and Dad, I've been denied entry into the States. I'm now being sent to Vancouver in 30 minutes. I will call you from there, all is good. Can you please leave a message on Mandy's cell phone letting her know I'm being sent to Vancouver, as she thinks I will be getting sent back to Colombia.'

As I hung up the phone my police escort arrived: two doughnut-loving, blue-uniformed officers in their early thirties. They were handed my passport and plane ticket, took me out to a car waiting on the tarmac and drove me to the departure gate.

The officers were friendly guys and I was having a laugh with them at the position I had got myself into. I told them how I was meant to be sent back to Colombia but that I had been allowed to buy a ticket to Canada. They sounded surprised at this, and told me that they reckoned it was a waste of $520 as there was no way Canada would let me in. They thought that I would be sent back to Atlanta, to spend another night in the cells until I could organise myself a trip back to New Zealand. Like in Korea with Mr Kim, once again I felt like the statue rather than the pigeon.

We arrived at the departure gate, but found out there had been a gate change. The officers thought it would be quicker to walk me through the airport as my flight was leaving soon. We made our way through the building with everyone around me doing what they do in airports: drinking coffee, hugging, crying, waiting, reading. As we passed Dunkin' Donuts I joked with the officers that I would buy them some, and while they ate them I could make a run for it. They had a laugh and told me that if I made them run, I had better hope they didn't catch me. They said, 'We wish you were staying, we're beginning to like you.'

When we finally got to the gate, the officers gave the head flight attendant my ticket and passport, which she would hold onto until we touched down in Canada. I said my goodbyes to the officers who said, 'Good luck, but we'll see you tonight.'

The attendant escorted my dishevelled body down the aisle

to my seat under the watchful eye of the passengers. I excused myself past the elderly lady in the aisle seat and slumped into the window seat, eyeing up the empty worn leather of the vacant middle seat. It looked so damn inviting I could barely stop myself from lying down right there and then, and sleeping.

I said hello to the sweet elderly lady with the grandmotherly smile. Her name was Jillian. Her husband had passed away the year before and she had just been visiting her son and grandchildren in Atlanta. She had had to call off her stay early as it was too hot for her at their house, so she was going back home to Canada. In a nice-old-lady way she asked me why I looked like shit, and I explained everything to her. Being the caring person that she was, she was appalled that I had spent the night in the cells, overlooking the fact that I had worked illegally and only had myself to blame.

She took me under her sympathetic wing like she was a mother duck and I was her wounded little duckling. Jillian gave me half of her home-made chicken sandwich and told me to eat it. She then told me that I needed to get some sleep. I lay my upper torso down on the middle seat, the first time that I had been able to relax for the past couple of days. With my eyes closed, I felt Jillian get out a flimsy little plane blanket and tuck it in around me, a caring gesture I will remember the rest of my life. Then, after the flight attendant had brought us our meals, half-dozing I overheard Jillian asking for extra snacks and juices for me.

Jillian woke me as we touched down in Vancouver. She gave me the bag of snacks. I wanted to keep in contact with her and let her know how I got on, but she said she didn't have email. We hugged and she wished me luck as she let me out of the nest into the wide world.

As she waited for all the passengers to exit the plane her parting words were, 'Don't worry, dear, they let anyone into Canada.'

## A Memorable Stopover

As I waited in the queue, I started thinking about what the officers had said, *There's no way Canada will let you in.*

Then I started thinking about Mandy, wondering if she had got the message from Mum and Dad that I was being sent to Vancouver. Knowing Mandy she would have probably already bought a ticket to Vancouver. I imagined her arriving here and me being stuck back at the Atlanta City Prison.

And then on my other shoulder, opposite the US immigration officers, was Jillian my guardian angel saying, *Don't worry, dear, they let anyone into Canada.*

'Hi, passport please. What brings you to Canada?'

'I used to live here. I'm visiting friends and picking up my gear that I left here.'

'How long will you stay?'

'Probably a couple of weeks.'

*Stamp.* 'Have a good stay.'

## Making the best of it

As I passed through the immigration booth, an overwhelming feeling of relief swept over me. I cleared the airport and hopped on the bus heading downtown. With my pack on my lap, a wave of emotion hit me. I felt lost and alone. I looked out the window, holding back tears, knowing I had to keep pushing. I had to get a hostel bed, get in contact with Lucy, who I knew was living in Vancouver, and had to earn some money.

I walked around the hostels, and finally found some accommodation. From the $77 I paid $33 for a hostel bed, the amount of money I had been living off for a day in Colombia. I entered the six-bed dorm room where all the other roommates were probably out taking in the beautiful sights of Vancouver.

I decided to take a shower. Like a sack of potatoes I slumped down on the bed and opened my pack to get some clothes out. On top of my clothes was a note scribbled on the pink-lined paper of Mandy's notebook. She must have taken my bag off the baggage carousel and put the note in there before the guard took it away again. The note read:

> Hap,
> I'm so scared. I've been waiting and the worst has happened. I just met some nice ladies from Guatemala who are letting me spend the night in their hotel room. I love you. I hope they weren't too horrible to you.
>   I love you and wish I could've done something.
>   It's so hard to do this. To go home without you. I hope you are okay, Mil besos, Mandy.
>   PS my cell phone number is xxxxxxxx

Then, like a flash flood after a drought, the tears came, unabated. All the emotion that I had been keeping inside to get me through the events of the past 24 hours came gushing out. I cried hysterically like a man who doesn't cry naturally, and I didn't try to stop it. The more I thought of Mandy the more I cried. So this is what love is? A word that had come a little awkwardly in Colombia flowed freely in my mind as I pictured my time with Mandy, and her warm smile.

The hot water of the hostel shower was a welcome relief to the travel grime on my skin. The Advil tablets I had taken for my headache were as effective as fighting a war with sticks. As much as I wanted to crawl into bed and wake up to everything being fine, I headed out the door into the overcast early afternoon with a tired determination in my stride.

First I went to a pay phone to ring Mandy. She mustn't have arrived in Denver as it went straight to her voicemail. I left a message, letting her know I was in Vancouver and not Colombia. Then I headed to an internet café and sent an emergency email to Lucy and all my friends who had previously lived in Vancouver. I briefly told them what had happened and asked if they had any contacts for a couch to crash on.

I then caught a bus to my old workplace where I had worked

## A Memorable Stopover

around a year and a half earlier, before heading to Banff for the snowboard season. The bus I caught went down Hastings Street, where all of Canada's homeless congregate. As I looked out the window I saw hobos, prostitutes, crackheads and lost souls with shopping trolleys full of cans. I knew that the only thing that separated me from them was the fact I had people to support me, who loved me and were willing to help me. I was lucky.

I arrived at the warehouse, which I saw had a new coat of white paint. It had recently been graffitied by a Hastings Street local, and the bright red spraypaint read: *Your mum goes to college.* A small smile managed to crack my lips as I thought that it must be rather offensive to tell a homeless person that their mother is educated—maybe it takes away from their street cred.

As I walked through the office door, I pumped myself up into a happy place, inflated the old Hap, put on the Hap they knew.

'Anyone there?' I shouted into the corridor of the new upstairs office that I had helped paint all those months ago.

'Hey mate, remember this face?' I said to the big healthy frame of the boss as he exited his office.

'Hap, how are you?'

I quickly told him my story, and asked him if he had any work so I could earn some money to buy an air ticket home.

'We'd love to have you back. We'll sort something out.'

'Can I start tomorrow?'

'OK, be here at 8 a.m.'

I sincerely thanked him and left, feeling a little better knowing I would have some money coming in. But I was unable to shake the feeling of loneliness. Back in the centre of town I looked at all the people going about their everyday lives and felt jealous of their little annoyances like the bus being late, or waiting at the traffic lights.

I made another call to Mandy and still no answer. I left a message, hung up and cried. I cried because I missed her, but also because I knew she would still be worried as she thought

I would be back in Colombia. I kept crying while I found some unoccupied grass to lie on in English Bay so that I could continue to weep freely without anyone noticing. I stayed here for an hour until I managed to pull myself together.

Back at the hostel I asked the front desk girl if I could book in for the following night as well.

'Sorry, we're booked out,' she answered.

'Would you be able to ring some other hostels and see if they have a bed?'

'No, sorry I can't.'

'Would I be able to store my bags here while I go to work tomorrow then pick them up after work?'

'No, sorry we don't store bags for non-residents.'

I headed to my bed like the dejected little stray dog that kept getting kicked when all he wanted was a belly rub.

After two hours of lying in bed, unable to sleep, I got up and decided to check my emails. I exited the hostel into the Vancouver evening and found an internet café that reminded me of the computer gaming rooms back in Korea.

I had an email from Lucy with her number and a message that read, *Of course you can come and stay, Crapster.*

There was also an email from Mandy. Her brother-in-law had picked her up from the airport. He had passed by her house to get her cell phone and then taken her straight to a Mexican restaurant to medicate her with some margaritas. As soon as she checked her voicemail messages, she had run across the road to a café and asked a random guy if she could use his computer to book a flight. With her depleted credit card she booked a return flight to Vancouver for five days.

As soon as I read the email, I went to ring her. Finally I heard her voice. All of a sudden I wasn't worried about my predicament. I didn't care that I had no money, no house, no plane ticket home. All I cared about was that the following day I would have Mandy wrapped up in my arms.

## A Memorable Stopover

The next morning I rang my boss and explained that my girlfriend was going to be in town for five days, and he was cool with me starting after she had left. At the airport I met Mandy and we kissed as though we had been separated for years, not days.

The five days with Mandy were spent lying in parks, drinking cheap red cask wine on beaches, walking in the mountains, basically doing activities that didn't cost money. We cried at the cruel nature of what had happened and tortured ourselves with the thoughts of how great it would have been if we had been happily back living in her apartment.

Instead, five days later I kissed Mandy goodbye. We had no more tears to cry. She walked through the departure gate with the stunning smile that had attracted me to her all those months ago in the Mexican bar, and with the little teddy bear I had bought her at the supermarket tucked under her arm. Now all we had was our plan.

Our plan consisted of travelling around the world together, but first Mandy would have to finish her school year and also complete her masters, not to mention save some money. The plan for me was to earn my plane ticket back to New Zealand and then try to sort out a way to get to the States on a work visa. Failing that, I would try to get work in the Australian mines, earn some money and meet Mandy back in Mexico for a holiday halfway through her school year.

But the dreams of world travels had to wait as I went back to my reality in Vancouver. I started work the following day, and I still had nowhere to stay. Lucy was working crazy hours on film sets, and living with an older guy who owned the house, so she had to get his permission for me to stay. I was waiting on a text from her, and if I could stay she had to organise with her flatmate to let me in that night as she was working until 2 a.m.

First I went to the laundromat and cleaned a month's worth of dirty clothes. With my black rubbish bag full of clean clothes, I went and sat on the beach in downtown English Bay and looked at the container ships in the harbour. Once again I felt lost. I felt as though I was making a nuisance of myself, even though Lucy would never have thought that. I was beginning to hate relying on people—here I was, 25 years old with no money. I was sitting on an inner city beach like a bum, with a rubbish bag full of my clothes (albeit clean clothes) and with nowhere to sleep for the night. I couldn't keep paying $30 a night for hostel rooms. I had to save $1500 to buy my ticket home.

After two hours of sitting on the beach, my phone rang. It was Elle, a friend of Lucy's who Mandy and I had met the previous day. Elle was one of life's kind souls. She was in her early thirties, sported short blonde hair, hung with a young crowd and always wanted to have fun. Her bubbly voice was a welcome relief from my thoughts. 'Hey Hap, Luce rang me and told me you need a place to crash. You can crash on my couch, no worries.'

She just so happened to be biking past and came to get me. Her act of generosity meant so much to me. I walked with my rubbish bag up to her apartment, which overlooked English Bay, and was just around the corner from the rainbow house I had stayed in with Barney and Bugz. Elle was generous; her house was my house. She cracked me a beer and we sat on the couch looking at the view.

Then Elle, my Vancouver angel, solved one of my problems. After knowing me for only a day, she offered me her apartment for the following six weeks! She was a geologist and was flying out in two days' time for six weeks in the bush. She refused to take any money. When she was away, I was going sleep in her bed, be the carer of all her possessions, have the key to her home. Angels come in all forms; in this case it was an effervescent short-haired blonde geologist.

For the following six weeks, I lived the life. I worked every day available at my old work, saving money. After work I would come home to Elle's apartment with one of the best views in Vancouver. On my days off I would hang out with Lucy and her friends. Every couple of days I would go to the pay phone and call Mandy. When we talked, it usually ended in tears. We decided that maybe it was better to talk less, get on with our lives and work towards meeting up.

The time came when I had enough money to leave and Elle was due home. I cleaned Elle's house like a maid possessed, filled the whole fridge with her favourite beer and left a bottle of whisky and a card on the coffee table.

Lucy picked me up in her car and drove me to the airport. I thanked her and gave her a hug.

'No worries, Crapster.'

Then she drove off to work and I checked in for my Singapore flight, where I had a 24-hour stopover before reaching New Zealand.

I was looking forward to seeing my family, and to being home. I didn't know how the next chapter would pan out, and never in my life did I believe it could be worse than the one I had just had.

## Chapter 11
# FALLING OFF THE LONG WHITE CLOUD
**AUSTRALASIA: Auckland and Nelson, New Zealand, 19 September 2007–14 January 2008**

Arriving back home in New Zealand, the familiar land of the long white cloud, was comforting as usual. Kindly, my aunty picked me up from Auckland airport as she always did and I settled into the spare bedroom and the luxury of her apartment.

I got on to the US embassy to see what my options were for re-entering the States. The straight-talking guy on the other end of the phone told me the visa process was lengthy, in some instances taking over a year, and being on record as 'denied entry' would not help.

During a teary phone call to Mandy, I shared the news that I couldn't come back to the States. After being together for only four months, we had set ourselves a short-term goal of meeting up in a neutral country for a holiday once I had earned enough money. The long-term goal was to reunite in ten months' time once Mandy had finished teaching and studying for her masters. With this goal set, being apart was easier, and it gave us something concrete to work towards in our uncertain future.

The Australian mining industry was booming, so I started sending my CV away to all the companies, applying for entry-level mining positions. I also sent off my CV to all the Australian and New Zealand oil and gas companies, but received nothing back. In these industries it was all about who you knew, and I knew no one.

I was feeling lost again. Nothing seemed to be working out. What was I doing with my life? Was I kidding myself that after being together with Mandy for only four months I was going to wait ten months before being with her again? Would I be better off cutting ties, staying in New Zealand and getting a real job?

What made things worse was seeing people my age who had respectable jobs. I spent a lot of time with Barney in Auckland. After we lost our jobs on the Canadian rigs, Barney had gone back to Auckland and helped manage his mum's beauty salon. Now he had just got a new job as a PR manager, the perfect job for him. He was excited. I was happy for him, but it didn't help my feeling of not knowing my dick from my toe. I had no direction. I would stay at Barney's flat some nights, sleeping on the lounge room floor. In the morning all his flatmates were off to work in the city's law and accounting firms wearing their smartly ironed shirts. They would innocently ask me what I was doing—a question that at that point in time ripped the enthusiasm out of my larger than life, live-the-dream demeanour.

To tell you the truth, I was jealous of them and their careers. They were somebodies in society's eyes. They had security. I had a girlfriend in a country I couldn't enter, no job, no career, no money, no direction—just some goal to live and work in every continent of the world before I turned 30 that no one gave a shit about. I was beginning to wonder why I gave such a shit about it.

After a couple of weeks in Auckland sending CVs off to drilling and mining companies, I flew back home to Nelson. I always found home a bit of a dream killer. I heard all the stories of sons and daughters doing well in their careers, parents becoming grandparents, people buying houses and new cars. I was no longer overseas travelling and working, surrounded by like-minded people.

I was at the local pub talking to a guy from school, and I remember his words.

'So Hap, when are you going to stop fucking around and get a real job?'

He had a point. What was I doing? I was soon to be 26. I had no assets and had spent the last four and a half years bouncing from one short-term job to the next. Working the world was just a stupid little challenge I had set myself. I was only halfway through it. No one would care if I threw it away now. But would I?

All I knew was that I had to earn some money, and I had to get out of my home town. I knew I had to surround myself with people who were on my wavelength, otherwise it was going to be hard not to start looking at myself and questioning what I was doing.

From my previous experience of trying to get work on the rigs in Canada, I knew it was a waste of time sending out CVs to Australian mining companies while I was still in New Zealand. I had to go to where the action was to have any chance of getting work. I had to show a potential employer that I was serious.

I booked flights to Perth, Western Australia, but before flying out I went away on a family weekend, a weekend I would never forget.

## Swinging times

Jim and Sandy were basically my second parents. Mum and Dad had met them at the squash club when they had first moved to

## Falling Off the Long White Cloud

Nelson. My earliest memories were of my sister Jarnia and I playing with Jim and Sandy's children, Ellie and Jason. Jason and I had been best mates. Our fathers had coached our soccer team as youngsters and I had spent my weekends staying over at their place. He was the same mate who had been there when I had shaved my head as a thirteen-year-old, the same mate who was there as I flew through the air on a four-wheel motorbike before hitting the ditch and getting stitches in my knee, the same mate who had been by my side in the back of a house bus at a rave when I had got my nipple pierced and fainted as the stoned blue-and-red-haired tattooist put the skewer through the nerve endings. Jarnia and I, Ellie and Jason had all grown up together, weekend barbecues, tramps, annual Christmas camping trips, boating, fishing and water-skiing.

While I was back in New Zealand, it just so coincided that all 'the kids' were at home at the same time. One last family weekend was planned because it would probably be the last time everyone would be here at the same time, as we were all settling down in different areas of the globe.

We headed to a remote part of the Marlborough Sounds, at the top of the South Island, to Jim and Sandy's bach. The bach was set in a tranquil bay one hour off the main road, with the last part of the trip along a dirt road through farmland.

We had a great weekend of barbecues, fishing and playing cards, then Sunday afternoon had arrived. After lunch, we decided to walk through the bush to check out the rope swing that Jase had made. Now this was a gnarly, backyard construction-type rope swing, in true Jase style.

The swing was a health and safety nightmare, but in this world of rules and regulations, it was a breath of fresh air. Looking at the old rope tied high up in a tree with an orange buoy fixed to the bottom of it made you think, *Shit, that looks dodgy*, but it added to the experience. Most rope swings go out over water, but this swing went out over New Zealand native bush. Due to the steepness of the hill you gained height quickly; at the apex you would be 20 to 30 metres above the forest floor.

The mothers had stayed at the bach as Sandy was on crutches because of recent knee surgery. The fathers and kids all had a go on the swing when my sister Jarnia stepped out for the last go of the day. All day, I had been helping everyone on and off the swing. The reason for this was because the ground was steep and unstable, and there was no level take-off point, but rather hillside covered in ferns, scrub and undergrowth with loose dirt that constantly made you lose your footing.

Jarnia took off, Dad getting a photo of her as she swung high in the air over the bush canopy. As Jarnia swung back I pushed her out for a second time, but my push wasn't strong enough, so on her return she was slightly short of the landing spot.

As I reached out and grabbed the rope, Jarnia had only half-dismounted, her hands clinging just above the buoy. With her feet short of the ground, the rope started to swing back out. I leant out, trying to take more strain on the rope; however, the momentum of the pendulum had turned against us and we were both being pulled from the land. In a split second I had to decide whether to let go of the rope and watch my big sister swing back out over the bush canopy wondering whether she could hold on. So with the rope about to leave my grip, I made a major decision and committed myself to the rope. I lunged and grabbed it just below Jarnia's hands. Both of us were now in it together, heading out over the canopy, holding on for dear life.

In hindsight this decision was totally illogical. But in a protective brotherly way I wanted to be with my sister. I could not have lived the rest of my life with the vision of my sister plummeting from the swing while I stood watching, powerless, from the landing spot.

The big old black rope was tied in large knots, holding the buoy on. It was too thick in diameter for me to get a good hold and as we arced out over the canopy, my grip started to slip.

## Falling Off the Long White Cloud

I slipped all the way down the rope, and in desperation to stop myself falling into the bush below, I grabbed onto whatever I could. This just so happened to be Jarnia's legs. Obviously she could not hold our combined weight, and Jarnia also lost her grip.

Dad lived his worst nightmare in that moment, watching his grown children fall more than 6 metres, out of sight, eaten up by the bush canopy. I remember the feeling of falling and thinking, *This isn't going to be good.*

Through a blur of native New Zealand bush, I remember falling feet first, then I hit a tree that spun me around and I landed with the base of my neck and spine taking the full impact. As I crashed into the ground, what seemed like a camera flash went off before my eyes, filling my vision. Jarnia and I then tumbled head over heels like rag dolls down the steep slope, crashing through the bush, until we came to a stop some 10 metres from where we first hit the ground.

Dazed like a patient coming out of a coma, I took in my surrounds. I could feel myself sliding on the rotting and damp vegetation below me and I became aware of a burning pain at the base of my neck as I inched to a halt on the steep slope.

I knew from first aid training that this was not good. But my first worry was my sister who had landed face down a metre away from me. She was moaning and groaning in agony.

*I had pulled my sister off the swing!*

Guilt and worry overwhelmed me. *Just let my sister be okay. I can't live a life knowing I disabled my sister. The guilt will kill me, please let her be okay. I don't care if I'm in a wheelchair, just let my sister be okay.*

Dad and our friends came crashing through the bush onto the scene. The concern on their faces was as clear to me as the scared look they would have seen on my face. Dad didn't want us moved because of potential spinal injuries so Jim took off back down to the bach to raise the alarm.

## HAP WORKING THE WORLD

My mother recalls seeing Jim running into the bach, out of breath, saying, 'There's been an accident.'

Both mothers asked in unison, 'Who is it?'

'Hap and Jarnia,' Jim replied.

Luckily Sandy's cell phone had reception and she dialled the emergency number to get the rescue helicopter dispatched. Jim and my mum ran back with blankets, water, a sledgehammer and stakes.

The stakes were hammered into the ground to prevent Jarnia and me slipping further down the slope. The smallest movement caused us pain. Ellie sat behind me, stroking my head and reassuring me. Jase, who was a keen photographer, had his camera and captured the terror that we were all experiencing.

Everyone was stunned and unbelieving as this unforgettable day unfolded, a day that could change my family's life. I kept going into shock, my breath quickening as my mind processed the possible outcomes. I tried hard not to focus on visions of family Christmases with both Jarnia and I in wheelchairs, drinking puréed Christmas ham through a straw, and knowing that it was me who had put us in the situation.

As Jarnia groaned with chest pain when a pillow was positioned under her head, I experienced the scariest moment of my life. Like a fuzzy signal on a TV, my vision started to blur, and then I lost reception. I couldn't see. I remember shouting, 'I've got my eyes open, but I can't fucking see! I can't fucking see!'

To try to explain how I felt is hard, but if you want, shut your eyes now and imagine living the rest of your life from this point on in the dark.

I'm not religious, but I remember reasoning with someone out there, or maybe I was just reasoning with myself, *Please give me back my vision, I don't care if I'm in a wheelchair, just let me see.* I could only imagine the concerned looks on everyone's faces. I was scared, I couldn't hide that. Ellie kept stroking my head.

At some point while I was lying on the forest floor, everything about my working-the-world goal got put into perspective. Even though the majority of adults I talked to supported me and told me they wished they had done something similar, I had been having major doubts about whether I was doing the right thing. This stupid little challenge I had set myself, to live and work in every continent of the world before I was 30. What was that about? Who cared about that? I was going to let this stupid little goal of mine rule my life so that when I was 30 I would have absolutely nothing to show for it? I would be in debt and bedraggled, while all my mates would be happily married, living in beautiful houses and would have great careers. And I would still be sleeping on their couches among their kids' toys as they read the morning paper before going to their high-rise downtown office. I was about to turn 26. What the hell was I doing with my life? I had nothing. I had a degree that I hadn't used. I had no career. I had no assets. I had no money. I had a girlfriend who I'd only really known for four months and now I couldn't even visit her country. I was travelling the world with no responsibilities; I wasn't living in the real world.

Lying there with the two basic necessities of sight and movement taken away from me gave me clarity.

It wasn't a stupid challenge; it was my dream. Right then I promised myself that I would do everything in my power to achieve my goal. Falling 6 metres was the best thing that could have happened to my working-the-world quest. But then reality hit—what job could I do blind and in a wheelchair?

After what felt like a lifetime, but was probably only a couple of minutes, the blurry green bush slowly came back and eventually I could make out the leaves, and thick strong trunks, the blue sky high above the native bush.

Later I found out that my loss of vision may have been caused by a number of things, for example, my semi-upright position causing a lack of blood to my head. Whatever happened, I had just been taught a great lesson: life can be taken from you on a sunny, comfortable Sunday afternoon while you're with your family, so you have to live your dream. You don't want to be lying on a forest floor contemplating a future of being blind and in a wheelchair *wishing* you had lived your dream.

With the return of my vision came the far-off vibrating sound of helicopter rotors. Like the morphine that was going to be pumped through Jarnia's veins, relief flooded through me. The helicopter landed on the stony beach in the bay, and ten minutes later the rescue team arrived, consisting of the helicopter pilot, paramedics and a police officer.

Their presence had a calming effect, a feeling that everything was under control. The paramedics assessed us: they weren't concerned with me, as my condition wasn't going to worsen if I was handled properly and I couldn't fall any further. They were more concerned with Jarnia's cracked ribs, the possibility of a punctured lung and other internal injuries.

The helicopter pilot had taken Jim and Jason to help him create a path through the bush to a small clearing from which he would be able to winch us up.

With everyone pitching in, the paramedic rolled me onto a spinal board with particular attention given to keeping my head in line so as not to risk further damage to my spine. Once on the spinal board all my extremities were strapped in and a helmet placed on my head that was then strapped to the spinal board so I couldn't move. Then, while the paramedics prepared to move Jarnia the 20 metres up through the bush, the men lifted and pulled me up their make-shift track like lumberjacks pulling a log. Once at the small clearing, I was wrapped in a blanket and left while everyone went back down to help Jarnia up.

After a long time, punctuated with intermittent screams that echoed in the otherwise quiet bush, Jarnia arrived at my side, hunched over with a trail of dried tears on her cheeks. Although we had arrived at the winching point, I was still anxious about her internal injuries. Even though I was trying to stay positive for her, I was worried sick about the injuries we couldn't see and which were causing her so much pain.

Jarnia was winched up first in a sling, and then I was winched up on my spinal board as the helicopter hovered above, the rotors sending the bush canopy into a frenzy like a tropical storm passing through. As there was no room in the helicopter, Mum and Dad had to drive the two hours back to Nelson Hospital where we were being taken. I can only imagine what was going through their minds. Would their grown children's lives be the same? Would their lives be the same?

The helicopter landed at the heli-pad and the orderlies and doctors came out to meet us. I will always remember the look on the orderly's face as the paramedic was debriefed. As I looked up at the sky, the orderly who was pushing from behind my head made an instinctive sympathetic face to no one. It was just a reflex expression of pity, but one that said to me, *This guy's a little fucked.*

## Lesson learnt

'Can you feel that?' asked the young doctor in his English accent.

I thought, *Of course I can bloody feel that, you have your finger up my bum.*

But I must admit I have never been so happy to feel another man's finger up my bum, as it meant I hadn't lost all feeling.

Trying to diffuse the awkward situation, as the four nurses held me lying on my side with the doctor's finger fully inserted, I answered him, 'Yip, is it as enjoyable for you as it is for me?'

Unfortunately, I just made it weirder, the doc not seeing the funny side, unlike the nurses.

In the ER room with nurses and doctors buzzing around, I kept up a jovial front. It wasn't until I got wheeled away and was by myself in the dark X-ray room getting a cat scan, with large, intimidating, robotic medical machines around me, that

## HAP WORKING THE WORLD

I became scared again. As I lay there on the plastic sheets in my neck brace, at the entrance to the cave-like scanning machine, I was overwhelmed again at what my future could hold. Even though the finger up the bum trick showed I had feeling, I wasn't home safe. The doctors were still concerned and treating me as a serious spinal patient. It wouldn't be until the specialists had the results of the X-rays and scans that they would know the full picture, and as it was a Sunday, that wouldn't be until the next day.

As cheesy as it sounds, as I lay there wanting any kind of help, making promises to the universe, I brought my right hand up to my mouth and kissed my ring, the Scorpio ring that Wheels, the paraplegic Native American man, had given to me that night in the Red Deer park. I kissed it, hoping that what he had said to me at the picnic table while we drank cheap whisky was true, that by me wearing his ring he would take all my pain and injuries as he knew how to fight after all he had been through. Then I thought, *Wheels himself would have been in this exact same situation after the car accident that left him wheelchair bound.*

I spent the night in the hospital staring up at the ceiling counting all the little holes in it, trying to take my mind off my future and the uncomfortable neck brace. The specialist walked into the room to give me my news. Like a politician awaiting the results on election day, I was nervous and anxious for it to be over.

In the fall I had fractured my T7 vertebrae, surrounding my spinal cord. The impact of falling on it had given me a 20 per cent compression fracture, meaning it had been squashed by this amount. But what did this mean? It depended what doctor or specialist you talked to, but the general consensus was that I would be very sore for a couple of months and wouldn't be able to do anything for at least three months, except rehabilitation, building up my muscles. One doctor even told me I was looking at eight months, and that once I was recovered I should not even think about work that involved heavy lifting. I wondered if I could still backpack.

Dad had rung Mandy to let her know that I was in hospital. Mandy later recounted the story of her being at the dentist, about to sit down for treatment, and getting the phone call from my dad. She knew when we were due back from the bach, so when Dad called straight away she knew something bad had happened. She could barely understand Dad's thuck New Zealand accent, but when he told her, 'Hap has fallen off a rope swing in the bush,' she knew it wasn't good, even though she cried into the phone, 'What's a rope swing?!' I had been against letting Mandy know about my accident, as I knew she would just worry and there was nothing she could do. She had no money to visit. She had to keep working and studying and was better off saving her money and putting it towards us meeting up.

Jarnia had been under close watch as the doctors waited for her results. Luckily she had been spared any internal damage, which was a relief. But she hadn't got away scot-free: she had a couple of broken ribs as a souvenir, and every time she laughed or coughed she winced in pain as though a red-hot poker had been thrust into her chest.

In the hospital I had gradually improved, from peeing in the bedpan to taking the walking frame to the toilet to finally hobbling like an 80-year-old. My body felt like it had been violated; not only did I hobble like an 80-year-old, I felt like one too.

There I was, back home in Nelson. I had cancelled my flight to Perth that was leaving in three days. After the hype of the accident had died down, and people stopped visiting, I was again left with my situation. I was about to turn 26, filling out a form for the sickness benefit, living with Mum and Dad, no money, no job, no direction and my girlfriend in a country I wasn't allowed to set foot in.

I had at least three months of rehab ahead; I had to make the most of this opportunity. When lying under that rope swing with Ellie stroking my head, I remember her saying to me, 'Hap, this is just another chapter of your book.' And it sounded right.

The past couple of years I had made small noises about maybe writing a book after mates had commented on my novel-length bulk emails. There was no time like the present, so I took a loan of $5000 from Jarnia and used it to pay off my credit card debt and with the leftover bought my first ever laptop, a cheap discontinued line (the one I used to write this book more than four years later).

On that laptop I created my blog, which documented my travels, country by country, up to that point. For those three months I lay on my back and tapped away at the keyboard.

I was also determined to have a quick recovery. I worked hard on my rehab, doing exercises religiously, going to physio and swimming every day. I was going to be back working the world in the new year in three months' time.

After being denied entry to the United States, falling out of a tree and getting a finger stuck up my bum, I was a changed man. Up till now my working-the-world quest had been more about having a good time, with no real plan, just ticking off continents as opportunities presented themselves. But from this point forward, my goal was going to consume my every thought. I had been given the lesson I needed to refocus on my goal: to see the world and live life without regrets. I imagined turning 30, having a great job and nice house, but with the feeling I would have cheated myself. Underneath that great career and house I would have known that I had let myself down, had quit my dream when I had the power to go on.

I had my health and my family and that was all I needed. I was going to live and work in every continent of the world before I turned 30.

## Chapter 12
# GLORIFIED BOY SCOUT
**AUSTRALASIA: Woodie Woodie, Western Australia, Australia, 17 January 2008–25 February 2009**

*All those travelling to Woodie Woodie please make your way to the departure gate.*

I walked out the departure gate of the small private airport in Perth, the rising sun blinding me.

It was my first day of work in the mining industry. I was excited and apprehensive. I was excited about the adventure of working as an exploration field assistant, to be back working the world, ticking off the continent of Australasia in the outback. But I was apprehensive as it had been just over three months since I had been lying on the forest floor wondering if I was going to be blind and in a wheelchair.

I had been eager to get back to work, and had used my marketing skills to make my health record look more appealing when applying for this job. But the reality was my back was still causing me discomfort, even though I was regularly doing exercise, stretches and strengthening routines. A friend of a friend who worked at the mine had told me about the position of exploration field assistant. With their help, I applied and became a part of the booming Western Australian mining industry.

I boarded the plane and sat next to a guy who with his high-vis safety clothing and steel-toed boots looked like he was ready to walk off the plane straight into work.

He extended a hand. 'Tony. How ya doing, mate?'

When I introduced myself and told him it was my first day and that I was going to be an exploration field assistant, he laughed a hearty down-to-earth laugh.

'It's my first day as well. I'm the exploration geologist. You're going to be my bitch.'

Straight away I liked this goofy-looking geologist with reading glasses that incorporated safety side shields. He had an air of knowledge about him, but he was rough around the edges; like it was with the boys back on the rigs, a spade would be a fucking spade with Tony.

Tony, who had worked in the industry for the last ten years, filled me in on the Pilbara, the outback region where Woodie Woodie was located. Woodie Woodie, commonly known as Woodie, was a manganese mine. Manganese is used as a hardener in the production of steel—it's where the name 'mag' wheels comes from. All I knew was that we were going to get heavy black rocks out of the ground which left you looking like a Gollywog out of a Noddy storybook by the end of the day.

The closest town to Woodie was Marble Bar with a population of 120 hardened folk. Marble Bar's claim to fame is that it holds the world record for the most consecutive days, 160 in total, at a minimum temperature of 37.8 degrees Celsius.

The flight attendant walked down the aisle of the small plane handing out sweets, but when she got to me I realised they were ear plugs.

## Glorified Boy Scout

Tony grabbed some and handed me a pair, saying, 'Put these in, these planes are shit boxes, you can't even hear your iPod on full volume.'

With ears plugged, I settled in for the two-hour flight north, taking a little nap to the drone of propellers in the background.

I woke with a nudge from Tony, telling me to look out the window. Like a little kid seeing snow for the first time I was in awe of what I saw. It was like nothing I had ever seen, just a red landscape as far as the eye could see and massive scrambling patches of a small pale green tussock plants that I was soon to learn was spinifex, which thrives in the harsh outback environment. Tony pointed out the trees on the dried-up riverbeds cutting through the landscape like green veins.

'You always know you're close to water or a riverbed, where there are trees and vegetation.'

The plane circled the earthen red landing strip. There was nothing but outback. Woodie was literally in the middle of nowhere. From the air, Woodie mine consisted of five or so big holes in the ground. Big Tonka trucks moved piles of black rock like little ants. In the middle was the mining camp, a place that 100 or so people called home at any one time. There was only one lifeline to Woodie, the 400-kilometre narrow black snake of a road that slid its way through the red dirt from the coastal town of Port Hedland. The road had been built so that the 50-metre-long road train could haul the black manganese from the mine to the ports to be shipped to the world—an umbilical cord that Mother Nature would cut off every now and then, when she hit the region with cyclones and flash floods.

We bumped our way down the red dirt runway and pulled up at a portable shed with a shadecloth awning—Woodie airport. I walked from the plane into the mid-January heat and felt like I was in a high humidity sauna back in Korea.

I followed Tony and we hopped into a mini-van that would

take us on the ten-minute drive to camp. I sat next to a dump-truck driver.

She gave me a friendly Woodie welcome and summed the place up wonderfully: 'Mate, it's a bit of a shithole but full of good people.'

What the Bundaberg T-shirt-wearing lass meant was that mining camps are usually mini hotel complexes, five-star outback resorts with full length swimming pools, fully equipped gyms and footie fields. But Woodie was only a small mine: internet coverage was patchy and there was no cell phone reception. A planned mine expansion would turn Woodie into one of those state-of-the-art camps with a new airport and facilities. But this wouldn't happen until over a year later after I had left.

We hopped out of the van and Tony popped up beside me. 'Mate, we have to go get our dongas.'

With a surprised look on my face, I asked for clarification. 'Dongas?'

Tony didn't even blink an eye at the word after a decade in the industry. 'Ya donga's the cabin where you sleep.'

We got our keys, and Tony and I walked across the green grass of the mining camp that contrasted with the surrounding red dirt. We rounded a corner and I leapt a mile high as a mini dinosaur-like creature scampered across my path. Tony lost it laughing; he had just found a way to entertain himself for the rest of his time at Woodie—scaring the shit out of Hap.

After he stopped roaring his hearty belly laugh, he explained what I'd seen. 'That's a bungarra. They are pretty harmless but if they bite you, you'll probably get a bacterial infection. They will run up the closest tall thing to them if they are startled, and you're pretty tall, Hap.'

I was unsure if Tony was bullshitting me, but I made sure to keep an eye out for any 2-metre-long bungarra lazing around.

I arrived at my donga, pleasantly surprised. It had everything I needed: a single bed, desk, TV, fridge and en suite. I was in heaven. Since I didn't have a house in Perth yet, this donga was my home, and would be for two weeks at a time, as I was working the standard mining swing of two weeks on and one week off.

Because of my early flight I had been drip-feeding myself coffee all morning to stay awake and I needed to beeline it to the donga toilet. With bladder emptied, I turned on the cold tap to wash my hands.

'Fuck!' The water was bloody boiling.

I thought someone had swapped the hot and cold taps over as a joke. I told Tony as we met up and walked towards the exploration office. He just laughed and pointed to the exposed black PVC water pipes basking in the scorching 40-degree-plus heat. I made a mental note to run the tap off before putting my hands under in the future.

We arrived at the office, a building that resembled two sea containers side by side with the middle cut out. The old air-conditioners seemed to be working overtime but the thermometer inside was still reading 26 degrees Celsius.

We met the rest of the exploration team. They seemed a relaxed bunch of people, and I was soon to find out that mines were pretty relaxed places, especially exploration departments. It seemed like everyone was hurrying to slow down.

## One of those days

It was in my second swing out at Woodie when I had one of those days when you wonder why the hell you ever got out of bed.

It was February, the temperatures were freakishly hot, the flies were like plagues of locusts and the lightning storms were better than any fireworks show I had ever seen. It was the time of year when the exploration department was preparing for the upcoming dry season. The dry season allowed us to get to isolated areas as rainfall was not an issue. We would set up tented camps from where we would base our drilling programs without the risk of being cut off by the flash floods that were a common occurrence in the sweltering wet season. While preparing for the dry season we also completed work in the surrounding areas of the mine.

On this particular day everything that could go wrong did go wrong, right from the start. Every morning we had to do a breath test for alcohol, and you had to be able to 'blow zero'. If you didn't you would be stood down that day without pay. Three strikes and you were out of a job. So when I blew 'numbers' at the 5 a.m. safety meeting I was very surprised as I had gone to the gym the night before instead of going for beers. Thirty minutes later I retried and this time I blew zeros.

After this second attempt, Tony came over to me and said, 'Hap, you don't by any chance use mouthwash do you?'

'Yeah,' I replied, 'I was gargling the stuff as I was walked over this morning.'

He laughed as he told me mouthwash contained alcohol.

Having passed my second breath test, I was to spend my morning walking geophysics gridlines. This involved walking down 2-kilometre-long lines and tying ribbons every 100 metres at specific GPS co-ordinates. The geophysics team would then come along, and send electrical currents into the ground. If the electrical current didn't bounce back immediately it meant there was a good possibility there was manganese below.

In the Land Cruiser I followed the needle of the GPS over the untracked red earth taking in certain trees and rocky outcrops as landmarks in this isolated landscape. The sun was still low in the early morning sky as a herd of camels trotted off in the distance and kangaroos jumped out from a nearby bush as the humming of my V8 engine alerted them that humans were around. My contented feeling was short-lived when I heard a hissing sound. Thankfully it wasn't a large venomous snake, but the air escaping from a tyre. The second lesson I was going to learn that day was to always check the vehicle had a high lift jack. A high lift jack is your best friend when four-wheel driving as it allows you to jack the vehicle out of tricky situations. But I only had a traditional bottle jack. This meant instead of being able to use the jacking points on the vehicle's roo bars, I had to lie down on the ground to place the jack under the axle. This would be no problem if I had been back in Perth, but I was in the middle of the Australian outback, surrounded by a sea of spinifex. Spinifex is the Satan of the plant world. It can grow needle-like tentacles over a metre high and spreads in the outback like a bushfire. As I lay down on the ground and pushed the jack under the axle, I indulged in some Aboriginal acupuncture, courtesy of a bed of spinifex. Luckily I was in the middle of nowhere, so no one could hear my cursing.

With the tyre finally fixed I arrived at the co-ordinates where I was to start my gridding. Now as you know Australia is home to some of the world's most poisonous creatures, and has no shortages of snakes. The outback is prime snake territory, home to quite a few deadly ones. Because I had grown up in New Zealand where there are no snakes, I particularly feared them.

One day, back at the exploration office, Tony had taken it upon himself to get me over this phobia, or maybe it was just for his entertainment, knowing my jumpy nature. Unbeknown to me he had gone to the trouble of tying fishing line to a rubber snake and then attaching it to a spade that was leaning against the shed. As I walked out of the office, Tony, who was sitting with the rest of the team, nonchalantly said, 'Hap, can you grab that spade for me please?'

I walked over and picked it up. All of a sudden a snake started coming towards me, and I yelled and jumped. In fright, I took flight, dropping the spade as I was fleeing. With adrenaline pumping, I glanced back over my shoulder to see everyone pissing themselves with laughter, and then I realised I had been set up—bloody Tony and his rubber snake!

Aside from the pranks, Tony did reassure me that when in the field the snakes would hear me and be long gone before I arrived.

Well, on this day, when I should have stayed in bed, a particular king brown snake hadn't got Tony's memo and chose to hang about. As I was walking along, concentrating on my GPS, my peripheral vision picked up a serpent-like slithering stick making its way over the exposed flat rock 2 metres in front of me. The adrenaline kicked in and in cartoon character fashion my arms and legs instinctively jolted into action, trying to get as far away from the snake as possible, but leaving my body behind. I sent the GPS skyward as once again I took flight.

I still had 3 kilometres more of gridlines to walk, and to say my nerves were shattered would be an understatement. Now, every sound was a snake, and every stick was a snake. So picture me walking in the outback, minding my own business, jumping at the cracking of sticks when out of nowhere, the bushy tree 5 metres from me erupts in a bashing, snapping explosion of sticks! A bloody kangaroo! I don't know who jumped higher, me or the roo.

By now the glaring sun was out in full force. I reached to get my sunglasses out of my pocket but they were gone. They must have fallen out when I had the jumping competition with the kangaroo. Trying to find something that small in this vast expanse of nothing would have been like trying to find love in a brothel, so I just kept walking.

As I finished my first line and went to start on the second, the batteries died on the GPS. Talk about frustrating. This meant I would have to come back again tomorrow and walk the same 2 kilometres with a charged GPS.

As I started my trek back towards the Land Cruiser I went to take a sip from my CamelBak, but it was bloody empty! What I thought was a heavy sweat, from all the jumping and adrenaline, had been my CamelBak leaking. No water meant I couldn't rehydrate, a potentially dangerous situation. To add to this array of misfortunes was the shitload of flies that were literally getting up my nose.

So as I trudged back in the mid-40s heat with the blazing sun in my unshaded eyes, no water, no GPS, and jumping at the slightest movement of a grasshopper, I realised just how vulnerable I was. In this environment, if I was bitten by a snake, or became dehydrated and disoriented, there wasn't much hope. It was a major lesson for me about just how harsh this country was. Even though I carried a first aid kit with a compression bandage for snake bites, I was 2 kilometres from the truck, then an hour's drive across barren land to the camp, then a further four hours' drive to the nearest hospital, or I would have to wait however long it took for the Flying Doctor Service to arrive. Even though I carried a SAT phone that allowed you to get reception in remote places via satellite, its usefulness was limited. During my time at Woodie, it became protocol to do field work in pairs to avoid these situations.

I arrived back at the exploration office thinking that surely my day couldn't get any worse. My afternoon was going to be spent rehabilitating the previous year's drill holes; locating them using GPS, plugging the drill holes, which had a diameter similar to a lamp post, with a concrete plug and covering them in dirt so the land appeared natural and undisturbed.

True to form the afternoon didn't start well. I spent the first hour driving around unable to find the drill holes. I would be standing at the correct GPS co-ordinates but there was no drill hole. The GPS was really starting to piss me off. I went back to the office to change the 'faulty' device, and bumped into Tony. I told him the problem. He laughed that laugh again. I knew the problem wasn't going to be the GPS, but rather me. He informed me that last year's holes had used a different GPS grid setting, of 200 metres difference. With a couple of pushes of a button Tony had solved the problem, and now all the holes would be where they were supposed to be.

I set out with my recalibrated GPS, my first co-ordinate pointing me in the direction of a disused mine pit. Procedure required me to do a call up on the radio before entering. I then proceeded into the pit following the arrow of my GPS.

Next thing I knew, there was a Land Cruiser flying towards me. It pulled up with the driver barking, 'What the fuck are you doing?'

Still caught up in trying to find the hole, I replied, 'I'm trying to find a hole to rehab.'

'Well, if you wait another five minutes you won't have to bother as we're just about to blow this area up!'

'You're bullshitting me,' I blurted out.

But he pointed to the waiting blast crew in the distance.

With my nerves once again shot, I decided to go give Tony a hand at a nearby drill rig to wait out the blast. I was now on full safety alert as I approached the rig, and gave it a wide berth by driving through some burnt-out scrub.

As I pulled up by Tony he pointed at my tyre, slapping his leg, laughing and saying, 'You've got another flat.'

I didn't take the bugger seriously, and thought he was having me on. Then he came around to the driver's side and erupted into further fits of laughter, bordering on an asthmatic attack.

'Hap, you have two flatties!' Tony then gestured to the scrub I had just barged through and told me that although it looked burnt out and brittle the stumps were as strong and dangerous as daggers.

Sure enough, I had two flat tyres, and to make matters worse I had to borrow the spare from Tony's vehicle, as I had already used one that morning. Then he really rubbed it in by bargaining with me, one spare tyre for a case of beer. That's fair game in mining. What could I do?

I got back to camp, my ordeal coming to an end. I didn't even contemplate going to the gym or for a swim for fear of dropping a weight on myself or drowning. I went straight to the wet mess and bought Tony the case of beer. With much laughter from the crew, I reflected on my day. A snake, an Aboriginal acupuncture session, GPS challenges, no water, nearly blown up, and three flat tyres. Shit, why did I get out of bed today?

## Farewell to the outback

No other day was like this but after twelve months working at Woodie it was time to move on.

Being an exploration field assistant was my favourite job while working the world. I loved being in places that felt like no man had ever stepped in before. At our remote regional camp, after a hard day's work, we sat around the campfire with the drill crew, cold beer in hand, with the sound and smell of dinner sizzling on the fire. After a few beers, we retired to our swags to sleep under the stars. There were the geophysics gridlines to be walked, kilometre upon kilometre through the wondrous landscape, along with helicopter mapping work and working with the local Aboriginal people conducting heritage surveys, looking for potential sacred sites.

In a sense my time in Western Australia had been a pit stop. It had been a time for me to regroup, to rebuild my working-the-world platform which had crumbled with my denied entry to America and the rope swing accident in New Zealand.

With dedicated rehabilitation, my back was as good as it would ever be. My credit card was paid off and my savings account was ready to once again work the world.

Mandy and I had endured our forced ten months apart. We had reunited in Bali, Indonesia, spending two glorious weeks island hopping and drinking afternoon beers. While there we had both gained our open-water scuba diving certification and discovered the underwater world.

In Perth we shared a room in a flat and spent time hanging with our great group of friends and taking road trips to the pristine beaches of Western Australia. But we had both developed a severe case of itchy feet.

# Chapter 13
# THE HEART OF SOUTH AMERICA

**SOUTH AMERICA: Asunción, Paraguay,
25 February–6 August 2009**

After a mate's wedding in Korea, Mandy and I made our way to Thailand. We spent a couple of months on the island of Koh Tao where I studied and worked as a dive master while Mandy worked at a beachside café.

During a visa run to Malaysia, Mandy and I were having dinner and we ordered a bottle of red wine, which happened to be from Argentina. We started talking about how cool it would be to do a snowboarding season in Argentina; Mandy could teach English and be surrounded by the Spanish language in which she was fluent and I would study Spanish. The more we talked about it the more excited we got.

Six weeks later, what started as a conversation on a Saturday night on the island of Penang became a reality when we hopped off the bus in the Argentinian ski resort town of Bariloche. Our excitement was greeted by the cool mountain air of the lakeside bus station.

I enrolled at my Spanish language school, but Mandy was unable to find work. The usually thriving tourist town was struggling with the global economic recession, a poor snow season and a swine flu epidemic. Ironically, five weeks later we were back at the bus station with our snowboards, heading off to a country with no mountains, no snow and stiflingly hot, humid weather!

After backpacking through Argentina and Uruguay we arrived in Paraguay's capital city, Asunción, and headed for the house of Mandy's former boss, Señora Sofia, where we would be living for the next couple of weeks while we settled into Paraguayan life. We drove through the streets in a beaten-up yellow Mercedes taxi with our snowboard bags hanging out of the boot tied on by tattered rope, football commentary blaring on the taxi speakers.

Mandy got off her cell phone and reported they were expecting us. Señora Sofia was still at work, but her husband, Señor Oscar, was at home waiting. Wanting to make a good first impression, which seemed like it was going to be hard judging by the number of prolonged looks my dreadlocks had already received, I started quizzing Mandy on Paraguayan greetings.

In Argentina the greeting had been one kiss on the cheek for guys and girls. Mandy informed me that in Paraguay they gave two kisses, one on each cheek. With my newfound knowledge of Paraguayan greetings fixed in my mind, the taxi bumped to a halt outside the security fence of her boss's home.

We rang the buzzer and the maid and Señor Oscar came to unlock the front gate. We said our hellos and pleasantries through the bars of the gate as the maid struggled to find the correct key in the evening darkness.

This gave Señor Oscar and me time to size each other up. He was a small man in his early sixties; his balding grey hair and glasses gave him an intelligent distinguished appearance. There I was on the other side of the bars, in boardies that still carried a sauce stain from Thailand, and shoulder-length mouldy dreadlocks with an array of seashells hanging from them. I was praying that the maid would hurry up and find the right key before he decided it was better for his family's safety and property's value that he didn't let me in.

Finally the gate was unlocked. I thanked God, picked up my bags and followed Mandy through the gate. Mandy naturally embraced Señor Oscar in a hug and they effortlessly kissed on each cheek.

After Mandy and Señor Oscar finished greeting each other, I confidently stepped forward to take his outstretched hand. I wanted to impress him with my knowledge of Paraguayan customs and put his dreadlock doubts to rest. I clasped his outstretched hand, placed my left hand on his shoulder, moved in and planted one kiss on his cheek. He didn't seem as into it as me, and I didn't blame him—getting a face full of mouldy dreadlocks can really take the passion out of a greeting. But I was determined to finish what I'd started, and he wasn't getting away that easily, so I quickly planted the second kiss on the other cheek.

Following that he recoiled and distanced himself from me with his hands in the air, stammering, 'No, no, no.'

I knew I had cocked up the greeting and looked to Mandy for help. But Mandy was as shocked as Señor Oscar.

I threw my hands up in an I-don't-know-what-the-hell-I've-done kind of way. I looked at Señor Oscar anxiously and said, 'Mandy told me that you give two kisses in Paraguay.'

He replied, 'Men don't kiss men.'

Mandy had now found her voice. 'Sorry Hap, I forgot to mention that it's not like Argentina where you greet men with a kiss.'

At least the ice was broken now.

# The Heart of South America

## Why are you going there?
Whenever I told anyone that I was going to Paraguay they always asked the same question: 'Why?'

They had a point. Paraguay is a small landlocked country, half of which consists of a barren inhospitable area known as the Chaco. Paraguay's temperatures range from hot to bloody hot, accompanied by stifling humidity with no beaches to cool off at. It is South America's second poorest country behind Bolivia. It's renowned for its corruption with the joke it was bribed out of first place.

At the time, Lonely Planet didn't even have a Paraguay guide book and apart from some Jesuit ruins and the world's second largest dam, there is not a lot to attract tourists compared to other South American countries. Although it may not have had the beaches of Brazil, the mountains of Argentina, the salt plains of Bolivia, the cocaine of Colombia or the Machu Picchu of Peru, it did have the friendliest people I was to come across during my working-the-world quest. And it isn't tainted with the desperation of a country that relies solely on tourism to put food on the table.

Paraguayans are happy with what they have. '*Asi es*,' they say: 'That's how it is.' If there is ever going to be an Armageddon and we have to rebuild our lives I will head to Paraguay. While the rest of the world complains about how life used to be, the Paraguayans will be getting on with life, still smiling, '*Asi es.*'

Paraguay is a country with an underdog feel to it, which is the main reason I fell in love with it. It has had a battered history which has given the people such heart. It gained independence in 1811 from the Spanish and refused leadership from Argentina. Since then it had been ruled by dictatorships or near dictatorships up until 1989. Today it has multi-party democratic rule.

The first couple of weeks there I took a small pack and went exploring. I caught a cargo boat up the muddy waters of the Rio Paraguay that cuts through the middle of the country.

## HAP WORKING THE WORLD

I headed into rustic camping grounds that had hidden waterfalls and I visited Jesuit ruins. The joy for me was not in the sights, but in reaching my destination. Tourist infrastructure didn't exist; there were no tourist offices, signposts or buses to where you wanted to go. I had to rely on my Spanish to ask directions and everyone seemed to give me different directions for the same destination. Sometimes I understood nothing as the locals could only speak their native Guaraní and you could forget about English speakers. The 6.5 million Paraguayans speak Spanish and the native Guaraní, and they are South America's only officially bilingual country.

The Paraguayan people I met along the way were a warm and friendly bunch. It didn't matter if you were asking directions or talking to street vendors. If someone approached you it was out of genuine inquisitiveness. They were humble, curious and not overpowering. There was only one price; it didn't matter if you were a tourist or local. I found it refreshing.

## Living and working in South America

We moved into Señora Sofia's brother Juan's house. He was a single man in his mid-forties, with a short round frame and thinning hair, but was young at heart with a love for playing music and listening to The Beatles. He was Paraguay's top lawyer, but you would never know when meeting him; like his house, Juan was humble. He happily opened up his house to us. He wanted nothing in return; his house basically became our house as he worked every hour under the sun at his law firm.

Mandy started working full-time at Señora Sofia's English institute and I went back to studying Spanish at a local school. I also joined up to take part in an upcoming production of *Fame* as I had always wanted to give acting a go. But I also had to find work. Not so much to earn money, as Paraguay was extremely

## The Heart of South America

cheap, but to tick off the continent of South America. Up to now I had spent a lot of time in South America, but I had never lived in a place long enough to find work.

In Paraguay I had several jobs including editing a company's website and tutoring a high school student who was heading to New Zealand on an exchange program.

The main job I had in Paraguay was as a storyteller, or more accurately an entertainer. A company that published children's English language books hired me to visit primary schools to read stories in English. The problem was that most of the kids didn't understand English. This meant I ended up acting out the stories, fooling around in front of the kids like Humpty Dumpty on crack. I was in my element. Most of the time it was pretty easy to entertain the kids; they had never seen a real live person with dreadlocks before.

One day, at a well-off school, this seven-year-old had been looking at my dreadlocks inquisitively. Towards the end of my reading, he gained the confidence to put up his hand.

In a distinguished but tentative voice he asked, 'Are you a hippy?'

I replied with amusement, 'What's a hippy?'

He quickly answered, 'Someone who doesn't shower.'

I laughed at the free and uninhibited reply that could only come from a kid. I told him that I had showered that morning, therefore I wasn't a hippy and that my name was Hap as in Happy, not Hip as in Hippy.

Although I was working in Paraguay, my thoughts were constantly consumed by another continent.

## The elusive white continent

At this time it was a couple of months before my 28th birthday, so I had just over two years left to get to my two remaining continents, Antarctica and Africa. Africa would be easy enough;

I could buy a plane ticket, live in a mud hut and find volunteer work. But Antarctica, that was to be another story.

The funny thing about Antarctica was that when I set myself the goal to live and work in every continent before age 30, Antarctica hadn't been on my radar. I'm unsure if I only thought there were six continents or if I just didn't even consider it as a place to be able to get work.

However, that all changed four years into the quest when I was in Colorado. Mandy and I were having dinner with one of her fellow teachers and her husband who had sailed the world. I was telling the husband about my goal and he asked me, 'What are you going to do in Antarctica?'

I replied I wasn't going to Antarctica, to which he said, 'Well, if you're going to live and work in every continent, you have to work in Antarctica.'

Shit, he had a point. And from that moment on my battle with the elusive white continent began.

I naively jumped into the task of finding work in Antarctica with the enthusiasm of someone who didn't know what he was getting himself into. My internet research showed that there were international science bases on Antarctica and it just so happened that New Zealand had one, Scott Base. Having no science background, the only job I was qualified for was as a cleaner. Surprisingly there was fierce competition to clean toilets in temperatures of -40 degrees Celsius. Over a hundred people applied at the annual recruitment for the one or two positions available. I didn't make the cut. I also tried the Armed Forces Canteen Council who run the shop and bar at Scott Base. I didn't make that cut either.

I also sought unskilled work at the 800-person American McMurdo Base and with an American Antarctic logistical company, but as I didn't have an American work visa and there were 300 million Americans who were capable of cleaning toilets, I inevitably got turned down. I tried the Australian bases,

## The Heart of South America

but they had no unskilled positions either. I tried the British Antarctic Survey and the Antarctic Heritage Trust, which looks after the heritage sites, but still no luck.

After these initial rejections I realised that because I was a New Zealander, Scott Base was my only real hope. I had to make myself more Antarctic-employable for the following year's annual recruitment. Hence when I arrived at Woodie, I realised a polar science base was similar to an outback mine as both are isolated communities. When there is an emergency the staff have to deal with it, essentially like a volunteer fire brigade does. I joined the mine emergency response team and airport ground crew, gaining experience and qualifications in fire fighting, high rope rescue, first aid up to the Emergency First Responder level, and aeroplane marshalling, fuelling and unloading.

But despite these extra feathers in my cap, I was rejected again a year later for the cleaner position.

With the Antarctic science bases giving me no love and another year to wait for the next annual recruitment, I had to get proactive. At this time I was in Thailand and expanded my research on getting employed in Antarctica. Tourism to Antarctica had quadrupled in the past decade, the majority of this through expedition cruise ships that left from the port of Ushuaia, at the southern tip of South America. I had now become obsessed with getting to Antarctica.

It was from Paraguay that I launched my Antarctica attack. I spent all my spare time contacting people and researching. Although I was doing the storytelling work and tutoring, my full-time job was finding work in Antarctica. The season was to start in a couple of months, sometime in October when the ice melted and allowed the ships access. I became more than obsessed. I was going to set foot on that continent that year if it was the end of me. Little did I know at that time that it nearly was.

I got hold of a list of all 52 companies that were registered to work in Antarctica and individually contacted them all, including some additional cruise ship recruitment companies. I contacted the Scientific Committee of Antarctic Research who advised there were 29 countries that had either Antarctic interests or actual science bases on Antarctica. So I contacted all of them too and then set about following up the leads I had got, contacting and recontacting people. Although people were supportive, it was just rejection after rejection after rejection.

Every morning I would wake and the first thing on my mind was Antarctica, and the last thing I thought about at night was Antarctica. Sometimes I would wake in the night and not be able to get back to sleep because Antarctica was still on my mind. Eventually the constant rejection was starting to get me down.

Then I got my break. Family and friends in New Zealand told me about two volunteer painting positions that had been advertised at Scott Base. Finally! This hope renewed my enthusiasm. It was the perfect job for me. I had painting experience from my time in Kentucky. I had worked in Canada's −40 degree Celsius temperatures, so I was used to the cold. And I was used to being isolated from my time working in the Australian outback. I poured all my heart and soul into the application form and made sure I dotted the i's and crossed the t's. Although I was out of the country I even booked flights back to New Zealand to show the organisation that I was serious about the positions.

Only 25 people applied for the two positions, and five people were shortlisted. I didn't even make the shortlist! I enquired why I never got shortlisted and was told my motivation to go to Antarctica didn't align with what the organisation was looking for. I was crushed.

## Meltdown

I couldn't face any more Antarctica.

I decided to put it on the back burner until the Antarctic season the following year. I kept up my part-time jobs, my

*Fame* rehearsals and put all my Antarctic energy into starting up backpacker tours in Asunción. I planned out the tours, talked to the restaurants and bars, and did trial runs. Then I started spending my days at the tourist office trying to recruit tourists for my tour. But there was one problem; there were no tourists. I knew I was flogging a dead horse but I just kept pushing myself to take my mind off Antarctica.

One day it all came to a head. I was in downtown Asunción, a place where Mercedes and horse carts shared the bustling roads. I was getting flyers for my tours printed. As I was queuing up in a busy little printing shop, it all just hit me: the constant pressure of putting myself forward and all the rejection. I quickly walked out of the printers before I was served. I walked up to a shop window and pretended to look inside to hide my face, oblivious to what was on display. I started crying.

I kept walking aimlessly, trying to leave this consuming feeling behind me. But it wouldn't leave, I wasn't myself. I couldn't go on. Words like *mental breakdown, depression, panic attack, anxiet*y were going through my mind. I was a mess. I had always believed in myself. I was confident, happy Hap. Right then I didn't even think I was capable of getting on a crowded bus and making it back to the safety of Juan's house.

What the fuck was happening to me? Was I a freak? Was I going to become a mumbling fool on a street corner unable to communicate and fit into society? The only time in my life I had been this scared was when I was lying under that rope swing thinking I was going to be blind and in a wheelchair for the rest of my life.

I managed to get on the bus, and luckily I was able to get a seat by the window so I could pretend to look out, to hide the tears I was fighting. I got home and climbed into bed with the midday sun shining into the room making it feel like a sauna. But I didn't care; the safety and comfort of the sheets were like a womb to a baby.

I had a meeting that afternoon with a book publishing company. There was no way I could attend. Shit, I wasn't even strong enough to ring up to tell them that I couldn't come. I rang Mandy and asked if she could ring on my behalf. Straight away she could hear in my voice that I wasn't myself and she asked me what was up. I just started crying, saying I didn't know what was happening.

She came home, walked into the room and saw me curled up under the sheets. I tried to be strong but as soon I went to speak I started crying again. She had never seen me like this before, and for that matter neither had I. I needed some answers and I needed help. I was scared, but I wasn't scared of asking for help. Mandy approached the ever-helpful Juan and I was booked in with a counsellor the next day.

As I waited in the counsellor's room, I took in the surroundings. There were no windows, the old concrete walls were painted grey, there was a painting on the wall that I think may have been Jesus. I thought to myself, *This is the most depressing room I've been in.* I may have laughed.

Then the counsellor came in and placed a typewriter on his desk. The last time I had seen a typewriter was in the mid-1990s in typing class at my first year of high school before our school got computers. Fifteen years later I was in a prison cell of a room with this counsellor clanking away at my patient card. He struggled with my New Zealand accent so I had to speak slowly and choose my words carefully. He prescribed me what he called 'tranquilisers'. All I could think was, *Shit, I'm not a horse. I've got to sort this out.*

He may have used a prehistoric typewriter and not been able to understand me very well but he gave me valuable advice. He told me to take a break from life and to have a good think about what was really important to me.

That is what I did. I called in sick to work. I didn't answer emails. I didn't write blog posts. I just let life pass me by while I sat on the footpath under the shade of a tree. What was important to me? How could I climb out of this hole that I had dug for myself? One factor kept coming back: Antarctica.

One day I went for a run in the rain. Due to the lack of drains, the roughly made cobblestone roads were in flood, but I just powered through the river that flowed down them. I was soaked to the bone, energised by the rain on my face. I got transported by an image where I was on the deck of a yacht with the sea spray hitting my face, and the yacht was headed for Antarctica. It was at that moment I realised that if I didn't continue trying to get to Antarctica, I would regret it for the rest of my life.

It was now late October and the Antarctic ice was just starting to melt, signalling the start of the tourist season. This was it, I was going to Ushuaia.

It was not an easy decision. I had to let a lot of people down and it killed me. But what was more important, making other people happy or my own happiness?

I threw away my tranquiliser prescription and pulled out of *Fame* just a month before the grand opening night. I had to quit my English tutoring job before the end of my contract. It would be Mandy's 30th birthday in about three weeks, but she supported me. I used my entire storytelling savings to buy her a beautiful dress that she had been looking at but couldn't afford. If I couldn't be there, I dearly wanted her to feel special on her birthday.

I finished my storytelling job and spent the last weekend away with Mandy. She was going to take some Paraguayan exchange students back to Denver over the Christmas break, and we would meet up back in Paraguay when she had got back from the United States and me from Ushuaia, or hopefully Antarctica.

After the weekend, and two days before my 28th birthday, I boarded a plane headed for 'the end of the world'.

# Chapter 14
# THE END OF THE WORLD

**SOUTH AMERICA: Ushuaia, Tierra del Fuego, Argentina,
9 November 2009–10 December 2009**

I looked out the rain-splashed window as we touched down and saw snow surrounding the tarmac. This was going to be my new home, for how long I didn't know. I looked down at my T-shirt which I had got printed in Paraguay before I left. It read *I will do ANYTHING to work in Antarctica*.

I was a man on a mission, a man possessed.

I pulled my beanie over my dreadlocks, which had been with me through the entire two and half years' battle to get to Antarctica. I walked into the airport terminal, with no accommodation booked as usual. I got a list of hostels and the first on the list was Antarctica Hostel. It seemed fitting.

Ushuaia, *el Fin del Mundo*, the acclaimed 'end of the world', was once a small mountain town but had now been swept up in the Antarctic tourism storm. The centre of town was the tourist

# The End of the World

heart, with overpriced restaurants, souvenir shops and outdoor shops selling all the top brands. Further up the hill, on which Ushuaia was perched, I realised the mountain town was still intact, with ramshackle boxy houses with smoking chimneys haphazardly lining the streets.

As I pulled up at the hostel in the taxi, a super-friendly manager Luis came out to help me with my pack. I entered the warm atmosphere of the common area and took off my jacket.

Luis looked at my shirt and read it aloud. 'I will do ANYTHING to work in Antarctica.'

I already knew that just because I was in Ushuaia it would still be nearly impossible to get work in Antarctica. Luis also warned me to not get my hopes up and he recounted numerous stories of people having failed. Just yesterday a guy had left after two weeks of trying, and Luis pointed to the sofa on which he had broken down crying.

I was under no illusions. I knew I only had around a 1 per cent chance of getting work. It was not like I could walk up to a cruise ship and ask for work. All the cruise ship companies had recruitment offices and HR departments in their home countries. All employees had to go through a rigorous application process, medical tests and have particular certifications before being employed. From my research I knew that the majority of the Antarctic cruise ship workers were recruited from the Philippines and Russia. There were only a handful of English-speaking Antarctic experts who were crew and who would give lectures and take the passengers ashore in Zodiac boats, but for that you needed a career that ended in 'gist': geologist, biologist, anthropologist, climatologist, marine biologist or ornithologist.

Although I only had a 1 per cent chance it was more than I had in landlocked Paraguay.

After putting my pack under my dorm bed I took my laptop into the common area of the hostel and sat on a comfortable armchair in the corner. This was going to be my office for as long as it took me to get to Antarctica.

I recontacted all the 52 Antarctic-registered companies, the recruitment agencies, the 29 countries with Antarctic interests and scientific bases, and other contacts I had made over the last two and a half years, telling them that I was in Ushuaia and could leave tomorrow if need be.

At times I ventured from the armchair and fought my battle on the ground of Ushuaia. I was glad I had learnt Spanish as this was a key weapon in my arsenal. I approached the local paper and they ran an article on my quest to gain work in Antarctica. I went to the offices of the two cruise ship companies in Ushuaia. I waited outside the security gate to the pier where the cruise ships were berthed and handed letters to crew members for them to give to their captains. I even asked the security guards and found out where ships' captains would have coffee, and then I personally took them letters. In the hostel I followed up leads with people who had just come back from Antarctic cruises and who told me of a possibility of an opening on board the ship they had just been on.

On one occasion I heard that adventurer Robert Swan was in town with his 2041 Organisation. He was taking a leadership expedition of environmentally aware young people to Antarctica. Swan is a strong advocate for Antarctica, and is the first man to have walked unassisted to both the North and South poles. I had read his book *Antarctica 2041: My Quest to Save the Earth's Last Wilderness* and knew if I could talk to him he would see my passion for Antarctica. I found out what hotel he was staying at and wrote him a letter.

I walked through the plush hotel foyer up to the front desk and told the receptionist I was there to see Mr Swan. I was expecting her to call security to throw out the dreadlocked hippy, but to my surprise she rang through to his room. The next thing I knew she was passing the phone over to me. Shit, what do you say to a

# The End of the World

famous Antarctic legend that you've just stalked and who doesn't know who you are? Well, I started with my name and then just let rip with my passion for getting to Antarctica.

Even though he was in the middle of a meeting, he listened to me, but said, 'I'm sorry, Hap, I have no berths available. But leave me your letter and I will read it. Take down my email address and email me with what you can offer my organisation and I will do what I can to get you on next year's expedition. I admire your persistence. Good luck.'

To this day, I remember his words: 'I admire your persistence.' Coming from someone like Robert Swan they meant a lot to me.

I visited all the travel agents hoping they would have contacts and dropped off my business card. I also went to the local naval base to see if they could get me work in Antarctica. I approached fishing boats. I approached the one company that flew planes to Antarctica. I contacted an Antarctic logistics company in Chile. And I contacted Patriot Hills Camp, the only private company to have a base on Antarctica from where their expeditions left.

After nearly three weeks I had made many contacts, everyone knew about me, but I was no closer to getting to Antarctica. December was now here. I had exhausted all my options.

I had tried everything.

It was at this point I wrote in my diary:

*Today I made a pact with myself, I will either leave Ushuaia having worked in Antarctica, or be arrested stowing away. Have nothing to lose.*

## The waiting game

With all the options exhausted, it was now a waiting game. I had put out all my lines and was waiting for the big fish to take the bait.

A couple of days later as I was walking out the door of the hostel to go for a run in the mountains to clear my head, the receptionist started speaking to me in excited rapid-fire Spanish. All I could pick up was that someone had been ringing for me that morning; someone was looking for me and something about a ship's captain at the hostel. I pretended I understood her, and knew I had to check my email.

As I went to get my laptop, the receptionist started pointing to a man coming down the stairs and saying, '*El capitán.*'

I was a little confused trying to piece all this together. I couldn't figure it out, why would a captain be in a hostel?

I stopped the older looking guy on the steps and asked him, 'Excuse me sir, are you a ship captain?'

He replied in a thick Australian accent, 'Yeah, mate. Why's that?'

'Were you looking for me?' I asked.

'Not that I know of, mate. Why?'

I told him who I was and how I was trying to get work in Antarctica, that I was hoping to get on a cruise ship and maybe he had work on his cruise ship.

He started laughing. 'Nah, mate. I'm a captain of a ferry back in Australia. I'm here to go on a cruise as a passenger.'

It seemed the receptionist had got the wrong end of the stick. Once again a door had been slammed in my face. But for some reason I still had this niggling feeling I needed to check my emails.

When I opened my inbox there were three emails from Sich. Sich was Richard Sidey, a young Kiwi photographer and videographer who worked on cruise ships in the polar regions. My good friend Hazel knew him and had told me to get in touch with him. I had emailed Sich from Paraguay, telling him that I would be in Ushuaia and it would be cool to catch up. When I first arrived his ship was in port so he came up to the hostel to have a cup of tea. Like me, Sich had worked all over the world so we chatted easily, but just as the jug boiled he was summoned back to the ship.

Now I had three emails all sent in the last couple of hours, two of which had the titles 'job????', and the other 'I really hope you check your email today bro'.

The first one I opened said:

*You gotta get in touch with me today asap bro. May have a lead. I'm having heaps of trouble trying to call you. Do you have Skype?*

The second one said:

*Basic story is dining room is short staffed and we come into port about 10 p.m. tonight. I talked to the hotel director and he says he needs a waiter . . .*

Holy shit! Then it clicked. It had been Sich on the phone to the hostel receptionist. Hope and excitement flooded my veins; this was as close as I had come, ever. Sich had given me the hotel director's email address to send through my hospitality CV.

Now I was faced with a problem. This cruise ship wasn't a normal cruise ship, it was the crème de la crème of cruise ships. It wasn't five star, it was six star! My problem was that I had never been a waiter and the closest I had come to working in hospitality was the toilet attendant job I'd had in Banff.

I looked at my T-shirt: *I will do ANYTHING to work in Antarctica*. Then I thought of Mandy's hospitality CV stored on my laptop. I couldn't squander this opportunity. I opened her CV, deleted her name and inserted mine. I changed a few dates, a few placenames and countries, and all of a sudden I had seven years' hospitality experience!

I sent off the CV, making sure not to mention my goal or to portray how desperate I was. A six-star cruise ship wouldn't care about my goal, they were just in dire need of an experienced waiter. I didn't leave my laptop the whole day, and set up camp waiting and waiting for a reply.

Finally it came that afternoon from the cruise ship's hotel manager. It read:

> *Your details have been forwarded to the office as we need to have all crew vetted through our HR department in Monaco.*
>
> *The biggest obstacle in hiring will be the necessary medical required by law for any crew on board as a health certificate needs to be issued by the home country.*
>
> *I will hopefully have a reply by tomorrow and will be able to give you details.*
>
> *Enjoy your stay in Ushuaia and hopefully we will see each other soon.*

Bloody hell. It sounded positive. It sounded like a foregone conclusion. If I could get the medicals completed in Ushuaia, and passed, then I would be on my way to Antarctica. But I couldn't count my chickens before they were hatched. I wouldn't allow myself to be crushed by further rejection by getting my hopes up too high.

The waiting game, oh the waiting game. I was a bag of nerves. I was so close. I didn't know whether to stay by my laptop or go for a run. I decided to stay, like a gambler too scared to leave his favourite pokie machine in case it hit the jackpot.

By the following day my patience had run out. I knew the cruise ship would be heading back to Antarctica for another eleven-day cruise. I emailed the ship's hotel manager for an update. A very long three days later, I received this email:

> *No news but this is not uncommon. Our mills grind slowly most of the time.*
>
> *I'll let you know if and when anything comes up.*

Shit. All my previous euphoria disappeared. I kept focusing on that last sentence of the short email: *I'll let you know if and when anything comes up.* I read and reread that message a hundred times, trying to figure out what it meant. *If* anything comes up. Was this single two-letter word going to slam another door in my face?

# The End of the World

Six days after Sich had contacted me I got an email from the HR department in Monaco. It said:

*I have been informed that you are currently in Ushuaia and you would be willing to join the vessel for a short period of time in the position of Asst Waiter. You would be required to complete a full medical exam before the vessel's arrival on 10 December, including chest X-rays, blood test, urine test, stool test etc. as outlined in the form.*

*Kindly confirm your interest and your availability.*

I replied, the content of my email along the lines of 'Hell yes, I'm keen.'

The ball was rolling, things were looking good now. But it was a Saturday in the small town of Ushuaia. This meant I would have to wait until Monday to find out if I could get all medical exams completed there, as people were telling me that I would have to go to Buenos Aires, which was out of the question. I had until Wednesday night to get all the tests completed and passed. Also Tuesday was a public holiday, and this was South America, the end of the world, where things don't happen quickly.

It was not only my medical tests that were going to be problematic. When I opened my email on Monday morning there was another message waiting from HR for me:

*As it is quite an 'unusual' situation please let me know how long you're available.*

*Please send the completed Personal Info form and a copy of your passport ASAP in order for me to issue your contract . . .*

By *unusual* she meant that her company had never recruited someone from a port before. But the part that worried me was that I had to send through a copy of my passport. My passport photo was a recent one, in which I sported my shoulder-length dreadlocks. Sich had been telling me that my dreadlocks would have to come off; appearance was everything on this cruise ship.

It's hard to explain to people who don't have dreadlocks how attached you get to them—they are like a favourite pair of shoes that you love but are not willing to throw out even though they are mouldy and smell musty. I would do anything to keep them, but I would also do ANYTHING to work in Antarctica.

Within a minute of me sending the copy of my passport through, the HR department emailed back saying:

*Would you be able to send me your current picture?*

*We have certain requirements with regards to hairstyle and I want to make sure yours is acceptable to the vessel's management.*

Shit, it was decision time now. I let out a sound like a wounded walrus while I pondered it, then I grabbed my jacket and ran out the door. I ran to a hairdresser a couple of streets away which was coincidentally called New Look. The well-groomed male hairdresser looked at me as though he was thinking, *What are you doing in here? Hippies don't get haircuts.*

I blurted out he had to cut off my dreadlocks and make me look like a 'six-star waiter' and if I started crying, to just keep cutting.

My dreadlocks slowly piled up on the floor like a pit of hairy snakes, and the guy in the mirror staring back at me started looking younger and younger as each dreadlock hit the ground. I now looked like someone who should be a waiter on board a six-star cruise ship, instead of washing dishes in the Greenpeace galley.

Not yet ready to totally give up my dreadlocks, I put them in a bag and ran back to the hostel. I took a photo of myself and emailed it back to Monaco, saying that my passport photo was from my earlier days. The HR department sent me through the contract.

It was now Wednesday morning and the ship was leaving the following day. I had spent all my time running around and queuing up to get my medicals. At one place I got an X-ray, at another I got my blood, faecal and urine tests, and then finally

## The End of the World

I found another place to get my cardiogram done. Then with all the results I still had to go and have my medical completed. Unfortunately some of the lab results would not be available until the following week, as they had to be sent to Buenos Aires. It seemed that Antarctica wanted to make me sweat. It wasn't going to let me get there until it had screwed all my nerves. With my new short back and sides, I read the following email from HR about my medicals:

> *I advised the ship (hotel director and the doctor) that you will show up tomorrow morning at the pier with all the paperwork.*
>
> *The doctor will check your medical exams and based on his judgement you will be allowed to board . . . or not.*

*Or not.* Why did she have to type that? It was cruel.

The next morning I woke early and finished packing. I put some of my belongings in the hostel's storage and went down to reception. Luis, who had first welcomed me exactly a month earlier, was waiting for me. He gave me a crash course on fine dining service, complete with lessons on how to pour wine, from which side to serve, which glass was the red wine glass, which was the white wine glass, how to set a table. I was so nervous I forgot it all. The hostel staff all came out and wished me good luck. I just hoped that I would be seeing them in eleven days' time when the ship was back in port and not in an hour's time.

I walked up to the security guards at the pier entrance to whom I had talked before and showed them my letter from the cruise ship allowing me entry. They didn't even recognise me without my dreadlocks. I put my bags through the X-ray machine and walked through the metal detector.

Then I was on the pier. The pier that I had looked at every night for a month, the pier that I had never been allowed on, the pier that had teased me, the pier that had been so close but so far away. I was tense. Would the doctor let me on with my missing test results? And if they did let me on, would they figure out that I was a fake? That I didn't have a clue what I was doing?

I walked up the gangway and was then escorted through to the room where the crew inductions were being done.

This was the moment of truth. Was I off to work in Antarctica . . . *or not.*

# Chapter 15
# MY EVEREST

Antarctic Peninsula, South Georgia Islands, Falkland Islands, 10 December 2009–February 2010

At the top of the gangway I was met by a well-groomed Filipino security guard. I introduced myself and he radioed through to get me an escort to the crew induction room. I was led through the passenger area of the cruise ship. The walls were lined with lush carpet and the freshly polished handrails sparkled. Then my escort opened an oak-panelled door off the hallway and we seemed to enter a new world, a world without daylight: the crew area.

The crew induction room was a hive of activity: walkie-talkies attached to people's hips were crackling, and crew members were coming in and handing over employee cards to a Filipino lady.

She asked my name and what position I'd be working in. I told her I was going to be an assistant waiter and handed over my paperwork. I wanted this to be quick, like pulling off a plaster. I wanted to know if I was going to be off to work in Antarctica, or not.

She went through the motions of checking my documents: employment contract, passport, X-ray, medical exam. She looked up from her paperwork and said, 'All is in order, you can collect your crew member card from the floor above.'

Was that it? After all the worry and doubt, there was no doctor, no medical checks—not even a single question!

I felt no elation, not even relief. Instead, a wave of fear and anxiety washed over me, the full extent of my fraudulent CV was hitting me. I was now an assistant waiter with seven years' waiting experience on a six-star Antarctic cruise ship.

I was shown to my crew cabin and introduced to my quiet yet smiling cabin mate, Narcisco. He was a waiter. He seemed polite, but that made me feel even more nervous. I would rather have an outback Tony welcome: *How ya doing, mate, you're going to be my bitch.* As I would soon find out, Narcisco, like the large majority of the ship's staff with the exception of the officers and expedition crew, was Filipino.

Suddenly a short, well-groomed gentleman in his late thirties appeared at the cabin door. His clean-shaven and smooth European complexion made me think he was somewhat feminine in nature. But when he spoke, his English had a heavy Eastern European accent which I couldn't put my finger on. I later found out the only feminine aspect to him was his manicured appearance; he had no warmth, and was direct and harsh. Narcisco's demeanour and posture stiffened. The gentleman told me his name was Herman, and he was my boss. He ordered Narcisco to show me around the ship and to organise my uniform and said I should get some rest for the remainder of the morning as I had a lot to learn later in the day. He then left us.

I asked Narcisco about Herman. He went to speak, but instinctively, he halted. I wasn't going to get a truthful Tony

## My Everest

answer: 'He's a bloody dickhead, mate.' Instead he replied, 'Herman is fine.' From that moment I knew that Narcisco and I would never be best mates, just cabin mates.

### Acting the dream

It was my first night of work. Now I felt like I was acting. My role was Mark the six-star assistant waiter who had seven years' hospitality experience. My tiny cabin was the dressing room, my costume was a black suit jacket, white shirt and black bow tie. I looked at the guy in the mirror. Clean shaven and short haired. I felt as though I was wearing a mask that I could pull off and see the real me, the dreadlocked, bearded Hap. But this was not a mask. This was not a movie. This was me, this was the dream I had been wanting for so long. I remembered the slogan on my T-shirt: *I will do ANYTHING to work in Antarctica.*

Gone were the days of 'Hey mate.' I had to address the passengers or guests as sir or madam, including the ship's officers. You were not allowed to ask guests, 'How can I help you?' You had to say 'Good morning, sir (or madam). How may I offer you assistance?' Then no matter what they replied you had to answer, 'Certainly, sir (or madam), my pleasure.'

I was lined up at the front of the dining room, Narcisco was beside me along with my fellow black and white penguin-suit wearing Filipino workmates. I'd never been so nervous on a first day of work. The only consolation was that the Beagle Channel was sliding by outside the dining room window. I was on my way to Antarctica.

But I still felt no elation—I knew the next five hours of work were going to be five of my worst. Like a crowd queuing at the box office, the guests were starting to gather outside the dining room doors. It was opening night, they were excited, this was the first dinner of their once-in-a-lifetime, eleven-day Antarctic cruise.

The guests waited until 1830 hours when Herman was ready. I could see that the dining room was Herman's ship, and that he loved the power of his role. In his presence I felt like a lowly deckhand on my knees scrubbing the floor. Playing the role of director trying to pump up his cast, Herman was walking up and down the line grilling us. His pep talk just made me feel more nervous.

'You're on stage out there, all eyes are on you, remember: six-star service. Here's your list of the 130 guests. I want you to be calling them all by name tomorrow, remember we are six star and that extra star is for the intimate customer service we offer. Mark, you're the new guy, you're with Maleah, do as she says.'

I nodded. 'OK.'

Lights, camera, action! The doors opened, the guests, bubbling with excitement, walked up to Herman. The mean streak I had seen directed at the hospitality crew was all of a sudden brushed aside with laughter and compliments that were as fake as my hospitality CV.

'Mark, please show Mr and Mrs Peters to table 15.'

I moved forward from the line and linked arms with Mrs Peters. I knew I would get this part right as I had been watching the other assistant waiters. 'Good evening, Mr and Mrs Peters, this way please.'

Then my mind lost the plot, kicking and punching holes in the wall of my skull. *Shit! Where is table 15? Were the odd tables on the left-hand or right-hand side?* Herman and I had quickly gone over the seating plan earlier, but now with the pressure my mind had gone blank; I had stage fright. Herman saw the confusion in my eyes and condescendingly said, 'Back left corner, Mark.'

I saw the unimpressed look behind his six-star smile with a side note that said, *That's why I'm your boss.* I could see trouble on the horizon when it became clear that I didn't have a bloody clue what to do. I would be in no position but to sit back and take the abuse.

# My Everest

As the night progressed the work environment became claustrophobic with intensity. I'd never been shouted at so much. Admittedly I deserved a lot of it and only have myself to blame, but even the veteran hospitality crew weren't spared. I really wanted to do a good job, but I clearly didn't have a clue. Maleah, the waitress I worked with, was getting frustrated with me and I didn't blame her. We had a packed section, there were orders for a million courses going left and right and I didn't even know how to place an order. When I asked Maleah for the second time how to place orders she looked at me as though she was getting a needle slowly jabbed into her eye.

'It's a lot different from the other restaurants I've worked in,' I offered.

This was not a learning environment. People were too busy rushing around to be able to help you. When you asked a question you were shouted the answer over a shoulder as the person ran to do their five tasks. All the while I was standing there not knowing whether to go left or right to find more garlic butter.

Now I was carrying a tray of crystal glasses that I had just cleared, but it felt like carrying a bomb that would detonate with the slightest movement. With my rigid movement and the slight roll of the ship I stumbled ever so slightly. My free arm shot out, trying to correct the inevitable. As the glasses impacted with the stainless-steel floor there was a crashing explosion. Luckily I wasn't on stage but backstage in the dishwashing area.

My rescuer came in the form of the Filipino dishwasher who was surrounded by towers of dirty dishes. I saw from the urgency in his eyes that my life depended on cleaning this up before Herman saw the crystal bombsite. As we were frantically cleaning up the glass I could see his look of pity. He was thinking what I was thinking, *If I'm struggling in the sheltered Beagle Channel there isn't much hope for me carrying trays in the coming two days as we cross the Drake Passage, renowned as one of the roughest seas in the world.* Then I remembered: *I will do ANYTHING to work in Antarctica.*

Then Maleah stormed into the dishwashing area, clearly agitated. 'Mark, where are the appetisers? I'm waiting for them, hurry up, and you need to clear the plates on table 11, table 15 needs their drinks filled up, and did you put in the order for their table? I shouldn't have to come back here to tell you this.'

I rushed to the appetiser station with a clean tray. The appetisers looked more like miniature works of art than food. The chefs, who had heard the crystal explosion, quickly showed me how to arrange the appetiser plates so I could fit all six on the one tray. Once again there was that look of pity in their eyes; they knew there was a very good chance they would have to remake these meals. As I bent down to take the weight of the tray and lift it up onto my shoulder, the slight sway of the ship unbalanced me again. I took my first tentative steps into the rocking dining room where all the guests' chairs had been chained to the floor to stop them from falling over when we hit the high seas of the Drake Passage. I was convinced all the eyes of the crew and guests were on me. Then Herman passed me.

He warned me, 'Be careful.'

I tried to focus on the 'care' part of that word, and not the 'ful' part. My steps were clumsy; the smashing of the crystal glasses still rang in my ears as the tray rested close to my shoulder. *Just get through the first night, Hap, night by night, it will get easier.* Then I realised, I was living my dream—I was going to work in Antarctica!

## Six stars: making simple complicated

After my first night it was blatantly obvious to everyone that I didn't know what I was doing, that I had the finesse of a drunken chimpanzee when it came to being a waiter. I knew this and I felt the burden of the pressure. I hate nothing more than being the weak link.

But in my working-the-world quest I had learnt one thing:

## My Everest

if you are willing to learn, are hard working and get on with people then you can do any job. I knew that I just had to put up with the abuse and belittlement until I had proved myself.

My shift had been a frenzied five hours that left me feeling shattered. Basically six stars takes something that is in theory very simple and makes it bloody complicated in practice! Serving a bowl of soup is a good example. In theory, you go to the table and place the soup in front of the guest. However, with six stars it is somewhat more complicated. A bowl is not sufficient to eat soup. The bowl is placed on a saucer, the saucer is placed on a slightly wider plate underneath, and the underneath plate on a slightly wider show plate! And you don't just place it in front of the guest, you have to serve the soup from the right-hand side.

Serving bread was also complicated for someone with the skills of a chimpanzee. The thought of serving bread would make my palms sweat when lining up for the dinner service. In six-star service you didn't just place the bread basket in the middle of the table for the guests to help themselves; oh no, that would be way too simple. Rather we had to squeeze the bread rolls into a tightly folded napkin which was then placed in a basket. You approached the guest from the non-soup side, that is the left-hand side, and politely asked, 'May I offer you a brown, white or wholegrain roll, sir/madam?' Then, very smoothly and elegantly using a spoon and fork in one hand like a claw, you picked up the bread roll that the guest had chosen and placed it on their bread plate. For me, it was like trying to pick up ice cubes with chopsticks. On countless occasions I could not clamp the dressed-up roll between the spoon and fork. I put the *roll* in bread roll, as I sent them hurtling over the table.

Finally there were the sugar sachets. One day after the breakfast shift, we were summoned by Herman. I could see the pained looks on everybody's faces as we knew the longer the meeting took, the less time there would be for rest before the lunch shift started in an hour. Initially, I thought that a serious incident had occurred during the morning's breakfast. But no, the meeting had been called about the sugar sachet bowls. Herman had noticed during breakfast that our sugar sachet bowls didn't comply with the six-star dining room guidelines. Every table had a sugar bowl that was filled with sachets of white sugar, brown sugar and three different types of sweetener. Herman asked me to get my sugar bowl. I brought it back, thankful that I had remembered to restock it. But Herman was the kind of boss for whom nothing was ever right.

'Mark, why doesn't your sugar bowl follow the guidelines?'

I tried to think what I had done wrong. I thought defensively, trying to pick his play. Maybe I hadn't polished the sugar bowl? But I couldn't think of anything.

I reluctantly accepted Herman's trap and shrugged my shoulders. 'I don't know.'

Herman puffed up his chest in triumph and pointed out that page 10 of the guidelines stipulated sugar bowls must have sixteen white sugar sachets, fifteen brown sugar sachets and six each of the sweetener sachets! Herman then announced, 'It's not just Mark's bowl that is unacceptable, and you should all know better. Now before we leave today I want all the sugar bowls restocked to the guidelines and we aren't leaving until I have checked them all.'

I wanted to put my hand up and ask Herman, 'What do we do when stores are running low on brown sugar? Do we go with an 18, 13, 6, 6, 6 formation? Do the guidelines have a contingency plan? How would you like a fistful of sweeteners rammed up your arse!'

But instead I replied, 'Yes, sir,' remembering *I will do ANYTHING to work in Antarctica.*

The cruise ship industry is one with a strong hierarchy, especially on a six-star ship. Officers have their separate mess where they eat in privacy away from the crew. When addressing officers you use their rank, or sir or madam. On one particular occasion, I was conducting the evening menu briefing. I finished by thanking the head sommelier for telling us about that evening's wine with a friendly 'Thank you, my good friend.'

Herman instantly reprimanded me in front of the entire dining room staff, barking, 'Mark, he is not your good friend, he is your head sommelier.'

I replied, 'Yes, sir.' I had grown to despise Herman.

The part of the job I really enjoyed was interacting and joking with some of the guests. I found there were two types. There were those who were down to earth, on a once-in-a-lifetime holiday to Antarctica and who were there to make the most of every opportunity. Being called sir or madam and the whole six-star service was a novelty to them. You could see they felt uncomfortable having someone waiting on them hand and foot, serving their bread rolls and placing their napkins on their lap. They were used to doing it themselves, but they appreciated it.

Then there were the others. They were on just another cruise, they expected six-star service and nothing seemed good enough. One of the most ridiculous experiences I had with this type of guest was with a snotty upper-class gentleman.

He came up to the dessert lunch buffet that I was running and asked me, 'Where's the crème brûlée?'

'My apologies, sir, it has been very popular today. We currently don't have any, sir, but if you like I can ask the chef if we can get some more for you.'

'What do you mean there isn't any? They should have made more. It's not good enough, I'm not moving until I get some!'

With that he crossed his arms and turned his head away with his nose in the air, standing his ground like a spoilt little kid not getting a chocolate bar at the supermarket checkout. After ten minutes my food runner arrived with his specially prepared crème brûlée. The spoilt old man rudely snatched it out of the runner's hand and turned on his heels, nose still in the air and victoriously marched off without even a thank you.

What I would have done to slip some laxatives into his brûlée!

## Living my Antarctic dream

*Beep, beep, beep.* It was my alarm. I'd been on the ship five weeks now; it felt a lot longer. The ship was heading back to Ushuaia after a week on the Antarctic Peninsula. I didn't know if it was sunny or cloudy outside. I never knew if it was sunny or cloudy outside. I would only know this if I went three levels above into the dining room to start my shift, where there were windows. I didn't know what day it was or what time of day. There were no longer seven days in a week; my body clock was run by laundry day which fell on every second day. If I missed that it meant I had to hand sponge the stains out of my uniform so Herman wouldn't notice and give me a warning. I knew we were in the Drake Passage though as the ship rose and fell in the swell. It'd been a long cruise, but we were heading back to dry land. The thought of being able to walk further than 100 metres made me as excited as a little kid about to enter a theme park. Also this time we had been promised more time ashore which added to my excitement, as on the past two trips we'd only a couple of hours ashore.

But I still had a full day of work to get through. I waited for Narcisco to get up. Our cabin was too small for both of us to get ready at the same time. It was barely big enough for one of us to get ready. We had fallen into an unspoken routine where he got up five minutes before me. I waited until I heard him exit the cabin. I pulled back the curtain that encapsulated me in my coffin-sized top bunk. Through experience I had learnt not to sit upright as my head hit the cabin ceiling. I rolled out of bed and dropped to the floor, my eyes still closed. I headed to the shower. Bugger, the shower door was locked. We shared our closet-sized shower and toilet with the cabin next door and they had forgotten to unlock the door. I squeezed past our wardrobe door into the passageway and entered the next-door cabin that was occupied by two Russians who worked in the engine room. It smelt of cigarette smoke. You weren't allowed to smoke inside, but they always snuck a cigarette in before work, blowing the smoke into the ventilation fan of the toilet. I didn't blame them as it was a long way to go outside in the bitter freezing cold to have a fag. I wondered if inmates in prison could smoke inside? I unlocked the shower door which allowed me back into my cabin.

I showered, the hot water bliss on my aching back. It slowly brought me to life and I knew that this would probably be the highlight of my day. I looked at the shower floor with the water rolling side to side in unison with the motion of the ship. I reluctantly turned off the hot water as if turning off a life-support system. I was running out of time. I dried off and stepped into my cabin. I put on my heavy-duty harness back brace and swallowed four ibuprofen. This was my morning ritual—the bending down and lifting of the trays stacked high with dirty dishes had caused my compressed vertebrae to flare up. It was causing me constant pain. But I had never declared it on my medical for fear of being rejected for the job so I hid it. *I will do ANYTHING to work in Antarctica.*

In the mirror I looked at Mark. Every day the bags under his blood-shot eyes were getting bigger and blacker, his face paler and gaunter. I'd seen crackheads on Vancouver's derelict Hastings Street that looked in better shape than me. I looked at my cheeks and wondered if I could get away without shaving until the next shift. But Herman had already sent me back to my cabin to shave once before, and I didn't want that to happen again. I decided to shave.

I put on my 'Mark' nametag and made sure it was straight. I was missing a button, and hoped Herman wouldn't notice. I had tried all of the previous day to get the tailor to fix it after it came back from the laundry missing a button, but our dining room hours didn't coincide with the tailor's. I sat down on Narcisco's bottom bunk, and spit-polished my shoes so Herman wouldn't have the pleasure of asserting his power over me. I started to put them on. As I put on my second shoe I realised I hadn't put on my trousers.

Once dressed, I walked down the passageway, swaying from side to side with the waves. I walked past the roaring engine room, its noise deafening, and just as I was about to enter the crew mess I saw Herman walking out.

'You have ten minutes, Mark, hurry hurry.'

I wanted to tell Herman that I was quite fucking aware that I only had ten minutes to inhale my breakfast, but instead said, 'Yes, sir.'

Then Herman pulled up short and said to me, 'Mark, what's wrong with your uniform?' Bugger. I started to explain about the missing button and the tailor's hours but Herman just looked at me like I was only slightly retarded.

'Mark, it's breakfast time, you're wearing your dinner uniform.'

Shit!

I walked back down the rolling passageway knowing that I now wouldn't have any time for breakfast. My mind started its battle, a conflict that had been going on for a while now. The conflict existed because I had wanted to work in Antarctica for so long, and so many people had helped and supported me to get here, but now I was here, I hated it. I dreaded going to work and when I was there I hated it beyond belief. When I finished work I was already counting down the minutes until I had to force myself to go back. When I started work I counted down the minutes until I finished. It was a crazy twist of ironic fate that my Antarctica job had ended up being the worst job of my working-the-world quest.

As I took off my dinner uniform and put on my correct breakfast uniform, I gave myself a pep talk: 'Hap you're living your dream, you're working in Antarctica. Just get through the day, you'll be in Ushuaia tonight, mate. Just make it through the day, it ain't that bad.'

## My Everest

I made it to the dining room in time for Herman's team meeting just before the dining room doors were opened.

Herman announced, 'I've just had word that tonight in port after we finish serving dinner we will go straight to loading cargo until 0200 hours.'

What I heard made me feel numb, destroyed my soul, made me feel like inflicting pain on Herman, on the cruise ship lifestyle. I wanted to scream, my blood was boiling, I felt so taken advantage of. I felt like a slave.

We would now finish work at 0200 hours. I would only have four hours to sleep before getting up around 0600 hours to unload the passengers' luggage. I would then have to load provisions while the new guests boarded. All the while I would be tortured like a prisoner looking out his cell window at the free world of Ushuaia. Then we would cruise back to Antarctica for another eleven days, with another shipload of excited tourists.

As the guests started coming into the dining room I was in a dark mood. I couldn't force any jokes with them and make them laugh. It wasn't fair. When I spent every waking hour in the restaurant working and every sleeping hour in my coffin-sized bunk, a couple of hours ashore seem like gold! I asked myself, *Hap, are you really living your dream?*

If I had learnt one thing from my meltdown in Paraguay, it was that happiness is everything. If you're not enjoying life, change it. I realised that I'd lived my dream, I'd worked in Antarctica, I'd achieved my goal. I had become a competent assistant waiter and was now the hospitality crew member who got the most mentions on the guest feedback cards. I'd even been offered a new contract to stay on the cruise ship to go through Europe and up into the Arctic, and was told a job could be arranged for Mandy. But I knew she would hate everything about it.

At that moment I decided to wave the white flag; the battle was over. I would hand in my notice. I had worked five weeks, I didn't want my dream to turn into any more of a nightmare.

I felt relief having made this decision; the next two cruises would be my last. In 23 days' time I would be leaving the beautiful continent of Antarctica and would also be walking away from the worst job of my working-the-world goal.

## My worst job

How did a job that sounded so glamorous become my worst job? There was a combination of three factors: the work environment and my psychological and physical condition.

When people think of cruise ships they think of floating cities with 5000 guests cruising through places like the Caribbean and the Mediterranean, stopping off at ports along the way. These ships can have up to a couple of thousand crew. They have access to 24-hour crew bars and gyms. Well, an Antarctic cruise ship is the polar opposite. It was an 'expedition' cruise ship, meaning it was smaller so it could go to less accessible places. It was around 100 metres long, and carried 130 guests and 120 crew. Crew facilities consisted of a small bar that was only open three times on an eleven-day cruise and the bar doubled as a storage space that had sacks of potatoes piled in the corner. The gym was a cupboard that barely fitted a bench press. There was no way for anyone to assist you during bench pressing, it was that cramped. We did have an alternative, a small guest gym that had a combination weight machine, treadmill and exercycle. We were allowed access to this between 2200 hours and 0600 hours when the guests were in bed. I never used it as my back was either too sore or sleep was a much higher priority.

The feeling of being caged in was not just because the ship was comparatively small but because crew didn't have regular port calls where the ship would dock and you could explore the town or city. Instead, once we left Ushuaia, the ship became a floating prison until we returned to Ushuaia eleven days later. Then the ship was only in port for less than 24 hours. During this time you served the guests' last meal, and then prepared the dining room for the following day. Then, as on all my cruises, I had to stay aboard to help load provisions. Usually I would not finish until after midnight when I could finally get ashore. But I had to be up by 0600 the next morning to offload the guests' luggage. After this I would continue loading the provisions for the next voyage. If we finished early I would get a couple of hours to sleep or go ashore. Before I knew it, it was time to go through the fire drill with the new guests, then it would be into serving dinner as the ship left civilisation.

Of these eleven days, we spent a total of four days in the Drake Passage: two days going to Antarctica and two days coming back. The Drake Passage is known as one of the roughest seas in the world with swells as high as 15 to 20 metres as an entire ocean tries to squeeze through the 800-kilometre gap between the bottom of South America and the tip of the Antarctic Peninsula. A large majority of guests got seasick and surprisingly a lot of the crew did as well. It's a regular occurrence in the Drake Passage to see waiters go out the back, throw up, clean themselves up, slap a six-star smile on their face and return to serving guests. Being seasick was just a part of the job. I was lucky I didn't suffer from this.

I found the lifestyle the hardest part of being an assistant waiter on a cruise ship. The 70-hour weeks, which worked out to be 10 hours a day, were in reality always longer. We would start breakfast between 0400 hours and 0700 hours, and then got an hour or two for sleep before lunch which we would start at 1200 hours. After the lunch shift you got another couple of hours sleep before the dinner shift which started at 1815 hours and usually went through to just before 0000 hours. Sleep was very broken and this affected my body clock. Also, much to the amazement of my crewmates, I would go ashore in Antarctica at every landing. This came at a sacrifice to sleep, and just added another shade of black to the bags under the eyes of my sleep-deprived body.

Also, there were no days off. You had a breakfast duty off

roughly once a week. If you finished the dinner service at midnight and got breakfast off, you would still have to start back at midday for the lunch duty. So a 'day off' was really only 12 hours, but during this time you had to tidy your cabin for a cabin inspection, do your personal laundry, miss breakfast to get more sleep, and then get ready for the lunch shift.

I also found the cultural situation difficult. My Filipino crewmates were diligent workers, very friendly and I got on well with them. But I was very much the foreigner. As soon as the guests left the dining room, my crewmates would all be cleaning and polishing, laughing and chatting away in their native Filipino tongue. But the Filipino crew and I did have one thing in common and that was an intense dislike for Herman.

Herman's leadership style was autocratic. At one meeting he yelled at us, 'I'm your boss, I demand respect.'

He got no respect from me. The Filipinos feared him; I despised him. As soon as the guests left the dining room Herman would sit down and bark orders at us. On his command we had to drop what we were doing to bring him whatever he requested, usually more food or another glass of wine. In Herman's dining room you were constantly walking on eggshells. You weren't working to do a good job; you were working to avoid doing something wrong. This left me fatigued.

As I walked down the gangway at the end of my stint as an assistant waiter, I was pleased to be leaving. The pressures of the work environment and my psychological and physical condition had all taken their toll. The stress caused by lying about being a six-star waiter, the verbal abuse and constantly being shouted at left me mentally exhausted. The sleep deprivation caused by the shift work and my opting for trips onto the ice added to this. With my rundown state I had picked up a virus that made me acutely ill and left me with bronchitis and weight loss. This illness was on top of my chronic back pain.

# My Everest

However, I would do it all over again just to work in Antarctica!

I walked along the pier and out of the security gates like a prisoner entering the free world. I went and sat on a seat at the water's edge, the same seat I had sat on and devised a plan of sneaking onto a ship and stowing away. I watched the floating prison majestically glide through the calm mirror of the Ushuaia harbour and head out into the Beagle Channel for another eleven-day sentence. I knew exactly what my crewmates would be doing, masking their tiredness with the same smiles they had used that morning to farewell the departing guests and to welcome the new guests aboard.

Now with the dread from my worst job gone, a warm feeling flowed over my body as I watched the ship depart. There was relief, but there was another feeling. It was a great sense of pride. I was proud of myself. I had done EVERYTHING to work in Antarctica. Now I was sitting here having lived and worked there. I had knocked the bastard off!

## The most beautiful place I have been

As the ship was swallowed up by the Beagle Channel I walked back up the familiar path to the hostel. I went through the doors, and there was Luis. He was as excited to see me as he was the very first day when the taxi had pulled up outside and he had picked up my flag-covered pack. The only difference was that now, when he came to give me a hand with my pack, there was a Port Lockroy, Antarctica, patch on it.

We hugged and kissed on the cheek, his smile saying a hundred words. He, like Sich and many other people, had played a big part in getting me to Antarctica. He wanted to know everything, and his enthusiasm was contagious. It made me realise how lucky I had been, given that two months previously I had been sitting in this same hostel chair willing to do ANYTHING to work in Antarctica. All of a sudden the ship lifestyle, the shouting, the sleep deprivation was gone. All I could think about was how spectacular Antarctica was.

I told Luis how I made nearly twenty landings on Antarctica. I recounted to him the very first time I set foot on the ice. I told him how it was like a desert of whiteness, with first the beauty hitting me, and then the serenity, the tranquillity, the silence just wrapped itself around me like a blanket as I lay in the snow and was consumed by the great white continent.

I talked about working in the dining room and having whales and icebergs floating outside the window and about the one afternoon I got to serve champagne to guests in the inflatable Zodiac boats as we zipped through the sculptural icebergs of the Lemaire Channel. It was as though we were floating past clouds in the sky with giant seals resting on them. I told him it was in this magical place, the Lemaire Channel, that I saw the most magnificent sunset I have ever laid eyes on as the sun set directly between the mountains at the channel entrance, blanketing the sky and sea in a luxurious, sparkling-crimson orange silk.

I told him how on one cruise over Christmas and New Year we visited the Falkland Islands, being careful to use the Argentinian name Islas Malvinas as the Falklands War is still too fresh in most Argentinians' minds. I explained how the island is like a little slice of England that had been cut off from the United Kingdom and dragged to the coast of Argentina. In the Falklands I managed to escape the ship and went and sat in an old English pub. It was the afternoon of Christmas Eve and I sat in front of a fire with a cold pint of beer, savouring the quiet, relaxed atmosphere, away from the demands of guests.

From the Falklands we then visited South Georgia en route to Antarctica. South Georgia is the resting place of the legendary Antarctic explorer Ernest Shackleton, whose grave I visited. At

# My Everest

St Andrews Bay on the island, I stepped onto the beach which is one of the biggest king penguin rookeries. It was like I had entered a penguin refugee camp: the smell of guano, the chorus of 200,000 squawking penguins filling the atmosphere, the elegant yet comical waddling birds. It made me forget about Herman and the upcoming dinner shift I had to rush back to.

I told Luis about swimming at Deception Island in the South Shetland Islands, about 120 kilometres north of the Antarctic Peninsula. Deception Island is an active volcano that last erupted in 1972. The onboard scientist called it a sunken caldera, meaning that the volcano had sunk into the ocean with only the crater protruding above water. Part of the crater wall has collapsed, allowing our small expedition ship to cruise into the middle of it. On the volcanic sand of the shore, which used to be home to an old whaling station, the expedition crew dug little pools that filled with steaming hot water. I took an icy polar plunge then jumped into the steaming hot pool.

I told him about one particular day when we were anchored in Paradise Bay on the Antarctic Peninsula. I had started a breakfast shift at 0400 hours and had finished at 0800 hours. Walking back to my cabin via the ship's foyer I felt my bunk calling me. My heavy eyelids drooped over my bloodshot eyes, my back pleaded with me to get horizontal, and my lungs fought the bronchitis the ship's doctor had diagnosed. The expedition crew were organising guests to take ashore. As always, I asked an accommodating expedition crew member if there was room for me. He told me if I hurried I could go ashore. Forgetting about the three hours' sleep I really needed to get me through the lunch shift, I ran down to my cabin, threw on my cold-weather gear and gumboots and headed for the Zodiac. I was here to see Antarctica!

On my way to shore I felt like I was on my top bunk dreaming as we entered the Antarctic wonderland. There wasn't a cloud in the bright blue sky, which cut a contrasting line where it met the pure white of the Antarctic mountains. Whales sprayed water in the air as they came to the surface among the idle icebergs that were floating like cereal in a breakfast bowl. There was no wind, just stillness, a calmness that slowed the mind and soul like a soothing meditation. The tranquillity gently forced me to see the true beauty of Mother Nature without the make-up of human construction to hide it. As I jumped from the Zodiac on to the shore I walked past the seals lying on the beach looking like slugs with puppy-dog faces resting serenely on a white lettuce leaf. I walked past penguins that were waddling in an organised fashion up the hill on what seemed like a penguin highway. I found myself a spot on top of the hill and lay back in the snow to take in this splendour. I looked out into the bay at the cruise ship lying at anchor in the sheltered waters. I could see this heavenly creation on canvas.

I thought, *This will be the picture my mind will paint when I remember Antarctica.* A painting that will have the caption: *Antarctica, the most beautiful place I have ever been.*

## Chapter 16
# PREPARING FOR THE FINAL CONTINENT

**AUSTRALASIA: Melbourne, Victoria; Tullah, Tasmania, Australia, 19 May 2010–5 June 2011**

After Antarctica I went hiking in Chile before going back to Paraguay. When Mandy returned from chaperoning her Denver exchange trip, I was there to welcome her at the airport. After a week of catching up and saying goodbye to Juan and our wonderful friends of Asunción, Mandy and I left for the next chapter, together.

We flew to Melbourne, the hip cultural epicentre of Australia. I had two things on my mind: firstly, to settle down for the year and have a place to call home; secondly, to dedicate the year to prepare for my final continent, Africa.

For Africa, I wanted to put the focus on paying back people's generosity, to take responsibility for my journey's carbon footprint and to have an adventure.

For the past seven years I had been amazed at the generosity of people, both friends and strangers—generosity that at times I had depended on to help me keep working the world. Like the friends who had let me sleep on their couches or the volunteer serving me at the soup kitchen in Canada. I had become aware of how many people were worse off than me, who had been dealt a rough hand in life, such as the orphans in Mexico.

I had also become aware of how humanity was impacting on the environment, and how I as an individual added to this impact. I had worked jobs that had put scars on the face of Mother Nature: the oil rigs, the mine and the ship that had cruised through the pure white wilderness of Antarctica while burning 10,000 tonnes of fuel a day.

As well as all this, I wanted my final continent to be an adventure. For seven years I had been turning up somewhere, finding work and then backpacking around. I loved it, but I had done that and wanted a new challenge.

I had come up with the idea of a Final Continent Expedition (FCE), which would incorporate human-powered travel, thus decreasing my carbon footprint while providing a new challenge. I also wanted to establish my own community project, allowing me to give a little back to the world. But first things first.

Mandy and I had arrived in Melbourne and had to play the usual setting-up game: find a house to live in, find bikes for transport and jobs for money. As Mandy was American she would have to wait at least six weeks for her de facto-partner work visa to come through. We needed money. A mate told me of a mining exploration job going down in Tasmania, working twelve days on in Tasmania and nine days off in Melbourne. I thought I'd do it for a month or two to get some money in the bank and get us on our feet. I got hold of the guy in charge and, with my oil rig and previous field experience at Woodie Woodie, I was employed. Before I flew to Tasmania we signed

## Preparing for the Final Continent

a contract on a shoebox-sized apartment in Melbourne's North Fitzroy.

It felt good to have an actual address to call home.

### Tasmanian fieldy

The following week I was peering out of the plane's window as we flew over Tasmania, Australia's island state.

My plane touched down at Devonport airport in Tasmania's rugged northwest. With every country there is always one part that bears the brunt of all the redneck jokes. In Australia, it's Tasmania.

I had heard all the jokes about inbreeding and people having six fingers, and as I walked through the terminal doors into the small airport I wondered what my new workmates would be like. I was collecting my bag when my arm was grabbed from behind. I spun around thinking, in backpacker mode, that I was being robbed. I was met by an athletic-looking cop-type with short Steelo hair.

Looking me in the eye, he said, 'Airport security. Come with me.'

I hadn't had much luck with airport security in the past and I tried to think what I had done or packed to warrant their eagle eye. My mind was racing. I no longer had dreadlocks and I wasn't working illegally. The night I spent in cell 210 in Atlanta City Prison flashed before my eyes.

'You must be the man. Are you Hap?' With a smile on his face, he said, 'I'm your senior fieldy. Nice to meet you.'

The bastard. He had me. I knew then I would get on with my new Tasmanian workmates just fine.

We drove an hour and half down the west coast and arrived in the small town of Tullah. From the 1970s to the early 1990s, Tullah's population was 2500. It had been a construction town for a hydroelectric scheme that saw a bunch of dams built around the area. Today only a couple of hundred people call it home.

When I first started, my intention was to do only a couple of swings, then try to get work in Melbourne. But as per usual, I ended up just falling into a routine. I worked with a great bunch of people, had a good roster, twelve days work, nine days off, which meant I spent two weekends in Melbourne and one in Tasmania. While I was away in Tasmania I wasn't distracted either and spent all my spare time preparing for Africa, and then on my nine days off back in Melbourne I put my nose to the grindstone doing the same. It was an easy way to save for Africa as I couldn't spend anything in Tullah.

My Tasmania job title was the same as that of my favourite job in Western Australia, exploration field assistant, but that was where the similarities stopped. In the outback I had worked in the hottest place in Australia; now I was working in one of its rainiest places with an average of 250 wet days a year. Red dirt and spinifex were replaced with rugged mountains, rainforest and snow; leeches replaced flies; merino garments and heavy jackets replaced lightweight clothing. At Tullah we were doing what was called mine feasibility—basically making sure there was enough of the good stuff in the ground to create a mine, as opposed to Woodie where we worked on an existing site trying to find other deposits in the surrounding area.

The job was located in Tullah township as opposed to an isolated mine. This meant we were a part of the community. Every Thursday night we would head down to the local pub for a team meal, play pool and have a good time with all the local characters holding up the bar.

During the whole winter there were only three days when it didn't rain and it wasn't unusual for it to snow. Compared to my outback experience the job became monotonous during this long, wet, grey winter, and a lot of the time I was stuck in the cold shed cutting up rocks. It was only the laughs with

## Preparing for the Final Continent

workmates and the weekly team dinner at the local pub that got me through.

Just after Christmas 2011, with the dry summer weather having finally arrived, the exploration season was upon us and we got to go bush. I was helicoptered with my crew out into the middle of untouched, pristine Tasmanian rainforest. We would set up fly camps and hike through the rugged country, taking soil samples. Spending time in the lush rainforest made me hope we didn't find any mineral deposits so the place wouldn't be turned into a mine—but unfortunately that's the nature of the beast, as we keep constructing and building.

Although I had seen out the tough winter and wanted to stay on for the summer fieldwork season, Melbourne was calling. I needed to spend more time with Mandy and organise the final preparations for Africa. With four months until our departure for Africa it was time to get work in Melbourne.

### The Final Continent Expedition (FCE)

Now instead of having to fly out to work in Tasmania, my full-time home was North Fitzroy, just up the road from arty Brunswick Street. I had been told by a volunteer I had worked with back at the Tapachula orphanage about the charity Bicycles for Humanity (B4H), which had a chapter in Melbourne.

Basically B4H fills shipping containers with around 400 donated disused bikes. Once the container is full it is shipped to another charity in Africa, Bicycling Empowerment Network, Namibia (BEN Namibia). BEN Namibia then ensures the container gets to a local community where the bikes are needed. The container is converted into a permanent bike workshop with work benches, bike stands, shelves and tool racks installed. The bike shop is then set up as a small business and run by five locals who are trained in bicycle mechanics and in running a small business.

They service the bikes and sell them cheaply to the local community. The income from the bicycle sales and the ongoing servicing is used to pay the five mechanics, buy new spare parts, and cover the cost of resupplying bicycles, thus establishing an ongoing sustainable business.

Both B4H and BEN Namibia seemed to tick so many boxes. Working with these charities would allow me to pay back the generosity I had received by helping a community, and the bikes offered an environmentally friendly form of transport. I also liked the idea of how an unused bike that had been collecting dust in someone's garage in the western world was given a new life in Africa. A bicycle can mean access to drinking water, food supplies, marketplaces, hospitals, schools and potential business opportunities. It allows people to travel around four times as far and carry five times the amount. Kids can cycle fifteen minutes to school instead of having to walk for an hour, giving them more time to do homework and chores. It means health workers can reach further afield, giving more people greater access to healthcare. Subsistence farmers can transport their produce to the market more easily, freeing up time for other tasks, therefore making their farms more financially viable.

The other aspects I liked were that bikes are not just given to the locals without charge; they have to buy them, thus giving them a sense of ownership. The workshop is set up as an ongoing sustainable business so bikes can always be fixed. But the best part is that the business is run by locals for locals.

Earlier in the year, when I had been on a nine-day break, I had met up with Matt McCullough, the founder of the Melbourne chapter of B4H. I explained my proposal to team up with B4H, raise the AU$10,000 to $12,000 to buy a shipping container, fill it with old bikes and transport it to Africa. I then wanted to go to Africa and help convert the container into a bike workshop, train the locals as bike mechanics and thus tick off the working aspect of my goal.

## Preparing for the Final Continent

I also wanted to make a documentary of the whole journey, from the packing of the container in Melbourne to the opening day of the bike workshop in Africa. I had already approached Sich, the guy who had given me my break in Antarctica and who happened to be a talented documentary maker. He was keen on the idea and was on board from the start. The wheels were starting to turn.

Although the idea of the FCE and original motivation for it was mine, it was now very much the combined effort of Mandy and me. We were a team and I couldn't have done it without her.

Having taken care of the repaying of generosity and the environmental aspects, I turned my mind to the human-powered part of the FCE equation. The solution was quite easy. Living in the cycle-loving city of Melbourne and having teamed up with the bicycle charities, a cycling expedition seemed to be fitting. Mandy and I decided we would cycle through southern Africa starting in Cape Town. We hoped the container would go to Malawi, around 5000 kilometres from Cape Town. The plan for the FCE seemed pretty simple. Raise the money through donations, send a container-load of bikes to Africa, gain sponsorship for our unsupported cycle trip, meet the container in Malawi, train the locals and convert the container into a workshop. Goal completed. And I would film it all, as Sich had had to pull out of the trip, mainly due to a lack of funds.

However, the reality of putting the plan into action was somewhat different. While we thought our FCE vision was pretty cool, when it came to potential sponsors our vision was put at the bottom of people's to-do lists. We were just another couple of idealists off on an adventure to save the world.

On the positive side we had set up a fundraising website that allowed friends, family and businesses to make donations to help pay for the shipping container. Family and friends had been generous and we were ecstatic when two mining companies I had approached donated a total of $5000. I also realised that if

Mandy and I were going to be cycling through southern Africa with no support and I was going to help train locals to be bike mechanics, I needed to know what I was doing. I managed to find full-time work at a local bike shop and enrolled in a bike mechanics' course.

By now it was February 2011. We had four months until we left for Africa. June had to be our month of departure. It was southern Africa's dry season which would give us enough time to cycle to our destination and to set up the bike workshop. I was also turning 30 in November.

For the next four months we lived and breathed Africa. Our shoebox apartment became FCE headquarters. We called on the help of our talented group of friends to help us ramp up support for what we were doing. We retargeted our sponsorship proposals to try to get gear. We did a PR blitz to get the word out, we burnt the midnight oil applying for grants.

At eight weeks out, we had most of our cycling gear thanks to the Australian distributor of Ortlieb, who make high-quality cycle panniers and equipment. As luck would have it they were located only five minutes away in a suburban warehouse. I had knocked on the nondescript door as I had found the personal approach worked the best. The guys were super-supportive of our cause and it resulted in some heavily discounted gear.

One major issue was that we still needed our bikes—kind of a biggie when you're expecting to cycle 5000 kilometres through Africa. I had done my homework and knew exactly what I wanted. It was an American-made, mid-range, tough touring bike that would hold up under the rigours of Africa. I had been talking for a while with a local bike shop, hoping to get hooked up at cost price on the back of our expedition, but it all ended up falling through. Mandy had been harassing the US manufacturer, again with no love. Then we contacted Dirtworks, the Australian distributor of the bikes, and they were more than willing to jump on board, offering us advice and the bikes at cost price. While they had my complete bike in stock, they only had a frame in Mandy's size. With the help of my bikeshop co-worker I ordered all the parts off the internet and with my newly acquired bike mechanic skills I was able to assemble Mandy's bike. We now had the bikes ticked off, although we still had to wait until the very last minute for all the parts to dribble in.

With sponsorship not being as successful as we had planned and our applications for grants declined, it meant we had to use a lot of our personal savings to purchase gear, which was money we had put aside to live off in Africa. We still needed to buy plane tickets and spend money on some high-quality camera gear that would be up to the standard needed for filming a documentary. Our funds were heading towards the red and we now knew we had to raise money to pay our way through Africa.

At this point we had raised nearly $11,000, enough to get the container to Africa, but it was looking like we would have to go into personal debt to follow through with setting up the container workshop. Mandy and our good friends created the fundraiser event Beer, Bikes and Bands to be held at the Workers Club on Brunswick Street in Melbourne. The brew pub Little Creatures, where Mandy worked, became a sponsor. Local bands and musicians volunteered their time for the cause and Fitzroy businesses generously donated items for a silent auction.

In among all this organising, we were also spending time filling containers with donated bicycles. It was a special day when we packed and closed the doors on our container with our friends and B4H volunteers. I was looking forward to the day we would open the doors of that container in Africa and see not just the bikes but recall everyone who had made it all possible.

We were now just six weeks from departure and we still didn't have a confirmed destination for our container, making it impossible to finalise the plan. Was the container going to Malawi, Zambia or Namibia? Finally we heard it was headed for Namibia's northeast, to a small community called Katima Mulilo. We received this information by email from BEN Namibia founder Michael Linke, who advised they had secured funding for a bike project in this community. So it was decided that I would complete the final continent by living and working in the town of Katima Mulilo.

With our destination confirmed, our plan started to become more concrete. We would fly into Cape Town at the start of June, cycle 2500 kilometres up through South Africa and Namibia, arriving in Katima Mulilo. We would take a couple of months to set up the bike shop and celebrate my 30th birthday and the completion of my goal on 11 November 2011 (11/11/11). We would then continue to cycle another 2500 kilometres through Zimbabwe, Zambia and into Malawi to finish on the shores of Lake Malawi in January 2012.

### Last-minute madness

Bike parts, cycling gear, camera gear, cases, cartons and camping gear were strewn all over the floor. A small path to the apartment door had been cleared amid all the carnage. The fold-up couch was out, taking up the remaining floor space, and piled high with Sich's bags and camera equipment. He had been couch surfing at our apartment for the previous ten days, pre-filming for our *Bikes for Africa* documentary. To top it off my parents were arriving and somehow we had to fit them into the apartment. Life was full on. I was really looking forward to landing in Cape Town and the simplicity of cycling.

Suddenly there were only four days until departure and it seemed that every time I ticked something off I would think of another ten things to be done. My mind was overflowing with things to do: pack up and move out of the apartment; get more packing tape; chase up spare bike parts, maybe sell the neighbours our kitchen table; thank people and donors for

## Preparing for the Final Continent

the Beer, Bikes and Bands contributions; get travel insurance; complete taxes; research what kind of electrical plugs they use in South Africa; tell employers the address to send tax forms to; get spare spokes; get more water purification tablets; meet Mum and Dad for goodbye lunch; call on my bike shop mate to fix badly damaged wheel and rear derailleur after falling off bike; check how much sunblock we need; see if I should take more chain lube, and so on. At 2 a.m. a couple of days before departure, we were packing bikes into boxes, our eyes shutting, with me still trying to make notes to self about packing.

It's hard to think we arrived in Melbourne only a year earlier with just two backpacks. Our downstairs neighbour helped load all our gear onto his truck and we distributed it among several of our friends. I rushed to the store to get some last-minute camping gear, and added to the Cape Town to-do list: still have to get bike pants, spare spokes and Vaseline.

We were now running on adrenaline, furiously cleaning the apartment for the 4 p.m. inspection with the property manager. We were relying heavily on getting the $1000 bond back. The carpet cleaner arrived on the dot at 2 p.m. We were racing against the clock.

'Have you cleaned the oven?' I asked Mandy.

'No.'

'Shit, we have no oven cleaner.'

I was belly-button deep in the oven with window cleaner as the property manager arrived. Bond retrieved, keys handed over, another place lived in.

Carrying a miscellaneous bag of gear, I walked to our friends Matt and Linnley's place where we would spend our last night in Melbourne. I desperately wanted to sleep but I knew I couldn't stop. I sent off some more thankyou emails and opened a beer. Friends came over for our goodbye dinner of curry, beer, wine, laughs, goodbyes, tears and thankyous. It was now 11 p.m. We decided it was time to book some travel insurance.

We woke up on the day of departure, the day we had been working towards for over a year. We still weren't organised, with thoughts racing through our heads like *Must ring cell phone company and cancel payments, where's my credit card?*

Then our station wagon taxi arrived and we had another challenge: the seats couldn't be put down, our bikes wouldn't fit in. The Indian taxi driver said, 'Maybe you miss plane?' But he was on our side, as it seemed everyone that day would be. He struggled to ram the boxes into the back seat as though we were already in Africa.

Finally he got them in, and with Mandy in the front seat I asked him, 'Where do I go?'

He smiled and pointed to the small gap between the bike boxes and the seat. I was glad I had the physique of a Kenyan marathon runner and not that of a Japanese sumo wrestler.

'Make sure no one see you,' he said.

What a legend, risking his taxi licence to get us to the airport on time.

We arrived at the airport, our driver stopping away from the main terminal entrance for me to squirm out from my backseat burrow. As we struggled to get the boxes out of the wagon a lady came up and offered us her prepaid luggage cart. We loaded the cart and headed for the sliding doors of the terminal but couldn't fit through. A friendly parking attendant approached us and helped to unload then reload the bikes on the other side of the sliding doors. At the check-in we taped up our flimsy $2 polyweave bags so the zippers wouldn't burst. We checked in, cleared immigration and boarded our flight.

Tomorrow I would be stepping onto my seventh and final continent—Africa.

# Chapter 17
# THE DARK CONTINENT

AFRICA: Cape Town, South Africa; Katima Mulilo, Namibia,
5 June–14 September 2011

The grey clouds that were draped over Table Mountain seemed to fit our melancholy mood. It was rather ironic as we had been looking forward to and planning for this moment for so long. But we couldn't be bothered doing anything; our bodies seemed to have shut down. The colds that we had been fighting off with pre-departure adrenaline caught up with us. The only thing that excited us was sleep.

I had been in bed all day and the thought of getting up and going to a restaurant felt like an expedition in itself. I was crippled with pre-trip anxiety. My expectations; other people's expectations; being underprepared; the *Bikes for Africa* documentary, never really having used the video camera before, would the footage I shot be good enough; what did the bike shop have to offer; did I have all the required camping gear; would we get eaten by lions;

could Mandy make the grade; could I make the grade? Even though I knew these fears were common before undertaking a trip of this nature, I was still bedridden, the weight of these thoughts upon me like an overloaded African truck. But there was also another anxiety that I couldn't quite put my finger on, a worry that was bigger than just this final continent.

I had been talking to a mate at our leaving party back in Melbourne, telling him we had just found out the shipping container had already arrived in Africa, and it would be at our destination in the Namibian town of Katima Mulilo much earlier than expected. My mate hit the stop button and asked me, 'If the container is already on its way to Katima Mulilo and it takes two months to cycle there from Cape Town, then you won't be there to meet it when it arrives, will you?'

This hit me like my polar plunge back in Antarctica. What had I been thinking? I hadn't been thinking.

The FCE planning was easy in theory. Send a container of bikes to Africa, cycle 2500 kilometres, arrive to a standing ovation of smiling African kids and hymn-singing mamas. As we dismount, taking off our helmets and flicking our sweat-soaked hair and flinging droplets through the air, Mandy and I embrace. Then someone hands us an ice-cold bottle of Coca-Cola and we guzzle the refreshing bubbly coolness with sweat gleaming on our tanned faces. The container arrives in town with hundreds of smiling African kids running behind it. Then Elton John pops up and starts singing the 'Cycle' of Life song and Michael Jackson floats down from heaven to join Elton in a duet. Lions, zebras and giraffes come skipping onto the scene and we all join hands and sing in unison as we open the container doors, laughter and singing filling the air as the glowing red sun sets over the village. Charley Boorman and Ewan McGregor ride in on their motorbikes on their famous *Long Way Down* African adventure and work alongside us for a couple of months to help establish the bike workshop. Nelson Mandela flies in on a private

# The Dark Continent

helicopter to cut the ribbon at the bike shop's opening ceremony. Then with the bike shop successfully operating, Mandy and I ride off into the African savannah on the second 2500-kilometre leg of the journey. We reach the golden sandy shores of Lake Malawi and under the setting sun I propose to Mandy. We adopt a malnourished orphan, open a shelter for amputee baboons, build a bamboo hut and live happily ever after. Simple.

But like the six-star service in Antarctica, it was a lot more complicated in reality.

It was always going to be a miracle if everything aligned and we arrived at the same time as the container. Plans were never set in concrete. They needed to be adaptable to an ever-changing situation. We only found out Katima Mulilo was the destination of our container six weeks before leaving Melbourne. But never did we think the container would beat us to the destination by two months. This was Africa, where things didn't happen with the same efficiency as the western world, or just didn't happen at all. I had always thought we would have to extend our bike ride to kill time while the container was held in customs or sat on the side of the road on the back of a broken-down truck.

So with the imminent arrival of the shipping container in Katima Mulilo, we had to adapt our plan and get our heads around not doing our entire 5000-kilometre human-powered journey. This was hard, but there was really only ever one option. I was in Africa to work, to complete my goal. If we persisted with cycling the entire way to Katima Mulilo then we would miss out on setting up the bike workshop. Mandy and I owed it to friends, family and strangers who had donated money and volunteered their time in order for us to complete this venture. Ultimately, it wasn't about me and my hunger for adventure, it was about me paying back all the generosity I had received over the last eight years of working the world. It was my way of saying thanks.

## The start of the road – Namibia

After a 30-hour bus ride from Cape Town, we arrived in the town of Rundu in northern Namibia on the border with Angola. Rundu is at the start of the Caprivi Strip, a thin sliver of land sometimes referred to as the pot handle in Namibia's northeast, squashed between Angola, Zambia and Botswana. At the end of the Caprivi Strip, 600 kilometres away, we would meet the container in Katima Mulilo, known as Katima.

We got up early on the first day, planning to get on our bikes and leave Rundu before the blistering sun rose in the sky. Well, after the sun had risen our gear looked as organised as if it had been strewn all over our apartment floor in Melbourne. The only difference was it was now laid out in the sandy yard of the house where we had stayed. After numerous goes at packing, unpacking, repacking and restrapping, we finally pushed our way out through the sand to the tarsealed road. Little did we know, the change of plans to start from Rundu instead of Cape Town was a blessing in disguise. It was the perfect training ground for two absolute novice cyclists in the middle of Africa. The climate was now hot instead of cold, the terrain was flat and the roads tarsealed and straight, with little traffic.

The moment as we pedalled away I couldn't wipe the smile off my face: we were here, we were doing it, we were cycling to meet the container. The start of the adventure. The first days were everything I had expected. We camped on the roadside, scared and apprehensive about animals and people. We visited existing BEN bike workshops and stayed in small villages. African ladies walked along the roadside with bundles of wood balanced on their heads. Excited kids ran out of mud huts shouting 'How are you?', expressing the same eagerness with which I used to chase the ice-cream truck.

But there was still something hanging over us. The melancholy clouds of Table Mountain seemed to have followed

## The Dark Continent

us. The excitement of our first days of cycling soon dried up like the riverbeds we were crossing. What was it?

After two weeks we arrived in Katima late in the afternoon. We went straight to the campsite bar as the red African sun set over the Zambezi River. Since hearing my high school outdoor education teacher talking about the Zambezi, I had wanted to see it. And here we were. We had made it. We had cycled here. Although it was only 600 kilometres on flat sealed road in what was a stable country compared with others, it was still Africa; it was our first baby step. I was proud, and I was really proud of Mandy—not every girlfriend would do that. We were now cyclists; we had pedalled the road.

Katima was no longer just a circled dot on the African map in the living room of our Melbourne apartment. It wasn't a nice-looking place, wasn't somewhere I would ordinarily go if I wasn't working there. But that had been the same with a lot of the places I had fallen in love with—Bucheon in South Korea, Tapachula in Mexico and Asunción in Paraguay. As I drank my beer, overlooking the Zambezi, I wondered if Katima would become one of those places.

Katima is located at the very end of the Caprivi Strip with the Zambezi River separating it from Zambia. It is a town of around 25,000, but it didn't feel that big as most of the population was spread among outlying villages and residential locations. They lived in mud huts and shacks, had no electricity and had to collect their drinking water from communal water taps that were located on the side of the sandy roads.

We found a room to rent from a local family. We expected to be staying in a mud hut, but this was Katima, the 'big city' of rural Namibia, and we lived in a newly built house in a residential neighbourhood where ours were the only white faces. It was the Namibian version of Pleasantville, identically built cubic western-looking houses, with square fenced properties, but instead of grass front lawns there was sand.

## HAP WORKING THE WORLD

Our small room was modern but sterile, with white tiles and cream walls and a barred window. We moved our bikes into the corner, unloaded our panniers and piled our clothes on the floor. We purchased a foam mattress from the local 'China' shop and put our sleeping bags on top. This was to be our home. But something continued to bug us; we still didn't feel happy.

A few days later we met Moses, a volunteer from Catholic Aids Action who had been selected as the bikeshop manager. He was one of five volunteers who would be trained as bike mechanics and then given paid employment in the shop. Moses and I were about the same age, and he was a tall good-looking guy with a big, immaculate, white-toothed African smile. He was charismatic and vibrant, a well-known member of the community and an integral part of the church. Moses was the ideal choice for the manager, and his aspirations and visions for the future of the workshop left me feeling inspired. Moses filled me with a sense of hope for Africa. If some African leaders had half of Moses's moral character and shared the same passion for their countries that Moses had for his shipping container, then the future of the 'dark continent' would be bright.

Moses had given us directions to the container, which we finally got to see at around nine o'clock on a Monday morning. It was a rewarding moment to find the container on the sandy ground of the fenced churchyard, looking like a tired dog after a long journey. It appeared content in its new home with kindergarten kids running around it laughing, a stark contrast to the dreary abandoned industrial estate where it had come from.

There was a buzz around the container. The Catholic Aids Action volunteers were busy raking up leaves, kindergarten kids were playing on a see-saw and people from the community were walking in, asking when they could buy bikes. The BEN trainer, who I would be assisting, arrived with a key to the container. I was given the honour of unlocking it, which was a little harder than it looked as someone had already taken to the heavy-duty padlock with a hammer.

Our first day was spent doing a stocktake of the bikes to see how many had made it through the 'inspections' of the customs officials, en route to Katima. We unloaded an expected total of 405 bikes and lined them up against the wall of the unfinished brick classrooms that some other volunteer organisation had only half completed the previous year. When I looked at these unused classrooms it made me determined to see this project through and not leave it half finished.

Foreigners working in Africa use the acronym TIA, This Is Africa, to help explain the way things are done or, more accurately, not done. Things happen a lot more slowly in Africa—9 a.m. is never 9 a.m., and the pace of life is a lot more laid back. That is never going to change and if you try to change it you will end up frustrated. It would be like an African going into the New York Stock Exchange and telling the brokers to chill out.

Mandy helped out during the first few weeks, preparing the lunches and working with kids at the kindergarten. I spent a lot of my time with the five volunteers, who had now become paid trainees in this business, teaching them bike mechanics.

I quickly learnt that this project wasn't about me coming in and transforming the shipping container into this amazing bike shop with the concrete floor and shaded work areas that I had told people back home about. It was about the five bike mechanics whose bike shop it was going to be. They had to be proud of it. From the start I realised I had to let them do it their way, otherwise this container would be like the unused classrooms in the churchyard. My role was to pass on my knowledge, help with the training, advise Moses and the mechanics of alternative ways of doing things. But the decisions had to be theirs.

There was a lot of laughter. The five trainees were eager to learn, and just as eager to have a laugh. Like any workshop I had been in around the world, conversation always fell back to ladies, except here we were laughing about the man with nine wives and our workshop was a bit of black plastic under a tree.

I was posting photos on my blog that showed this idyllic African setting, working on bikes under the shade of a tree, laughing with the locals, making a difference, changing the world. People would email and comment, saying what an amazing thing Mandy and I were doing, and how incredible it must be. Little did they know there was another story behind the photos, and it involved a thief.

## Worries about tomorrow — what next?

I'm beside myself. I'm crying, blubbering like I have never done before. There is no way to explain how pathetic and useless I feel at this very moment. I want to hug Mandy, to hold her, to console her, tell her I love her, but I can't say those words to her as I have just broken up with her. But I do love her. I cry.

I'm walking around the house. It's mid-morning, a Tuesday maybe, it's sunny and hot outside, but my world is dark and gloomy, my head can't think straight, I've just taken the biggest leap of my life, one that I thought would be the answer to the way I was feeling, but instead is probably going to keep me falling for a long time.

I put my hands through my hair, just crying. I can't stop crying. I can't even talk properly. I'm trying to calm Mandy down. She's crying now, not crying, wailing and groaning as though a piece of her body has been severed from her, and I suppose it has. I've done this to her, me—what an arsehole. How could I break up with this caring, loving soul who has unconditionally loved and supported me through everything? And now that I have broken up with her all I want to do is hold her in my arms and tell her we'll get through it together.

When Mandy and I had arrived in Cape Town we were

## The Dark Continent

in a sombre mood. This mood had made Africa into our own 'dark' continent. The quote that inspired the two black sinister characters I had tattooed on my back in Canada all those years ago was now in my head: *Regrets over yesterday and worries about tomorrow are the twin thieves that rob you of the moment.*

That 'worries about tomorrow' thief was playing with our heads, teasing us with 'what next'. It constantly lingered above us like a rain cloud over a picnic. Ever since we had first met on that beach in Mexico this thief had always been robbing us. As one chapter unfolded we were constantly trying to find a new chapter that would work for both of us, a chapter where we could both get visas, could both earn money, could both find work, would both be challenged and, most importantly, both be happy. Up till now we had always been able to hop to the next continent, the next country, the next chapter, and when we had decided what we were doing next, only then was the thief locked up and we would enjoy the moment.

However, we both knew the big 'what next' would come in Africa with the end of my working-the-world goal. The goal that had been a guiding light for the last eight years was about to go out and I would be left in the dark.

In Melbourne, that 'what next' question had kept raising its head. Anyone in a relationship with someone from another country knows the added pressures that come with it. Visas are always a financial and stressful burden, and being denied entry into the States made permanently living there a significant barrier. However, the greatest stress I could see was one partner was going to have to miss out—one partner would have to give up their home, give up a part of themselves, give up sharing the joys of their children with their family. One family on the other side of the world would have to watch their grandchildren, cousins, nieces and nephews grow up through Facebook photos and updates.

I had found the previous year in Tasmania and Melbourne

hard. I had had a gut feeling that I needed to end our relationship, but I fought it. I decided I wanted to give it my best shot with Mandy and that was the least I could do after all she had sacrificed to be with me. Mandy always said that Africa would either make or break us, and she thought that if we could make it a success, then we could have that big house with a kitchen and some little kids crawling around in it. I always wanted a family and the last thing I wanted was to be single and trying to pick up girls. I could have all that with Mandy by saying four easy words: 'Will you marry me?' Four easy words that would make her the happiest girl in the world. But even though I knew that's what I wanted, I knew that I was not ready.

When had life become so complicated?

Mandy was also unable to enjoy living in the moment in Africa, as she too was wondering what was next for us. As much as we both wanted to be in the moment, or looking to the future, that thief 'worries about tomorrow' was weighing too heavily on our minds. Like me, Mandy was holding onto hope that we would make it. One morning as we lay in bed with that thief, we were crying. I whispered to Mandy, 'I love you.' But she replied, 'I know, but soon that won't be enough.'

I knew that she deserved more.

There were days when we were cycling along and then all of a sudden we were on the side of the road, having an emotional discussion, trying to find the answer to the 'what next' question, an answer that would make us both happy. We came to the conclusion that after my 30th birthday we would go home to our respective countries for the holidays.

Mandy would go back to the States to spend time with her family and get some bar work and I would go back to New Zealand to finish writing my book. This felt right, and we thought the time apart would help us figure out an answer to the 'what next' question, where we would live, what we would

## The Dark Continent

do, how we could make it work, and for me especially to sort my shit out.

This made us feel better, momentarily, until we both realised how much it felt like we were going our separate ways. Why were we making plans to be apart? Shouldn't this be the time that we were making plans to be together?

I was coming up to a pretty big transition in my life. After eight years of chasing my goal, I was struggling to think about life afterwards and to deal with the uncertainty it would bring. So I found myself under an unbearable amount of pressure. Not pressure from Mandy but pressure from myself. How could I think about starting a family with Mandy, supporting that family, going to live in the States at some point when I didn't even know where I was going?

If I didn't know now, after four and a half years, would I ever know? I couldn't keep dragging Mandy along with me, I couldn't endure any more sadness. I had to man up. I loved Mandy. She deserved more. I had to set her free from the shackles of my uncertainty. I had to make the hardest decision of my life. If I couldn't say 'Will you marry me?' I had to say the other words, the harder words.

But I couldn't say them. My head was fighting for Mandy right to the bitter end. *Your gut feeling is wrong, fight the thief, this girl is amazing, you just need time to sort things out.*

Like a man about to jump off a bridge, about to make the biggest decision of his life, I sat Mandy down in the lounge. I had to grow some balls and tell her. I knew that once I said those words, there was no going back to the bridge.

I didn't know how to say it. How do you say such a thing? I can't remember my exact words, but they came out bloody cowardly sounding, not at all how I wanted them to sound.

I said something to the effect of 'Do you want to leave?'

What a coward. Of course she didn't want to leave; if she had wanted to she would have left already. If we couldn't have a break, I had to break us. I had to jump. The tears rolled through my hands as they held my face. I said the words, 'I'm breaking up, Mandy. I'm sorry, I'm sorry.'

I had jumped.

'Don't follow me!' Mandy shouted. 'Don't try to see me. Don't call me.'

And with that I watched Mandy wheel her bike through the sand and out the front gate. The sun had set. Darkness had fallen.

## The end of our road – Zambia

Africa had broken us but there was no better place for it to have happened. In Africa we had no family or close friends; we had to help each other through this. After all we had achieved and experienced together it would be a shame to part on bad terms. Mandy was able to forgive me, and also agreed that it was probably for the best in the long term. We had a farewell luncheon for her at the workshop as she felt guilty for leaving before its completion. But I didn't think anyone would see it like that.

The following day we got a bus to Victoria Falls in Zambia. Mandy had invited me to go with her to spend our last holiday together, as a celebration of our relationship. It seemed that now our future had a definite path, we could finally enjoy the moment. That thief was locked up at last. We could both start planning, and stop living in that limbo land, that uncertainty.

We spent our time doing what Mandy and I did best— drinking beers, eating, hanging out, playing cards, laughing and poking fun at each other. It was as if nothing had changed. The way I looked at this time was that we may as well make the most of our last three days together to celebrate all that we had achieved and experienced together. We made love with passion, knowing it would be our last time. But we also laughed, reminisced, and were united in our heartbreak.

Then came Sunday morning. The day Mandy would hop

on the bus, I would wave goodbye and we would probably never see each other again. We went and bought some beers, and found some grass close to the bus station. We sat down and drank in the afternoon sun, watching Sunday in Zambia roll by. It was surreal. Was this really happening? Was this the last hour I would spend with Mandy, maybe ever?

We walked to the bus station. We sat on a small brick wall under the shade of the large tree that acted as the bus station. We got out the video camera and talked openly to it, which we had done since Cape Town. We cried. We drank some more beer. I hoped it would give me strength, or at least a little comfort. It didn't.

I was dreading the time we had to say goodbye. And then it came. All the passengers were called. We hugged, we kissed, we cried, oh my God, we cried. I told Mandy she was the most amazing person I had ever met. I thanked her as I already had a thousand times previously for all she had done for me, all the support. Then the moment came and Mandy and I walked to the bus.

I hoped it was for the best.

'Take care, Pooby.' Now we weren't together that was going to be the last time I could call her by the stupid little nickname I had for her.

I waved as the bus left. Mandy was going to walk back into her old life in Denver, Colorado, into the same school she had been teaching at when I first arrived four years ago. She would be with her family; it would be like the last four years were a dream.

Now I was all alone in Africa. From that point on loneliness and sadness were going to take on a whole new meaning for me.

## Business as usual

If the sun doesn't rise, does the day continue?

I woke the following morning back in Katima. The skies

were bright blue, but someone had pulled a black curtain over the sun. Life on the dark continent continued. Business as usual.

It was a Monday, the start of the two weeks' small business training. The trainees had successfully completed their four weeks' bike mechanics training. Also Michael Linke, the expat Australian founder of BEN Namibia, was on a road trip from the capital Windhoek up to northern Namibia and into Zambia to check on existing bike workshops and meet prospective new project start-ups in Zambia. We had been in communication a lot about the project while I had been preparing, but this was the first time I would meet him.

I tried to act like my normal bubbly, happy self, but that was exactly what I was doing, acting. I just felt so damn lonely. I threw myself into the filming, trying to keep my mind occupied and to be around people. After leaving the workshop, I would feel even more alone. I would go to the supermarket and try to figure out what to have for dinner. Mandy had always been the cook, I had always been the dishwasher. In that supermarket all I could think about was Mandy—I didn't even want to eat. I just stood there staring at the shelf in a trance.

It was a Tuesday night, only two days since Mandy had left, when I hit rock bottom. I was back in the empty house and hadn't bothered with dinner. I flopped down on the cheap mattress that Mandy and I had bought. Mandy's indentation was still visible in the foam where she used to lie beside me. I looked at her bike sitting in the corner of the room and cried. I missed her so much.

At that point I felt like I had back in Paraguay when I had my meltdown. But here I was, all by myself in the middle of Africa.

I knew I had to keep going. If I pushed it, I could get the bikeshop project and the filming for the documentary done in a total of three weeks; two weeks of small business training and a week for the shop to be open.

The thought of doing all this seemed impossible in the state

## The Dark Continent

I was in, let alone cycling solo through southern Africa. At that moment the thought of being alone on the road with all that time to think everything over was unimaginable.

People ask me what my secret is for being so resilient. My answer is the support of the people close to me. It is in the times when you cannot fight by yourself that you will lose the battle. My father had always told me a problem shared is a problem halved. I had no problem with talking—I knew the benefits of it from my experience in Paraguay—the problem was there was no one in Katima to be a sounding board.

My family, and some close mates, had pulled me through that time. Although I tried to come across as positive on the phone to my family so as not to worry them, I was still down. They gave me the strength to prop up myself and to pull me through. The piece of advice that got me through that time was 'Just get through the next five minutes. Just take it one day at a time.'

I made it through that first week and then the following week I went to film with Michael in Zambia, where he was meeting prospective bike shop partners. He was also checking on the two existing shops, one of which was a Melbourne container at an orphanage I wanted to visit. I had met the charismatic Zambian manager in Melbourne before leaving on the FCE.

That week of laughter, and being around someone who spoke my language and who I felt relaxed with, was vital for getting me over that first hurdle. We never spoke about Mandy as he had never met her. Also we shared a dry sense of humour and laughed a lot. With every bit of laughter, the curtains were pulled back a little bit more. Slowly light started to come in.

Like all good things, that second week came to an end. We arrived back in Katima and I needed to start packing Mandy's belongings. I had organised with Michael to ship them back to the US for me and he was leaving the following day.

I texted Moses telling him that I would be at the bike shop

tomorrow. He replied with a text message that would see the curtains pulled closer again, but would help put my situation with Mandy into perspective:

> *Welcom back 2 namibia bt tomorrow we shal b at Kongola 4 buring rodrick and u a free to go take picture and see how we bury our fellow volunteer when he dies and it wil take place moning at Kongola 110km away*

Bloody hell, I was shocked! Roderick was one of the five bike mechanics I had helped train. I knew he had been sick, but I was stunned at the sad news. Roderick was softly spoken and a polite gentleman. Unfortunately the HIV and AIDS epidemic that ravages this part of Namibia where over 40 per cent of people are infected didn't care if Roderick was polite. Who was I to be feeling sorry for myself?

You can talk about the statistics of HIV all day long, but it is not until it's close to you that the reality of it actually hits home. I realised that being the only white man attending the funeral and then filming it was going to be a very delicate matter. But something Moven, one of the other bike mechanics, did gave me the motivation to film it. Moven said that I had to film it to help portray to the rest of the world the effects of HIV. And then he made a courageous offer. He also lived with HIV, and he offered to share his story with me. There is still a lot of stigma around the disease in Namibian communities, even though the rate of HIV is so high. Attitudes are getting better, but sufferers are still victimised and treated as outcasts. If Moven was willing to tell his story, I was willing to film the funeral despite it feeling intrusive and totally against all my natural ethics.

The following morning I woke at 5.30. I biked out to meet Moses at the morgue, a small concrete brick structure. At the morgue we piled into the back of a pick-up truck with thirteen other funeral-goers. Then in a four-car convoy we drove for an hour to Roderick's village.

# The Dark Continent

It was around 8 a.m. when we arrived at Roderick's village. The scene was set for the funeral ceremony. Colourfully dressed African ladies sat on woven mats spread over the sand. The men were off to one side, with the elders sitting on chairs.

I was the only white person out of the 120 attendees. It was an honour, but I was also tense. I felt like an outsider, and even more conspicuous with my camera. Moses, who was to lead the funeral, wanted me to take some photos and video footage. Even though I had his permission I still felt like an intruder. I made sure that he had the permission of the elders and Roderick's family before I took out my camera.

The grief-filled atmosphere, the loss of Roderick, the past couple of weeks without Mandy and the knowledge that I was capturing something on camera that few white men got to experience had a strange effect on me. Tears were welling up in my eyes as the families grieved and I thought of Roderick and the funerals of beloved ones that I had attended. My legs were shaking uncontrollably as the emotion of it all passed through me.

I didn't think I would be this affected. I had grown up seeing war and famine ravaging Africa on the six o'clock news. I had arrogantly thought that death was just another part of everyday life here.

How naive was I. It doesn't matter if you come from a neighbourhood with streetlights and hand basins with running water or a small African village where the chickens and dogs play on the sand floor of your hut, death is death.

I can only describe the funeral as a beautiful ceremony. The vibrant colours of the women's clothing and the bright flowers on the coffin contrasted with the dusty weathered earth. Their singing was heartfelt. Their grief was expressed with no reserve, women openly wailing, wailing like I had never heard before. It was also special for me to see Moses, who I was used to seeing fixing bikes, dressed in his white robe, leading the funeral in a commanding way, well beyond his years.

# HAP WORKING THE WORLD

## An elephant corridor and a makoro adventure

Two weeks had passed since Roderick's funeral. It was evening and I was sitting at a riverside bar, drinking a beer after a day at the workshop. I liked this bar—it was out of town and different to the overpriced lodge bars that were frequented by safari tourists in their big kitted-out 4WDs. This bar reminded me of Thailand with its laid-back atmosphere. Couches were placed on the sand and you had a view out over the Zambezi as you sat beneath the thatched roof. I also liked this place as Mandy and I had never been there; it was a place my thieves didn't know about.

The bar was empty. As I ordered another beer from the friendly African bartender, a pint-sized Englishman dressed in khaki safari clothes came running into the bar. He attempted to do the splits while throwing a hand in the air, doing a Michael Jackson impersonation with a high-pitched 'Yahoo!'

As he cracked open his beer he turned to me and in his English accent said, 'Fuck me, I've been in the bush for a month! Man ain't a camel, I need a beer!'

Then he reached into his trouser pocket and pulled out a bag of biltong, the South African dried meat. 'You like kudu? Caught out by my place, just smoked it. By the way, I'm Simon.'

His place was a small camping ground from which he ran safari boat tours. He had just set it up the year before with a local community, just down the road from Roderick's village. From his grand entrance I knew there would never be a dull moment with Simon around. I was right.

When I woke the next morning I had vague recollections of watching a bunch of fights breaking out at the local nightclub and then Simon and I heading to a ghetto area with a load of locals in the back of his truck, driving the sandy roads and looking for an illegal shack of a bar that would be open.

He had crashed the night on my mattress. As he walked out the door he said, 'I gotta fly, I have a trip to organise, but hitch

## The Dark Continent

out tomorrow and give me a hand building a mud hut and I'll show you my backyard.'

The backyard he was talking about was the Bwabwata National Park which his camp bordered on the other side of the Kwando River.

With the bike workshop now open and Moses and the team functioning well, I thought a week with Simon out among nature, building a mud hut, would be good for the soul. The following day I hitched out to the camp.

Simon was just collecting some firewood. He welcomed me, 'Hey mate, want to have a beer and then go for a sunset fish?'

Next thing I knew we're cruising the maze-like tributaries of the Kwando River, which Simon knew like the back of his hand. We were on his pontoon boat with two outboard motors, buzzing past hippos lazing in the channels and elephants walking on the riverbank before we found a spot to fish and have a sundowner.

We returned to camp and it was time for me to pitch a tent. Simon then asked me, 'Do you want an exciting night's sleep?'

Without waiting for my answer he started walking and said, 'We'll put your tent outside the camp in the elephant corridor.'

The elephant corridor is basically what it sounds like. It's a pathway that the elephants use to go from the river back into the bush. The corridor is easy to spot with ravaged, broken trees and rock-sized elephant crap everywhere. Wanting the full experience, and because it was so bloody hot, we just put up the inner mosquito netting part of the tent. Then off we went back to the camp to light the fire, have a few more beers and dinner.

With the fire dying down it was time for bed and I made the trek back along the elephant corridor to my mosquito netting. Now in the darkness, with my fading head lamp and no visible path to follow, all the bushes looked identical and I wandered around trying to find where I had pitched the tent. I was also in fear of coming across an elephant, hippo, lion, pack of hyenas or any other wild animal that called this area home.

When I finally got to the tent it dawned on me how small, flimsy and insignificant the mosquito netting was, especially when you compared it to a 5-tonne bull elephant. Unluckily for me the apprehensive feeling only grew when I went to zip up the net. The zip didn't work. There was no way I was sleeping with the tent open, because Simon had seen fresh hyena tracks in the camp the night before and this area had a large population of them. They are rather harmless compared to lions, but they have been known to attack sleeping people.

I tried the zipper again and then to my relief I heard the sweet sound of it closing. I lay back and looked out at the trees silhouetted by the half moon. This was what I had envisioned Africa being like. The blissful moment slowly morphed into one of vulnerability. There is nothing like lying down on the ground in the middle of an elephant corridor to make you feel vulnerable. All the sounds of the bush turned into a hungry lion or a sleepy elephant that was going to innocently walk right over my tent.

I had asked Simon what to do if an elephant came by, to which he replied, 'Just don't act like a dickhead!'

So there I was lying in the middle of an elephant corridor under the African night sky trying to not act like a dickhead.

In the early morning those beers woke me up with my bladder knocking at the tent door wanting out. Simon had told me to grab a 5-litre water bottle to pee in if I was too scared to get out of the tent to answer the call of nature. As this would be my first night all alone in the African wild I had thought it was a great idea. But now, unscrewing the bottle, I quickly realised it had been used for petrol storage as strong fumes filled my nostrils. But putting the old fella in the petrol bottle seemed like a better option than going outside in the wild and having the zip fail on me when I returned.

With my bladder empty and my groin burning I lay back down. My thoughts were suddenly interrupted by the sound of rustling bushes. Then to my left, through the netting, I saw the

## The Dark Continent

unmistakable bulk of two elephants come into view. I couldn't believe how such giant creatures could move so silently and gracefully. I wasn't scared of these beasts, I was in awe of them.

I was surprised at how calm I felt as they made their way closer to my tent. I was up on one elbow looking out at them, unable and not wanting to move, transfixed. Then the leading bull quietly came to halt, 5 metres from where I was lying. His giant ears flared out as if in warning, his trunk went into the air, horizontal to the ground. He had picked up my scent. An elephant's sight is poor but its sense of smell makes up for this. As quietly as they had come into my world, they turned and walked out of sight to find another path in the corridor. Amazing!

The next morning as I was waiting for the water to boil on the campfire, Simon asked me if I had seen elephants. I told him I had been visited during the night and told him what a great experience it had been. I asked him about the elephants and how they know you're there, and what happens if they have a blocked nose and can't smell you. Isn't it dangerous? His answer once again filled me with confidence.

'Yeah, just last year down the road at another camp a German girl had her tent trampled while she was asleep.'

That day we spent digging termite dirt with Simon's workers. Termite dirt is used in the construction of mud huts. At around 4 p.m., Simon called it a day and said, 'Hap, do you want to go and explore in the makoro?'

Makoro is the local name for a dugout canoe, and Simon's plan was for us to meander through the narrow reed channels that he hadn't yet explored because his pontoon motorboat was too big. He wanted to navigate the uncharted tributaries around his peninsula of land and then end up behind his camp, where we could walk back along the sandy road to his place.

From the start I wasn't filled with the greatest of confidence in this mission. When we got to the makoro it was fully submerged and had algae growing on it. Simon assured me that if we bailed all the water out, and made sure we kept our weight towards the back so water didn't enter the sizeable crack at the front, we would be fine.

I hesitantly hopped into the makoro, which immediately started taking on water. My attention was channelled into my stress levels, as Simon told me to look for hippos coming up behind us.

Hippos are Africa's most dangerous animals and kill more people than any other. Even though they are herbivores they are extremely territorial. Floating through the reed channels in this hollowed-out log, I felt as vulnerable as if I had put on a seal suit to go swimming with a pod of killer whales.

Since arriving at his camp I had seen plenty of hippos motionless in the river like ticking timebombs disguised as large rocks. Every muscle in my body was tense with the anticipation of spotting a hippo's head. Every water lily or fish ripple became a hippo. Simon's running commentary didn't really help either as he paddled us down the narrow reed-lined channel, pointing down at the water below us. 'See the white sand down there, that's a hippo trail.' We were following it.

The later it got, the deeper into unknown territory we went. Although Simon had lived here for four years this was his first time in this part of the swamp. Making me feel further at ease, he exclaimed, 'I'd never do this with a client!'

The channel we were following forked. To the right was a deep narrow channel heading into the reeds, while the left went into swampy grass that was a little closer to our good friend, dry land. We took a left, but it wasn't long before we couldn't move due to the thick swampy grass. We both hopped out and started to push. Yes, this was also crocodile country.

To try to reassure myself, I nervously said to Simon, 'No crocodiles in this swampy area, eh Simon?'

In a Steve Irwin accent, but being serious, he replied, 'Crikey! There are, mate, but I'm more worried about the pythons.'

## The Dark Continent

'Cheers, mate,' I responded as we entered waist-deep water.

Twenty metres later we were both back in the makoro, clear of the swamp grass. We had been on the water over an hour and the sun was close to setting. Simon was unsure of how to navigate the remaining impassable maze of reeds that lay between us and the tree we were aiming for, about 500 metres away. We had three options: to try to navigate the channels and make it to our destination; get the makoro to dry land and walk back to camp; or turn back and retrace our route against the current.

None of these options really stood out as a favourite. Going into a place that Simon had never been in the fading light, with no cell phones or flashlight, could only end up with us being stranded. Getting to dry land and walking back wasn't an option because Simon had no shoes on and the fallen thorn branches that lay over the ground were similar to planks of wood with nails hammered through them. Our only option was to turn back.

To my relief we turned back but I would only be able to relax when I was in camp, seated by the fire with a cold beer. We were in the middle of untouched wilderness with the sun reflecting off the glassy water and not a soul in sight. But it was hard to truly appreciate it as I felt so vulnerable sitting at water level, knowing we were in hippo territory.

Simon reassured me that I had every reason not to be relaxed. 'Hap, I'm bricking it too. Now the sun has set, this is the time the hippos leave the main channels and come down these narrow side channels to get out and graze for the night.'

Simon's usual joking mood had also changed, his tone of voice more serious. 'If we get tipped, don't swim on the surface or they will get you. Dive down and swim to dry land.'

I was now on full radar alert, facing the front of the makoro, panning the water ahead as we headed back up the channel as that would be the direction the hippos would come from. Finally we hit familiar territory, 100 metres from camp. A place we had fished the evening before, a place I hadn't seen any hippos. Finally I could start to relax.

Suddenly my radar went off. 'Is that a hippo?' I nervously asked Simon. I waited for his reply to let me know that it was just another water lily.

Simon's tone was grave. 'Fuck, it's a hippo. Fuck, it's a big bastard. Fuck, it's moving towards us.'

The hippo was about 20 metres away in the wide lagoon. But the V-like ripples made by his eyes above the waterline were heading our way.

Simon was now in survival mode. 'Quick, we'll pull the makoro onto the island.' The island he was talking about was a low lying grassy patch with a single tree in the middle, which was joined to the riverbank by swampy grass.

We pulled onto the tiny island. The hippo was coming around behind, its eyes still firmly focused on us.

I was hanging on Simon's every word. As he made himself look big and clapped his hands above his head to try to scare the hippo he said seriously, 'Stay calm, let's get to dry land.'

We started off through the swampy grass with water around our knees, no longer worried about crocodiles or pythons. We had one more grassy channel to cross and luckily it didn't look too deep. All I wanted to do was run as quickly as possible through the swamp to the bank, but Simon was all about staying calm and doing a fast walk. I looked back, the hippo was still moving towards us. Then his eyes went under the water.

Fuck this walking business, I had seen hippos move through the water like torpedoes. Simon could calmly walk all he wanted, but I was last in line, therefore first on the menu. I went to run the last 10 metres when Simon disappeared, falling forward with a splash and going under. I followed straight behind him. The once knee-deep water had dropped off into a deep grassy channel.

Scrambling over each other, we desperately splashed and swam our way to the bank, not bothering to look behind. It was every

# The Dark Continent

man for himself. We scampered up the bank on all fours. I didn't stop running until I hit the bushline 30 metres from the swampy edge. We stood there looking at each other. All I could do was swear. My whole body was shaking uncontrollably. The swearing slowly merged into laughter, but I was still unable to form sentences.

Finally I recovered, the adrenaline slowly residing. Then, with a smile, Simon said, 'Hap can you go and get my shoes, they are only over there where we launched the makoro, just past that tree.'

I shakily walked towards the tree, jumping at every noise, oblivious to the reason why Simon had been smiling. My approach spooked the hordes of giant birds that lived in its branches and all of a sudden they burst into flight, squawking at the top of their lungs to warn the animal kingdom of my presence. I jumped so damn high in the air, squealing. Long after the birds had squawked off into the distance, I could still hear Simon's uncontrollable laughter as he gasped for breath.

We got back to camp and cracked a beer. As I took my first sip we heard a hippo just 15 metres from us out in the river. That's it, no sleeping in the elephant corridor or going out in the makoro at sunset for me. But my God, I had never felt so alive!

## The light at the end of the dark continent

After the week out at Simon's place, I returned to the workshop. I watched the guys sitting on the black plastic beneath the tree, fixing bikes and dealing with customers. I felt so proud, not of myself, but of the mechanics. With the profits they had already made Moses had bought them heavy-duty blue work uniforms and work boots, and I sensed this made them feel good about themselves.

Moses gave me a tour of the workshop, even though I had only been away a week. And from the tour he gave me, I could have sworn Moses was showing me around his brand-new bike shop on the main street of Melbourne and not a shipping container in the middle of Africa. He told me how he had got a local builder to come out and give him quotes on renovating the container. He was planning to put in windows and air vents with the profits they were already making. I felt proud that these men had such a great sense of ownership for their workshop. Because they felt proud of the workshop, I felt proud of what Mandy and I had done, of what we had achieved and all the support we had received along the way.

On my last morning before departing Katima for the rest of my cycle journey, I dropped by the workshop with my bike packed up. The guys presented me with a wooden animal that they had carved. Because they had carved it themselves, had made it with their own hands with love and gratitude, it was worth more to me than some perfectly sculpted gold ornament.

I strapped it onto my bike and we said our goodbyes in front of the container, the container that Mandy and I had helped pack in Melbourne five months ago. I was now by myself, standing in front of a sustainable bike workshop that was running successfully under the leadership of Moses and would continue to sell bikes long after the names Hap and Mandy had been forgotten.

As I pushed my bike out of the church compound, I felt ready to leave Katima. This chapter had seen some of the darkest moments of my working-the-world quest. I thought back to the night after I had broken up with Mandy when I didn't even think I was capable of completing the workshop or filming the documentary. The thought of cycling another 2000 kilometres through southern Africa seemed an impossibility; it terrified me. Now six weeks later I was excited about the journey that lay ahead. It seemed that adventure was able to keep those thieves at bay.

As I got on my bike I felt more adventure was at my fingertips. This was the Africa I had dreamt about. Finally, there was light at the end of the dark continent.

## Chapter 18
# THE FINAL CONTINENT
**AFRICA: Botswana, Zimbabwe, Zambia, Malawi, Tanzania, 5 June–23 November 2011**

'You going by bicycle?' asked the serious immigration lady at the Botswana–Zimbabwe border at the start of the Zambezi National Park.

'Yup,' I answered.

'That's a bad idea.'

Then the lady beside her chimed in. 'There are lions, leopards, cheetahs, buffalo, elephants, hyenas and jackals in the park.'

I didn't know what a jackal was but assumed it was more dangerous than an angry sheep.

Another uniformed official came up to the ladies. They told him that I was planning to cycle through the park to which he added, 'You'll become a statistic.'

Umm, now I was feeling very nervous. All I wanted was a positive second opinion.

I had just met a retired American couple, and as I cycled to the entrance of the park I wondered whether I should ask them if I could put my bike on their 4WD roof.

Unfortunately my positive second opinion was not going to come from the young guy on the security gate. As I approached he was in fits of laughter, slapping his leg and getting the attention of all the other fellas lazing around in the shade of the shacks. 'You going to cycle through the park, ha, ha, ha.'

It seemed that this white fella on the bike about to cycle the 70 kilometres through the park was one of the funniest things he had ever heard.

He lifted the boom to the gate and let me through. I pulled off to the side of the road to get a photo of my bike under the *Welcome to Zimbabwe* sign.

At this point I was still in two minds. It wasn't too late to hitch a ride with the American couple, but I had that burning desire for adventure. While I was setting up my camera on the tripod, another smiling local came up to me in that friendly Zimbabwean way. We started talking and he asked me what my plan was. I told him I was headed for Victoria Falls and asked him if it was a stupid idea to cycle through the park.

He answered, 'I haven't heard of anyone being attacked on a bicycle.'

Perfect, that was the answer I wanted to hear.

I should have left it at that, but then asked, 'So people cycle through the park?'

He burst out laughing. 'Ha ha, no one cycle through the park!'

When my optimistic friend left me I was still tossing up what to do. Then I looked at my watch. It was 8.45 a.m. I thought to myself, *What would I rather be doing right now, sitting down at a desk in front of my computer for the nine to five grind or cycling 70 kilometres through a national park in the middle of southern Africa?*

It was a no-brainer. I hopped on my bike. At first I pedalled timidly, still not fully committed, knowing that I was able to turn around. Two kilometres into the park I was past the point of no return and pumped on the pedals with adrenaline-induced vigour.

Every bird that took flight made me jump, every breath of wind made me spin my head. I was tense. I rationalised that at least the heat of the day meant the animals wouldn't be so active. If I came across a lion under a tree I hoped it would just look at me and think that it was too hot and I was too skinny to bother giving chase. I also thought that a chance of a lion attack was very low, as long as I didn't see one. Unfortunately I couldn't ride with my eyes closed.

The thing that made it even more nerve-racking was the lion-coloured metre-high grass that came right up to the roadside, the perfect camouflage for a preying lion. Three metres beyond the lion-coloured grass was four-metre-high bush, just perfect for disguising elephants.

The tensest moments were when my peripheral vision detected a flash of lion-coloured fur. My heart would miss a beat, then it would calm down once I saw that it was only one of the abundant species of African antelope—gazelle, kudu, impala, waterbuck, reedbuck, puku, lechwe or springbok—which would leap into action as I went past and were probably more scared than I was.

I couldn't help but think as I cycled along the road that I felt like one of those defenceless antelopes. These creatures live their entire life under the constant threat of being eaten, like a chicken hanging out at KFC.

I took small comfort in the fact that if a tourist bus came across a lion attacking me on the side of the road they wouldn't be oohing and ahhing and uploading videos of it onto YouTube. But if I were a little gazelle they would be praising the Lord for giving them every safari tourist's most prized encounter—a lion kill.

The only potentially dangerous animals I encountered in the park were an elephant with two calves and a handful of buffalo. I passed within 20 metres of them. I didn't see the buffalo until I was right by them. I surprised them and was thankful they took off in the other direction. The elephant and calves I spotted early and I froze, but after fifteen minutes I decided to cycle on the other side of the road, while keeping an eye on them for any signs of agitation. Once I had passed them I proceeded to put as much distance between them and me!

After covering the fastest 70 kilometres of my life on a bike I arrived in the town of Victoria Falls, making it a total of 84 kilometres for the day. When I came flying down the hill into the town with a sense of achievement, I heard cheering. I looked back and it was the American couple I had met at the border that morning

After spending two nights in Victoria Falls, Zimbabwe, I reluctantly had to leave as I still had 265 kilometres to cycle and only three days to do it if I wanted to catch the Lake Kariba ferry, which ran once a week overnight from the western tip of the lake to the eastern shore. Lake Kariba is the stunning man-made lake that acts as the border between Zimbabwe and Zambia.

The trip didn't start too well. The cold that had been biting at my heels finally sunk its teeth in. I woke with a headache, and my nose was congested and running, along with my bum. For breakfast I had my malaria medication, ibuprofen, cold and flu tablets and an Imodium while watching the hostel TV. Then the TV went black because of the power going out, signalling that it was time I got on the road.

Much later, with the sun getting lower in the sky, I arrived at the crappy-looking mining town of Hwange, my destination for the night. As I cycled in, my GPS clicked over 100 kilometres and I gave a little whoop. I pulled into a rundown petrol station and asked the attendant where the cheapest hotel was. He pointed

## The Final Continent

to the top of a hill. Bugger, why did it have to be at the top of a hill! But the thought of flopping down on a bed motivated me to push up the hill.

My heart sank as soon as I saw the hotel. Like most places in Zimbabwe it had seen better days before the country had turned from the bread basket of Africa into Mugabe's basket case. It still looked out of my price range and my enquiry at reception confirmed this—US$90! There was nowhere else in town. So with the sun about to set, I had to put as much distance between me and the town and try to find a concealed spot off the side of the road to camp. As the big ball of red slipped below the horizon I waited until no traffic was in sight and hurriedly wheeled my bike into the bushes with my GPS now showing 115 kilometres for the day. I set up my tent, cooked some rice, and then fell into a cycle-induced coma oblivious to the sounds of nature outside.

I woke around 6 a.m. feeling pretty good. When cycling I found the best part of the day was the first kilometre. The sun is low in the sky, the temperature perfect and your body feels good. Then you realise you have to do this the whole day and your butt starts to hurt.

The previous day had taken it out of me and today it felt like my wheels were square and God had turned up the thermostat. Having covered 50 tough kilometres by lunch I took refuge at a truck diner shack. I had the filling African staple meal of white stodgy porridge that in Zimbabwe was called *sadza* and also splashed out on three bottles of Coke. After a couple of hours hidden from the midday sun, reading my book and with three bottles of Coke in my veins, I felt like a new man.

My vigour didn't last long though as my postcard-sized map of Zimbabwe didn't show the mountainous topography ahead. It should not have surprised me as the 265 kilometres I was covering was only a centimetre on the map.

There was one special moment when I was flying downhill,

leaning into the corners. As I came around the last corner I entered an oasis, a tranquil river valley where the silence was deafening. I parked my bike in the middle of a bridge and stood there taking it all in, my new surrounds and not a soul around. I fought the urge to set up camp here and instead pushed on so I only had a short ride the next morning to the camping ground from where the ferry left.

With the sun setting on another day, I tried to find a place to camp but there were mud hut villages scattered all along the road. This meant it would be hard for me to sneak into the bush unnoticed. I spotted a respectable-looking mud hut and decided to go in and ask if I could pitch my tent next to it for the night. A big African woman with a ripped shirt and warm smile welcomed me. Miriam was her name and she fed the chickens and yarned to me while I set up.

Then Miriam's husband Andrew arrived home. Andrew looked a little unsteady on his feet and confirmed what I was thinking when the first words out of his mouth were 'I'm boozy, he he.' Andrew was pretty sozzled. A nice man but a whole Sunday of drinking meant he had a tendency to keep saying 'like ABCD'—to this day I still have no idea what he meant.

The day of boozing had left Andrew in a very chatty mood which was the last thing I really felt like doing. It had also left him with a personal space discrepancy. There was a lot of repeated hand shaking and back slapping. Then Miriam brought me out a bucket of water for a splash bath. Under Andrew's orders she handed it to him and he led me around the back of the hut. There was a brick on which I had to stand so I wouldn't get sand on my feet. Then in one of those weird travel moments I found myself butt naked, perched on a brick splashing water on myself while Andrew sat there against the wall muttering in English interspersed with the odd 'like ABCD'.

In the morning I made Miriam and a very hung-over Andrew coffee and shared my biscuits with them. Then I eagerly jumped on my bike ready to tackle the last 50 kilometres of the first leg of this journey.

Midway through, I stopped off on the side of the potholed road for some jam sandwiches. This was day five of cycling since leaving Katima. I looked at my shirt which was covered in five days of snot, sweat, and apricot jam from cleaning my knife on it. I took a big swig of Zambezi River water that I had stocked up on at a nearby village. Then as I opened my new loaf of stale bread a cockroach scuttled out of the bag. This was exactly what I had been wanting, African adventure. I was loving it.

## Zambia—the road to Chongwe

Most of the time I spent cycling through southern Africa was on sealed roads. Villages were scattered along the roadsides where I could get water. There was a constant stream of colourful people walking along, carrying 20-litre buckets of water on their heads. There were stalls selling tomatoes, bananas and onions. One thing people tell you about Africa is that no matter where you are, even if you think you are in the middle of nowhere, you will see people. That's what I thought as well, until I took the road to Chongwe.

My little micro-adventure started because I wanted to avoid Zambia's sprawling capital, Lusaka. Therefore I decided to take a 'shortcut' that would bypass Lusaka and get me back on the highway at Chongwe. I had checked four different maps from people I'd met and each one was different. On several maps my shortcut road didn't even exist, on another it led straight back to Lusaka. On yet another map my only option of missing Lusaka was to cycle through a national park. Then on some maps this magical 'road to Chongwe' existed. Bugger it, there was only one way to find out.

After spending the night camping at a roadside truck stop, I arrived at the Zambian border town of Chirundu, just across the Zambezi River from Zimbabwe. From the sea of trucks transporting all kinds of wares and fares to the landlocked countries, I now turned off the main road and headed down a dusty red sand road which the locals told me I needed to take. Unfortunately the locals were as reliable as the maps. Four different people gave me the exact four different answers the maps had.

I arrived at the 30-metre-wide Kafue River and waited for the barge to take me to the other side. The helpful barge operators drew me a map of the road I was going to take, which, by the way, they were adamant did not go to Chongwe, but went to Lusaka.

I got off the barge on the other side of the river and followed their directions. I cycled about 9 kilometres on the sandy road, turning left at the banana farm as shown on the map. There I was, on the road to Chongwe—or was I?

I guessed it would be roughly 150 kilometres from Chirundu to Chongwe. If it was a tarsealed flat road I could easily cover it in two days, or one very big day. My biggest day cycling had been 153 kilometres, but this road wasn't going to be flat or sealed. I carried 15 litres of water on my bike, which was enough to last me two days for drinking and cooking. But there were villages everywhere so I could fill up, or so I thought.

I started off down the road, taking my time. It was late morning and I wasn't worried about the distance, which I could comfortably cover in two days. I passed a couple of mud hut villages with the locals waving and kids running full tilt alongside me, shouting in their usual relentless machine-gun barrage, 'How are you, how are you, how are you!' I passed another village and little did I know at that point it would be the last sign of humanity I would see that day.

I was in high spirits, flying down the undulating dirt road, pumping on the pedals to give me more speed like I was on a mountain bike and not a fully loaded touring bike. I was

## The Final Continent

dodging the ruts and tennis-ball-sized rocks on the road but then I hit one and came crashing off my bike. I'd had my first crash. I used a litre of water to wash my grazed knee, thinking villages and people were everywhere and getting more wouldn't be a problem.

At about 3 p.m. I hit the mountains. Slowly but surely the mountains, coupled with the rutted rocky road, became unrideable. I got off and pushed my bike. It was bloody hard work; I was grunting like a Korean taxi driver, swearing like Mac on the Canadian rigs and drinking water like I was in the Australian outback. I was buggered. I decided it would be best to find a flat spot on the mountainside and camp overnight rather than pushing on.

I saw what I believed to be a flat spot on top of a hill with a view over the valley below, where I had just come from. I hid my bike in the bushes, grabbed all my camping and cooking gear and puffed my way up the final incline to my resting spot. The spot wasn't as magical as my expectations. It was rocky and high dried grass covered the view. But it was flat. I was on the side of a mountain, I was hungry and wanted to sleep; it would do.

I set up the tent, and got the cooker on straight away. As I had my rice, potato, soya mince, tomato and beef stock bubbling away with the sun just dipping behind the mountain, I pondered my situation. I hadn't seen a person since midday, something unheard of in Africa. Except for the one the barge operators had drawn, I had no map so I did not know what lay ahead of me. Did the mountains continue? Was it flat? Was there a village over the hill? Was it another 30 kilometres of pushing up and down hills until a village with water appeared? I felt very much in the middle of nowhere. I had only covered 50 kilometres on the road so far. The last 2 kilometres had been steep hill and had taken me over an hour.

Water really worried me. After washing my grazed knee, cooking and drinking a lot more because of pushing my

60-kilogram bike uphill in the African sun, I now only had 5 litres of water left. Under normal circumstances this would usually last me a day but this mountainous road to Chongwe was scorching.

I knew that if I went another day into the unknown and didn't come across a village then I was in the shit—big time. On top of the hill I knew I was only a half-day bike ride to the last village I had seen. If I continued on this road, I would eventually reach that point of no return, the point where it was over a day to get back to the water source and safety of the last village. I made my decision. I would set off before sunrise, while it was cool, and hopefully on the other side of the mountain there would be flat savannah and a village where I could fill up on water.

My beefy soya stew was ready. I took it off the boil and willed it to cool down as I burnt my tongue with the first spoonful. I had worked up quite an appetite. I sat with my back to the valley as the long grass covered my view.

I felt truly alone; not in a sad, lonely way, but in an isolated way. I had the huge feeling of knowing that I had to rely on myself and not to take any stupid risks. There was no one with me to raise an alarm, and no one around to help; it was just me and Africa. Just what I had wanted.

As I pondered my isolation, movement caught my eye, a movement that would usually have excited me, but in my situation one that made my knees shake uncontrollably. About 150 to 200 metres away in clear view of my open camping spot I saw the unmistakable shape of a leopard stealthily making its way up onto a rock. I watched it. Was it watching me? I froze, half in awe, half in fear. I willed it to stay there, to turn around and head back up over the rocky outcrops and off through the skeleton of trees. I felt exposed, as though I was waving a flag saying 'Hey kitty, down here.'

From the rock where it stood, it surveyed the dusky valley below with the arrogance and elegance of an animal that is scared of nothing. Then it made the move I feared. It slid down over the rock in the graceful way that only a cat can move. I had chosen the 'maybe' road to Chongwe instead of the 'definite' road to Chongwe so it avoided the nearby Zambezi national park that lay 50 kilometres away.

As it glided over the rocks I felt locked into its predatory radar. I knew that I hadn't seen any wildlife all day so I assumed the pickings were slim. The fact that I was skinny wouldn't bother it too much—meat was meat. I thought about how humans are a pretty easy meal: our claws are laughable, our teeth are blunt and we move at the pace of a turtle in comparison to them.

Then my attention turned to the pot of beef-smelling stew on my lap. All of a sudden my hunger had disappeared. I was unsure if leopards liked beef stew or if they could smell it, but I didn't want to find out. I wasn't sending out any dinner invitations. I jumped up from my camp stool, keeping one eye on the predatory figure, the familiar rolling movement of its shoulders as it moved closer, metre by slow metre, towards my spot.

Now I took my eyes off it and focused on getting that stew away from my tent. I quickly and quietly made my way through the grass with the stew. Each metre I was calculating how far I could go without putting myself in danger of being cut off from the 'safety' of my tent. My heart was pounding as I waited to be confronted by a snarling leopard, or perhaps I wouldn't even know until it was upon me.

I made it about 20 metres from the tent. In a panic I threw the stew in a discus-thrower motion to disperse it, just like feeding chickens. The last thing I wanted to do was leave an inviting pile of cat food. I gently placed the pot on the ground, trying not to make a metal-on-rock sound that would give away my position. I retraced my footsteps back to the tent with urgency and fear. I was in survival mode. I genuinely thought *I* was going to end up as cat food.

What compounded my fear was that I was alone. I had no

one to share this terror, to talk things over with, to rationalise, to support. All I had was the thin fabric of a tent to separate me from the wild. To say I felt vulnerable was an understatement. I was shit scared, scared in a way that only a wild animal can make you feel.

I raced the rest of the way back to the tent. I grabbed my pannier with the food in it and hung it on a tree away from my tent. Did leopards like rice, biscuits and bread? I didn't know. All I knew was I didn't want to be sharing the tent with it. The whole time I was scanning the high grassy surrounds, 360 degrees like a periscope. With all the food-related items away from the tent, I unzipped it. The sound seemed to pierce the silence, saying to the leopard 'Hey ya, pussy, I'm over here.'

I didn't bother taking my shoes off. I didn't bother brushing my teeth. I didn't bother removing my sweaty cycling clothes. I shakily zipped up the tent in a way that was meant to be stealth-like, but in the noiseless mountaintop, where even the breeze in the grass seemed like a racket, it was pointless.

I tried to control the shaking, tried to lie motionless, hoping that sleep would whisk me away into a world where I was not in the middle of the African wilderness with a prowling leopard outside.

When I was alone in the wilderness with no background sounds, every noise became that leopard circling my tent. I imagined I could hear the leopard scratching at the pannier in the tree. What a fool I was to put my food in the tree. Leopards can climb trees, for shit's sake. They carry dead animals twice their size up trees to eat them. If I was to get attacked, no one would hear my screams, no one would know where I was. I was in the middle of nowhere land. The maggots would find me before people. Even if a nomadic wandering villager came across me, what would they do? Would they think to get my identification and take it to a policeman? Did they even know about such things as identification and passports? Would they see all my gear and think that God had handed them a miracle. My mind was becoming overactive. This was when I needed someone to rationalise with.

I fretted my way through the night but as time wore on my fear of the leopard waned. When I needed to pee I didn't dare get out of the tent, I unzipped the door just enough to fit the old fella out. I didn't care that my pee ran back under the tent. Piss on your tent beats becoming cat food.

At some stage I fell asleep and woke before sunrise. I was very wary that the leopard was still around. I knew I was being paranoid, but I also knew animals were most active around dawn and dusk. By now I should have been on the road, making the most of when the sun was lowest and the heat not draining me of my energy and forcing me to consume more water. But I couldn't get that silhouette of one of nature's great killing machines out of my mind.

I waited in the tent until it became an unbearable sauna and it was still only 7.30 a.m. My head was pounding. I had a massive headache, due to anxiety, no dinner, bugger-all sleep and dehydration.

Like a turtle poking a cautious head out of its shell I emerged from the tent. I scanned the long dry grass for a circling leopard. I felt more relaxed with the caring embrace of daylight. I was still cautious, and stayed close to my tent with the door zipped open ready for a quick entry. With the hard day ahead I had to eat. I couldn't eat my rice or pasta as I couldn't afford to use water to cook it, but luckily I had a safety ration of baked beans. I put my camp stool in the door of the tent, my back covered by the tent, and devoured the beans like one of the emaciated African dogs that came running out of the villages I passed on my bike.

As Mother Nature's beaming, sunny smile warmed me, an ibuprofen deadened the thud in my head and the baked beans filled my stomach, my paranoia started to be replaced with that sense of adventure.

I packed up my bike and started to push it up the rutted dirt track. It was 8.30 a.m. and already so bloody hot the sweat started instantaneously. The kilometres were painstakingly slow. But I loved it. The activity of pushing had dulled the worry of the leopard and coming across other wildlife. The possibility of what lay on the other side of the mountain fuelled my engine, an engine that was rather thirsty. I was trying to ration my water, only allowing myself a drink when I had pushed to the next shady spot 20 to 50 metres away. Once at the shady spot, I would collapse on the ground with my bike and cherish the two mouthfuls of water I allowed myself. This is what I wanted from my little African adventure: to be challenged.

When I hit the top of the hill, the sight of flat savannah with villages and the golden arches of McDonald's that I had wished for was not to be. Just more mountains with no clear end in sight. Having reached the top of the mountain was a small accomplishment and I wanted to push on. Like a gambler, just one more mountain; maybe there is a village on the other side of that one.

A couple of hills on, I was flying down the steep rocky dirt road sounding like a herd of buffalo. I bounced through a dry riverbed at the bottom of the valley, which was overgrown with bushes. From within the bushes, a movement caught my eye, one that filled me with ecstasy, not fear. It was a person. I jumped off my bike and quickly made my way through the bush, so excited at the thought of seeing a person. I didn't even care if the person was a poacher, I just wanted to be with someone.

I reached a clearing and there were three local boys cooking the white stodgy southern African staple on a campfire. They looked surprised to see me.

I tried to get information from these boys about how far away the next village was and what the road was like. From the hand signals and the odd word of English I interpreted it to be 50 kilometres away, and the next 20 was mountainous. This didn't quite seem to add up, but since I had no real map it was all I had to go on.

I set off again, feeling recharged after my human encounter, thinking I would bump into more people. After another hour of pushing my bike up hills in the midday heat, slipping on the loose gravel, flopping to the ground exhausted, I looked at the number of kilometres I was covering. I was averaging 2.5 kilometres an hour, 2.5 bloody hard kilometres. Judging from the local boys' estimate of the next town being 50 kilometres away, it would take me 20 to 25 hours. My drinking water was very low and wouldn't see me through the day. I had to face reality. I would be stupid to keep going into the unknown mountains. From where I was I knew if I pushed hard I could probably make it back to the last village I had passed the previous day at sundown. Reluctantly, a little pissed off at not having made the decision earlier, I turned my bike around and started to re-cover the ground I had just struggled over.

I was now retracing my steps. I would have to return to the point from which I had started, taking the main highway up through Zambia's capital, Lusaka, adding four long days to get to Chongwe. At least there would be no 'maybes'.

As I came over the second hill I was surprised to meet one of the three local boys from the riverbed camp nonchalantly walking towards me. I asked where he was going and got the feeling that he was going to his village, then I understood that he was walking to Lusaka after that. Then it clicked. When they had been talking about the next town being 50 kilometres away, they were talking about Lusaka.

I asked the boy if he minded if I tagged along with him and if he could help me push my bike up the hills. Here I was with all my camping gear, water bottles, CamelBak, camera and quick-dry clothes. Here he was with tattered clothes, odd shoes, a battery-acid bottle of water, a little backpack and a reusable shopping bag, and he was helping me push my overladen bike.

After a couple of hours, the hills became fewer and then we came across a village. This was my helper's village, and I was invited to a well. I dropped the bucket down and pulled up the glorious water. I filled all my bottles up and drank like the bartender had just announced drinks were on the house.

In the villages, with access to water and with people around, I felt safe. I thanked my helper and waved him goodbye. Further along on the roadside I cooked a massive feed of pasta. The rough dirt road gradually became better and the number of villages increased. About an hour before sunset I hit an intersection, and then, like a mirage, there was a sign pointing down a long graded dirt road that said *Chongwe*.

I slept the night in a schoolyard and the following morning I cycled the 40 kilometres into Chongwe. I celebrated with a bottle of Coke. I had made it. The road to Chongwe had given me my fix of adventure in Africa. It had also reinforced my travel motto, the same motto I had used when going to the bathhouse in Korea all those years ago: 'You lose much by fearing to attempt'.

## Mount Kilimanjaro — destination or journey

Poet Ralph Waldo Emerson once said, 'Life is a journey, not a destination.' And so far that's what working the world had been. But now I needed a destination.

After Zambia I made my way into Malawi. The country was in the middle of a petrol shortage and I rode past petrol stations with hundreds of cars lining the sides of the road. They had heard a rumour that maybe this particular station was getting petrol.

I enjoyed cycling through Malawi; because of the petrol shortage there was little traffic on the road, and the scenery was green and the people friendly. I eventually arrived at my destination, the idyllic Lake Malawi. It felt like I was back in

## The Final Continent

Mexico, the golden sand tricking me into thinking I was at the beach, not at a lake in the middle of Africa.

I had made it. After all the emotional turmoil I had been through with Mandy and the pressure of filming the documentary and completing the bike shop, I had achieved what I had earlier thought was unachievable. I had broken my bicycle trip into 500-kilometre sections with a destination at the end of each leg as a reward. Once again I felt proud, but it wasn't long before the loneliness set in. I now had nothing to drive me and my mind kept wandering back to Mandy. I still loved her. Malawi was where Mandy had wanted to end our cycle trip because she had helped a school group back in Denver to raise funds for a Malawian charity.

Now I was here, lying in a bamboo hut and listening to the waves of the lake lapping onto the rocks below. I was in the same hut that Mandy had stayed in just over two months ago, after we had said our goodbyes at the bus stop in Zambia. Mandy had told me that the Nkhata Bay hostel was a relaxed place with lots of friendly people. Now I was lying here in a double bed that felt spacious. Mandy and I could have been here together. We would have played cards on the balcony and had sunset beers, but now it was just me. I was exhausted both emotionally and physically. But I had done it.

Although I had completed my bike ride, I needed a new destination to celebrate my 30th birthday on 11/11/11. Mandy and I had planned to celebrate it together on the shores of Lake Malawi. Now we weren't together, it didn't feel right for me to celebrate here.

I had heard about Mount Kilimanjaro in Tanzania's north. It is the world's highest free-standing mountain and the highest point in Africa at 5895 metres. The thought of watching the sunrise while standing on Kilimanjaro's summit on my birthday now became my goal. But there was one problem; I had no money.

I tried some cyber-begging and sent out a few emails to Kilimanjaro trekking companies that had been recommended to me. Zara was the company that was most accommodating to my last-minute needs and offered me a great discount. With my credit card and birthday money from family, my dream to be on top of Kilimanjaro would now become a reality.

I locked my bike to a tree at the Nkhata Bay hostel, bought a $1 polyweave bag from a stall, packed what clothes I had into it and started the trek north. Hitchhiking and cheap local chicken buses were to be my mode of transport into the north of Tanzania, home of Kilimanjaro.

After a three-day 'pick-a-path' chicken-bus marathon I finally arrived at Moshi, the town at the base of Kilimanjaro. I made my way to the hotel and met my guide. I hired hiking boots and all the cold-weather gear as the thin summer clothing I had been sweating in during the past five months wouldn't suffice. Due to the last-minute nature of my trip I was the only person in my group, but I would be meeting John, another climber, on the third day and trekking with him to the summit. John reckoned he was one of only two Danish sheep shearers in the world. Never did I think when I boarded that plane as a wide-eyed 21-year-old off to teach English in Korea that I would be ending my working-the-world journey climbing the world's highest free-standing mountain with a Danish sheep shearer!

Most people climb Kilimanjaro for the experience, for the 'journey'. I was doing it for 'the destination'. I was doing it to be on the top of my final continent and to watch the sunrise on my 30th birthday. Standing on that summit would be the culmination of everything I had worked towards since planting the seed of this idea ten years earlier in that Gold Coast factory. It would be the end of my goal, a celebration.

I hadn't done any research on Kilimanjaro. I had booked it as a final challenge. I was expecting the mountain to be crowded and littered with rubbish from the estimated 35,000 people who attempt to summit it each year. However, I was doing it in the rainy season, the worst time of year. But there was one benefit: there weren't as many people crammed on the trails and I was pleasantly surprised at the cleanliness and natural beauty. I was doing the seven-day Machame route which is one of six routes to the summit. It is commonly known as the 'whisky' route as it is harder than the more commonly used Marangu Coca-Cola route, where you have the luxury of sleeping in huts.

Although the Machame route is meant to be one of the harder ones, we weren't exactly roughing it. It was five-star camping. On arrival at camp, your tent is already set up. A porter has carried your duffel bag for you and deposited it at your tent. You are welcomed with hot drinks and popcorn, and all your meals are cooked for you. If you weren't doing it on the cheap like me then porters would carry up a mess tent complete with tables and chairs. The more glamorous camping parties even had porters to carry up a portable toilet and shelter so they didn't have to use the trail toilets.

The first couple of days I loved the mountainous alpine scenery. It took me back to landscapes I had known growing up in New Zealand. It was totally unexpected. It was beautiful. Every day would start with glorious sunshine and then like clockwork would end in cold rain.

I hadn't given much thought to the effect the altitude would have on me and never realised that there was medication I could have started taking prior to help combat it. Altitude sickness, also known as acute mountain sickness, generally occurs above 2500 metres, and in the early stages you experience dizziness, exhaustion, headaches and nausea. In more serious cases it can become life threatening with cerebral and pulmonary oedema. It can affect anyone—it doesn't matter if you are super-fit or if you have dedicated your life to computer games and pies. I got my first real taste of it on day three and from this point on, like the afternoon rain, the pounding headache and nausea were going to be just part of the journey.

From this day on my objective was simply to make it to the next camp, where I would peel off my wet clothes, force some food down, flop into my rented -30 degree sleeping bag and focus on not throwing up. I was determined I would do everything in my power to get to the top of that mountain. The thought of spending my birthday 200 metres from the highest point of my final continent wasn't an option.

One highlight of my trip was on day four at Karanga camp. The usual afternoon rain was buffeting my tent. I was feeling like a bucket of Kilimanjaro long-drop excrement with my headache and nausea. The camp was only at an altitude of 3900 metres, but once again I was lying down wondering how I was ever going to complete this trek. The summit was still a towering 2000 metres away. At that point it seemed like Everest, and to some degree it was, as Everest base camp, which is another non-technical climb, is located at 5364 metres—600 metres lower than the summit of Kilimanjaro.

By evening my nausea had stopped along with the rain and the headache was just the normal dull thump that was going to accompany me for the rest of the trek. The camp was quiet as many groups had pushed onto the summit camp. The curtain of rain clouds had opened and let in a beautiful vista from the roof of Africa with the soundtrack of silence to accompany it. The peak of neighbouring Mount Meru rose through the clouds that separated us from the world below. John and I perched on rocks with the early evening moon in the sky, slurping at our soup, taking in the splendour laid before us. I felt like I was on top of the world.

The following day was a leisurely four-hour hike to the summit base camp, where I managed to make it into my tent before the rain drenched me. I had the afternoon to relax in my sleeping bag before getting up at 11 p.m. for the gruelling seven-hour night trek to the summit. It was rather intimidating lying in my tent realising it was an effort just to get out of my sleeping bag, let alone knowing I had to trek 1200 vertical metres in the dark to reach the summit for sunrise the following morning.

That afternoon and evening I didn't get much sleep. I was excited and nervous and so were my bowels, throwing me a send-off party which saw me making numerous rushes to the long drop. Finally the time arrived. I got up and pulled on every single layer of dry clothing I had, including four pairs of socks. I popped some Imodium tablets that John had prescribed me, hoping they would 'bung me up' for the seven-hour trek. It had been raining, but half an hour before departing the rain stopped and we had a glorious full moon that lit up the way.

Like the whole trek, the theme of the summit trek was '*pole, pole*', which basically means 'Go slow or you will end up in an altitude-affected pile of headaches and vomit.' So '*pole, pole*' it was, although I didn't really have much choice.

Anyone who has experienced altitude knows that the higher you go, the less oxygen there is, and therefore everything becomes harder. Walking becomes slower to the degree that you can only walk a couple of wayward metres before having to suck in lungfuls of air. I was hoping my altitude sickness wouldn't worsen and stop me getting to the top.

Eventually after a couple of pathside bowel-relieving breaks and six hours on a narrow track putting one foot in front of the other I made it to Stella Point. Stella Point is located at the edge of a crater rim and is the start of the ridgeline leading up to the summit a couple of hundred metres above. I had expected the top of Kilimanjaro to be just a peak, like standing on top of a triangle. So when I reached Stella Point it was like I was stepping onto another planet.

The landscape was out of this world and with my altitude-induced stupor I literally felt like I was out of this world. All of a sudden I felt overwhelmed. I staggered away from my guide as I felt tears welling in my eyes. He asked if I was okay. I heard him ask, but I didn't register that I had to answer him. I was just overwhelmed by the moment.

As I looked out over the clouds from the rooftop of Africa, the sun was about to rise on 11/11/11, and, like a pyrotechnics display before a big performance, the sky was backlit with a bright crimson. I was unsure why I was so overwhelmed, where this emotion had come from. Was it the altitude? Was it the surreal environment of this Martian landscape and ice fields on the top of Africa? Was it because I knew now that I was actually going to make it to the summit? Or was it because I had completed my final continent?

I had been working towards this moment for nearly nine years, and now it was here. I had almost bloody done it. I had lived and worked in every continent of the world before 30. I was now 30. I was no longer working the world. I had worked the world.

Altitude sickness was creeping in, and I didn't really know what I was feeling. It was like I was on drugs—euphoric, but it was so overwhelming it felt fake like a chemical high. I dried the tears from my cheek, making out that I was scratching myself, as I didn't want the guide to see me crying. I knew he was very concerned about me and could no doubt see the symptoms of altitude sickness taking hold. I turned and slowly made my way back to him.

'Let's go to the top,' I said.

As we made the last push to the summit, the sense of euphoria left me. My co-ordination went downhill as I kept trying to push uphill. Every step became a wayward one in the general direction of the summit. I was now just focused on getting to the top of the mountain. I staggered from side to side, repeating *pole, pole* to myself. Really I had no bloody choice. My legs were like lead, and I just mechanically put one foot in front of

## The Final Continent

the other, my body having no option but to follow. The sun had pierced the clouds; it was officially 11/11/11. I could see the summit sign in the distance and a few people having their photo taken in front of it. I took out my video camera and gave it to my guide to film my last 30 metres. Before the trek I had visions of giving an inspirational speech at the top. Instead all that came out of my mouth was a vacant emotionless, 'I'm knackered.' Looking back, it perfectly summed up everything: I was knackered. This goal had been my life. I had achieved it with no regrets, but it had taken its toll on me, especially Africa. I was knackered.

Fighting altitude sickness, I made it to the sign that read: *CONGRATULATIONS, You are now at Uhuru Peak, Tanzania, 5895 metres. Africa's highest point. World's highest free-standing mountain.*

This was the pinnacle of my working-the-world quest, but I felt no elation. The only thing I could think about was getting that bloody photo that everyone gets in front of the sign. It would be the photo that I would be able to look at for the rest of my life and know that I had lived my working-the-world dream, that I had set myself the challenge and I had made it.

I forced a smile for the camera, trying to look triumphant. But that smile was really a lie. I was ready for my goal to be over. I think I had been ready for a while.

As I was leaving the summit, a young couple about the same age as me came up to it. Under the sign the guy got down on one knee and pulled a ring from his pocket. I didn't hear what he said, but I knew he had just made the girl the happiest girl in the world. Like me, they would remember 11/11/11 for the rest of their lives. I thought of Mandy. I wanted to get off that mountain. I looked at my guide and said, 'Let's go.'

The guide was now very worried about me. As we started our descent, my state also declined, and pretty rapidly. I was disoriented, more confused than usual, my headache was out of control, and I knew I was in a bad way. My guide was checking my pupils and asking me questions: where was I and did I know my name. I knew where I was but I didn't really know how to answer.

Then I collapsed onto his outstretched arm.

We both knew I had to get out of the danger zone above 5000 metres. My guide grabbed me and ran with me, past the concerned people pushing to the summit. He ran as fast he could with my disoriented bag of bones leaning on him. We were racing the clock, and had to descend over 1000 vertical metres to get back to base camp at 4600 metres. I knew that it was paramount to get down before my brain started squeezing itself out my ears. I just kept going as fast as my legs and my guide could carry my leaden weight, with a stop every now and then to check my pupils and take in liquid.

We made it to camp where our porters ran to us and supported us into camp. There was talk of cerebral oedema and getting me back to Moshi.

John calmly appeared and was the voice of reason. I trusted him. He fed me some pills and told the guide to let me rest for half an hour to see if the lower altitude would cure me before reassessing if I needed to be taken lower.

I lay there fully clothed on top of my sleeping bag. I had nothing left. I had given this mountain my all, I had given this goal my all, and I had given this goal my life. But the mountain was different to my working-the-world goal. The mountain had been about getting to the summit, the destination. My goal had been about the people I'd met, the experiences I'd had, the lessons I'd learnt, the places I'd been, the journey itself. I was scared about going to sleep and not waking up. But I couldn't battle it any longer. I drifted off.

I eventually came to, my head booming, but I was thinking clearly. Thinking, *Get me the hell off this mountain.* I was fed some more headache pills and a few cups of tea before making the descent down to Mweke camp at 3000 metres, where we would spend our last night on the mountain.

I spent the night of my birthday drinking cups of tea with John. Then at 7 p.m. on 11/11/11, I could think of nothing better than going to bed!

## The end

I had finished with Africa, but Africa was not finished with me.

I started my chicken bus mission to Malawi where I was to fly back to Melbourne. I had four days' bus travel and a day's cycle before I reached Malawi's capital, Lilongwe, where I would fly out from.

I arrived in Tanzania's capital, Dar es Salaam, where I had to change buses. I decided I would take a risk and stay for two nights as I wanted to check out the city. But it meant that I couldn't afford anything to go wrong with my trip back, which was rather silly as one thing that you can count on in Africa is things going wrong.

Arriving in the heaving frenzy that was the Dar es Salaam bus station, I jumped from the bus with my $1 polyweave bag that was now held together by bungy cord. Feeling confident now that I was used to Tanzanian currency and the cost of buses, I haggled with one of the abundant unmarked motorbike taxis to take me to the central city hostels. I climbed on the back with my bag between us and we sped into the traffic, the fresh air and open space a welcome relief from the cramped bus.

I checked into a basic hotel room as there were no hostels. I had a cold shower and then headed outside with the excitement that only comes when you have an unexplored, culturally diverse African city at your doorstep. Having spent the past months cycling through southern Africa, it was the first time I had been on the eastern coast. It was also the first time since leaving Cape Town that I had been by the ocean. A sunset beer by the Indian Ocean to reflect on all that had happened in Africa seemed fitting.

Since I had no map or guidebook, I found myself wandering aimlessly through the hustle and bustle of the Arabic-influenced streets in search of the ocean that I knew was close. I approached a well-dressed young guy who was walking up to an ATM.

'Excuse me, mate, which direction is the ocean?'

'I'll take you there, just let me go to the ATM,' he replied as he ran to the bank.

As per usual in Africa, there was a power cut and the ATM wasn't working. He came back and told me to jump on the back of his motorbike as the beach was out of town. It went through my mind that this was probably a bad idea since I'd only known this guy for ten seconds, but my travel mantra went through my mind: *You lose much by fearing to attempt.* I jumped on anyway.

I noticed his motorbike was not the usual Chinese make that resembled a two-wheeled motorised Christmas tree with imitation chrome bars and lights that seemed to serve no other purpose except to add to the festive theme. I knew he must have had money as his bike looked sporty, built for speed. My thoughts were confirmed as he accelerated and swerved onto the wrong side of the road to avoid the peak-hour traffic that was bumper to bumper as everybody headed out of the city after work. Maybe I should have considered how he came to have the money to afford an expensive motorbike. I didn't.

I relaxed into the back of the seat, taking in the beeping of horns, oncoming cars, the blur of lights and the glow of the setting sun while the wind swept through the matted bird's nest that was my hair. I had only expected to be dropped off at the port, which I thought was close by, but now we were on the open road heading out of the city centre. I thought, *This is what travel is about. I go in search of some crappy polluted harbour to have a sunset beer beside and now I'm on the back of this complete*

## The Final Continent

*stranger's motorbike weaving through rush-hour traffic on my way to the ocean . . . Hang on, where the hell are we going?*

My paranoia settled as the coast and the ocean appeared on the right. Finally, I set eyes on the Indian Ocean and I had an epiphany: it looked like any other ocean. After ten more minutes we pulled off into a beach car park that had a few cars in it. We walked through to a beachside bar situated right where the waves were lapping on the golden sand beach, palm trees towering above like tropical high-rises. I offered to buy my new friend a beer, forgetting that he probably didn't drink because he was Arabic. He ordered a Coke.

The complete stranger told me he was 23-year-old Samir, and he worked for a hardware wholesale company, six days a week. His father passed away when he was ten and now he lived with his mother and younger brother. He loved motorbikes and was very proud of his city. I thanked him for taking the time out of his night to show me the ocean. I enjoyed his company; he wasn't one of those pushy types who has an ulterior motive. He didn't want to sell me jewellery or book me a tour, he just wanted to show me his city—or did he have an ulterior motive?

We finished our drinks with the sun having well and truly set behind the 25-odd container ships waiting out at sea for their time to enter Africa's second largest port. I hopped back on Samir's bike, assuming we were heading back to the city. Unbeknown to me, Samir had a different plan. He stopped along the way and showed me some famous cliffs, a boardwalk area, and took me on a tour of the flash five-star hotel complexes which were a far cry from the mud hut villages that I had been camping in.

A couple of hours since first hopping on Samir's bike, we arrived back in the city but his tour had not finished. I'd only been in this city for six hours, so nothing looked familiar and I was totally disoriented. He pulled into a back street and parked his bike. I thought that this would be the perfect spot for me to be mugged, but luckily I was with Samir, my new friend. I hopped off and followed him back onto a street that during the day was bustling with business, but now had been taken over by wooden benches and locals drinking strong black coffee and smoking cigarettes.

He approached a group of local men wearing Arabic-style little hats, sitting on roughly made wooden benches around a square knee-high table. A young kid was serving coffee from a large stainless-steel pot with a black handle. Samir introduced me to the eclectic group of men, from the old man missing teeth and smoking a cigarette to the well-dressed young professional. Everybody was friendly and welcoming. He ordered us two small cups of coffee and picked up a packet of sweet menthol cigarettes from the table, offering me one. The old man with bugger-all teeth passed me some of the fresh leaves of spinach that he was munching on. So there I was in the old town of Dar es Salaam, drinking strong dark coffee at 9 p.m., smoking sweet menthol cigarettes and eating fresh spinach leaves. This is what travel is about, these random moments, the rare snippets of insight into a foreign culture. You do lose much by fearing to attempt.

We left the group of men without paying. Samir told me not to worry about it as it was his local coffee hangout; it would be put on his tab. After a tour of the old city we arrived back outside my hotel. Samir gave me his cell phone number and told me if I needed any help while in Dar es Salaam to call him. I offered him some money for petrol, but he didn't want anything. I sincerely thanked him from the bottom of my heart for an unforgettable night and he drove off.

I went back to my hotel room, filled with the euphoria of travel, the kindness of strangers. When travelling independently you have to constantly rely on other people. Sometimes you get it wrong, that's just the way travelling is, but the majority of the time, no matter where in the world you are, people want to help and give you a good impression of their city. Because of Samir's generosity,

## The Final Continent

I now shared the same passion that he had for his city. I had heard from other travellers that Dar es Salaam had the reputation as one of Africa's most dangerous cities, second only to Nairobi. But I, thanks to Samir, had fallen in love with Dar es Salaam.

I lay on top of the white sheets in my bare concrete room with the ceiling fan above me buzzing around like the thoughts in my head. I slowly drifted off feeling content but excited about further exploring the city.

The following morning I woke with the usual sweaty layer covering my skin and the overhead fan still blowing humid air over me. The first thing on my day's agenda was to withdraw money and buy a bus ticket departing for Malawi the following morning. The day didn't start well as I turned my bag inside out and couldn't find my credit card. Luckily I still had my debit card which I could use to withdraw cash. But now the first thing on my day's agenda was to Skype the bank to cancel my credit card.

Before exiting the room I looked for a new place to hide my money belt. My room was basically a glorified cell, no hiding spots. I reluctantly lifted my shirt and clipped it around my waist, going against my travel protocol of not taking my valuables with me. At the last minute, as I was walking out of the room, I turned around and took my video camera out of my backpack, deciding I best not take everything of value with me.

I left the hotel like a walking gold mine, laptop in my backpack, money belt with passport, money and debit card strapped to my abdomen.

As I was walking along, feeling at home in this foreign city, a local guy came up to me. His name was William and he was roughly the same age as me. Like most guys who would come up to talk to me he knew that the capital of New Zealand is Wellington and New Zealanders are called Kiwis. But William was different. William was a local musician specialising in African music. He was in his fourth year of music studies at the local university. He had dreams to take his music to the world.

As I told him that I was making a documentary and looking for local African music, he became very excited. He was bubbling with passion and enthusiasm about his music and the possibility of the world hearing it. He wanted to give me his CD so that I could use his music for the documentary, and asked me if I had time to wait while his manager brought in a copy of his CD.

He got on his phone and called his manager. He was speaking in Swahili and all I picked up was the repeated mention of CD.

He told me his manager was at the studio and would come and meet us with a copy. As we continued to talk and walk in the direction of the meeting spot we crossed the main road and headed down a side road. As William was showing me his wedding ring and telling me how he met his German wife while playing a gig on the island of Zanzibar, a large white car pulled up beside us. The driver of the car was one of William's friends who also just happened to want his new CD. He offered to give us a ride. William said that would be fine just as long as he promised to drop me back at the internet place I had been heading to. The friend was all smiles and assured William that he would.

For some reason the part of my brain that should have been sending out warning signals didn't trigger. Just like the night before with Samir on his motorbike, I quickly assessed the situation. I felt comfortable with these two, so I accepted their offer and hopped in the back seat.

As I settled into the spacious, faded maroon interior of the back seat I thought how friendly everyone was in this city—another amazing travel moment. You lose much by fearing to attempt.

William was concerned for my backpack, which was lying on the unoccupied backseat beside me. He told me that there were many thieves in Dar es Salaam and they could easily open the door and snatch it.

I thought to myself, *I've been travelling for nearly nine years, and apart from nearly losing my camera in Guatemala, I've never been robbed. I feel safe from thieves in this car. I'm with two local guys, the windows are tinted so thieves can't see in and I have my hand on my backpack beside me.*

But I didn't want to be arrogant so I took William's advice and placed my backpack safely between my legs. I then told William how friendly everyone had been and about the amazing time I'd had with Samir the night before.

William got on his phone again and told me that he was going to call his manager and organise for us to meet him at the studio. Apparently there were a lot of cool musicians hanging out there and I might be able to get some more music for my documentary. William, who was riding shotgun, got off the phone. He started talking to me, but I couldn't hear him as his window was down, so he jumped into the back seat with me. With William now in the back seat, I noticed his forehead was covered in beads of sweat. I supposed it was bloody hot. He started singing to me in Swahili; I'm tone deaf but he sounded unbelievably talented.

Next his phone rang and he was talking away. Then the driver's phone rang. The driver passed William his phone and William passed me his phone mid-sentence as he started talking into the driver's phone. With William's phone in my hand I looked to the driver to try to figure out who I was meant to be speaking to. He said 'Sister.'

'Hello, who's this?'

A sweet female voice with only the slightest hint of an accent answered me. 'This is William's sister. He tells me you are making a documentary and are going to use his music.'

The small talk continued until William hung up on his conversation and I passed his sister back to him.

We'd been in the car heading out of town for about ten minutes. William told me we were close to the studio and seemed a little stressed that he was going to miss his lecture.

## HAP WORKING THE WORLD

William got another phone call and when he got off he was cursing his manager, who'd misunderstood the previous phone calls and had left the studio, with the CDs, to meet us. William told his mate to turn off the main road, and we bumped onto a dirt road. That little stranger-danger alarm bell started up an annoying, barely audible beep like a smoke alarm that is running low on batteries. But then it stopped as William pointed to a heavily trafficked main road ahead of us. We parked beside a local eatery-come-bar that was situated on the corner of the busy main road and the dirt road. We waited for the manager.

The manager finally arrived on the back of one of the many motorbike taxis that work the streets of Dar es Salaam. He was a big hulk of a man who walked with an arrogance that indicated he thought time should stop for him. He sauntered over to the car, and opened the passenger door before lowering his bulk onto the seat. Straight away I was not feeling the love from him, my low-battery stranger-danger alarm started up again, but my good friend William seemed in tune to my mood and tapped the manager on the shoulder.

'Meet Hap, he's the one who's going to put my music on the documentary.'

The behemoth manager gave me a welcome you would expect from a concerned father meeting his sixteen-year-old daughter's 30-year-old boyfriend who's a DJ at the local strip club. As I was being introduced, the car moved off from the parking spot and was doing a three-point turn back into the maze of dirt roads.

The stranger-danger alarm was more constant and beeping more loudly. As the driver finished his three-point turn, I got more panicked and asked 'Where are we going?' while trying to open my door before we picked up momentum. Fuck! My door was kiddy-locked. Then on cue, I heard the *clunk* as the driver locked all the doors and the tinted electric windows rose, separating me from the outside into my nightmare.

# The Final Continent

In an instant William changed from my best friend into a gangster. He pushed me against the door, shouting at me, 'We going to kill you, motherfucker!'

Now my stranger-danger alarm was wailing like a World War II bomb siren; all I could think was, *You've cocked up this time, Hap . . . and the bastard didn't even give you any lollies.*

In my infinite wisdom I had also figured out that my good friend William was probably not a musician, was not married to a German woman who he met while playing a concert in Zanzibar, that I hadn't talked to his sister and he didn't have a CD. In a weird twist of fate I realised how extremely lucky I was that I had lost my credit card as it had a $6000 limit.

I weighed up my situation. I was in a locked car with tinted windows bumping my way down a rough dirt road into the heart of the ghetto with three guys who I didn't really want to be in a locked car with. The guy beside me was shouting that he was going to kill me and wanted all my money. I cursed myself as I felt the weight of my money belt around my waist. I knew it had my passport, my debit card and $70 worth of Malawian money in it. My backpack was between my legs and held my new laptop that I had bought before the trip and had all the *Bikes for Africa* documentary footage and photos on it, plus my camera's SD card I had forgotten about. I did a quick mental check and I was pretty sure I had backed up of the majority of the footage, and thankful that I had decided to leave my video camera in the hotel room.

Although I was scared, I was also very calm. I started calculating my options. The doors were locked so I couldn't escape. There were three gangsters against one foreigner who had the upper body strength of a ten-year-old girl.

Stories of dead tourists flashed through my mind, such as the 29-year-old Australian who six weeks earlier had been found dead in Nairobi with his bank account records showing his credit card had been stolen.

I knew they wanted my money. I hoped they didn't want my life. I set myself a single goal: to get out of that car—preferably with all my limbs and organs intact.

I was brought back to reality as William seemed to have read my mind.

He shouted, 'You want to call for help? You want to call for help, motherfucker?'

The driver opened the electric window, letting the blinding sun pour in and the oppressive humid air of the inner-city wrap its sticky film around me in this shrinking back-seat world.

'Go on, call for help! Everyone here fears us. They're scared of us. No one cares about you.'

I made eye contact with the disinterested faces of the shantytown locals who were walking along the side of the dirt road, going about their everyday business. My eyes were as wide as saucers as I tried telepathically to tell them I was in danger. They looked through me. I was a *mzungu*. A white man. In a black man's world. They knew if they interfered their lives would be made a living hell. Fair enough.

I agreed with William that nobody was going to help me and he got the driver to close the window.

With his point made, William shouted at me, 'Give us your money, motherfucker!'

Ironically I thought to myself, *He really should tone his language down.*

He grabbed my bag from between my legs and passed it to the intimidating hulk of a gangster in the front seat. The stony-eyed giant opened it up and took out my laptop. He then pulled out my Swiss army knife. The knife was engraved with my name and the number 1994, the year my aunty gave it to me for my twelfth birthday. Just six days earlier I had celebrated my 30th birthday; the knife was in my pocket, the knife had been to all seven continents.

William reached over me and grabbed at my pockets, turning

them inside out. He seemed annoyed that I only had some small change. 'Where's your money, motherfucker? Is it in the hotel? Don't fuck with us.' My money belt felt glaringly obvious underneath my sweat-soaked shirt, but I tossed up whether to give it to him. I decided not to. Would this be my second poor decision of the day?

In an apologetic manner I spread my arms out, showing the palms of my hands. Hoping like hell I was convincing, I poured everything into my words: 'Look at me, I haven't shaved or had a haircut in six months. Do I look like I have money? I'm not a rich tourist driving around in a 4WD; I told you I'm riding my bicycle through southern Africa. I've been volunteering here in Africa, trying to help your people. I was setting up a sustainable bicycle workshop and making an independent documentary about it. When we first met I told you that I was off to the internet café to report my lost credit card. I have no money, I told you that.'

Unfortunately William was good at his job. He patted down my torso. His strong hands tore open my shirt to reveal my money belt!

'Motherfucker, you lied. We're going to fucking kill you!'

So after nearly nine years of working the world, this was how it was going to end, killed in a ghetto of a notoriously dangerous African city because I had hopped into a stranger's car. I could see my death certificate now, cause of death listed as 'Being an Idiot'.

William was now pushing me, getting in my face shouting, 'We going to fucking kill you, motherfucker!'

William's physical and verbal assault was interrupted by the hulk's giant arm thrusting my debit card at him. He stopped with the death threats and turned his attention to my debit card.

'Motherfucker, what's your PIN number? Don't fuck with me, don't fucking lie, if I go to the ATM and you've given me the wrong PIN I'll come back here and we'll kill you.'

In poker, I'm all about calling bluffs, but with my life on the line and two poor decisions already, I was not so confident. I was unsure how much my life was worth, but I valued it slightly higher than the remaining $300 left in my account. I gave him my PIN.

As the car pulled to a stop in the vicinity of an ATM, William asked, 'You sure you're not fucking with me? I'm not going back twice.'

I visualised an ATM key pad and tapping in the PIN number.

'Yes, that is correct. But William, the credit card I lost is the one I use to get money out. This one doesn't have much money on it and sometimes doesn't work.' Maybe we could discuss lay-by options?

With William out of the car at the ATM, the driver and the giant felt obliged to entertain me. The driver got into the Christmas spirit and started doing his shopping. Like picking candy canes off a Christmas tree, he took my sunglasses, tried them on, liked them. He reached for my right hand and tugged at the silver ring Mum and Dad had given to me before I boarded the plane to Korea on my working-the-world quest. He couldn't get it off and, as I had visions of my thumb being chopped off, I grudgingly assisted him. As I handed it to him I told him that my parents gave it to me, but he didn't care. He tried it on a few fingers before settling on his right middle finger. He rested his hand on the steering wheel, tilted it back. He nodded, another satisfied customer. Then the giant took over. He was the boss of this operation. He coldly stared at me and in a low frosty tone of a voice talked to me in Swahili, never shifting his focus. I squirmed in my seat. Not too sure what the hell to do, I just put my hands up in the air and apologised for not understanding Swahili.

The car door opened and I had never been so happy to see someone who had just stolen my debit card and ten minutes before had been threatening to kill me. William handed my card back to the giant and we started driving. William asked me when I was planning to leave. I was unsure how to answer this question. I knew I was leaving in six days, but I was paranoid about them holding me for ransom. I tried to figure out if it was better to say I was leaving tomorrow or in a couple of months. I ended up saying 'In two weeks.' Why? I have absolutely no clue.

The car bumped down memory lane as I saw the corner eatery where we had met William's 'manager' about 40 minutes earlier. As the car started slowing down my hopes rose; this could be the moment that I'd been waiting for since this ordeal started. Then like being handed a winning lotto ticket the giant gave me my passport and debit card. But just as he was about to hand it to me, he talked to William in Swahili.

He translated, 'Motherfucker, if you go to the cops we kill you. When you get out of this car, don't look back and keep walking.'

Then I felt the plastic cover of my passport in my hot little hand. God bless and all that kind of stuff.

The giant then handed William 500 Tanzanian shillings, the equivalent of 30 cents. William explained to me that this was for me to get a local bus back into town. Wow, the people of Dar es Salaam are so friendly.

The giant quickly opened my door from the outside. I got out; the sun was bright after the tinted car prison. The late-morning heat, which was usually oppressive, was like a motherly hug. I got out, started walking, feeling violated but extremely relieved. I went into James Bond mode. I was taking in all the characteristics of the car: four wheels, four doors and it was white. I stopped and tried to memorise the number plate as the car was doing a three-point turn heading back into the ghetto. It stopped mid-turn and the giant's passenger window slid down with his eyes burning into me. *Get out, keep walking and don't look back.* I decided I'd made enough stupid decisions for the day and crossed the busy road, putting four lanes of traffic between them and me.

I arrived at a major four-way intersection, where there was a heaving, beeping congregation of local buses with guys hanging from the doors shouting place names that I didn't know as the rest of the traffic rushed by. On the opposite corner I saw a police booth with a uniformed officer sitting in it.

I approached the immaculate officer. 'I've just been robbed.'

He looked at me with as much enthusiasm as if I'd told him I'd just shat my pants. He replied, 'Okay.'

This was followed by a long silence that I was hoping would have been filled with sympathetic consolation and helpful advice. He went back to reading his paper.

'Umm . . . can I file a police report?'

'Go to town.'

'Ummm, where's town?'

Like a weightlifter going for the Olympic record, he raised an index finger with excruciating effort and pointed to my left.

I walked towards the congregation of people. I was the only white man entering the chicken fight of local buses heading to town. I asked a few people about which bus to catch until I found one man who kind of understood English. He pointed around and said, 'Danger.'

I nodded, 'I know.'

On the bright side at least I had nothing of value on me.

He led me across the road. I followed, really hoping he was not a local musician.

He shouted out to a young guy with a stack of money in his hand hanging from the door of one of the many crammed buses that had slowed briefly at the side of the road to announce its intended destination. He confirmed what my new friend had asked. I jumped in while shouting *'Asante'* back to my helper.

I gave the young guy my last 500 shillings, he gave me no change. I knew he should give me 200 shillings back, but I was over this shit, just get me back to town. I wanted to have a cold shower before spending the afternoon in the police station which

# The Final Continent

I knew from previous experiences would be more painful than a dentist visit. I had to do it that day as tomorrow I would be getting up at 4.15 a.m. to start my four-day local bus marathon to Lilongwe to catch my flight home.

But Dar es Salaam was still not finished with me. After five cramped minutes with some miscellaneous body part pushed against my butt the bus made a left-hand turn off the main road that led to town. I tapped the young guy with the stack of money and pointed to the bus and said 'Town.' He shook his head. Wrong bus!

I wondered what I would be doing now if I hadn't met William. Then I started to think where my journey could have led me if I had taken different paths. Where would I have been if I had given up on this goal after being denied entry to the States, or when I had my meltdown in Paraguay? I tried to imagine where my path would have led if I had taken Mr Malikov up on his $120,000 job offer. But I was now rich, even though I couldn't afford a 30-cent bus ride. I was a millionaire with the experiences I'd had. I had invested in friendships with people from all over the world, I had memories that no amount of money could buy, I had experienced moments of happiness that no drug could give. I had nothing, but I had everything.

I started the long hot walk back to my hotel. With no money, I wasn't sure how I was going to be able to pay for the four days of buses and accommodation en route to Lilongwe. It felt like my final continent was going to chew me up and spit me out.

## Chewed up and spat out

The morning after my mugging, I was up at 4.15 a.m. to go to the bus station. Luckily William had given me back my debit card. Although he had withdrawn my last $300, I was able to get online and transfer some money from Mandy's account, which was still joined to the debit card. I bought a ticket and caught the usual overcrowded un-airconditioned hurtling coffin of a bus to Mbeya in Tanzania's south. It was a twelve-hour journey and I was pleased to get off the stale-smelling bus and into the cheap hostel close to the bus station, where I freshened up with a cold bucket shower.

The next morning I was up at 5.30 a.m. as I had to catch a collection of chicken buses and motorcycle taxis, clear the Malawi border and arrive in Mzuzu, a large city in Malawi's north.

The following day I got the bus back to Nhkata Bay where I had locked my bike to the tree two-and-a-half weeks earlier before climbing Kilimanjaro. I got all my gear from a storage locker, and prepared my bike to cycle the 55 kilometres back to Mzuzu the next day where I would pack it up.

The following day, I arrived exhausted in Muzuzu in the early afternoon sun. But I had no time to rest, I had go in search of cardboard boxes to pack my bike in for the bus trip back to Lilongwe tomorrow and my flight back to Australia the following day. Ten cartons and three rolls of tape later, my bike was packaged. By the light of a candle I used another roll of tape and two bungy cords to tape up the damaged $1 polyweave bag that contained all my bike panniers.

At 5 a.m. the next morning I arrived at the bus station. Two men in tattered clothes carried my bike and tied it to the roof of the bus using string that back in the developed world would have been thrown out years before.

'You sure that's going to stay up there?' I enquired.

'Yes sir,' they replied.

I wouldn't have minded taking out some insurance on that reassurance as my bike was now my only asset in the whole world. But TIA—they'd been doing this for years; it would do.

Even though I was told the bus would leave at 6 a.m., we pulled out of the station at 6.30 a.m. Once again, TIA.

I could now relax. I was on my way to Lilongwe. Tomorrow

# The Final Continent

I would fly out to Australia. But Africa would not let me relax. In Mzuzu the bus pulled into the petrol station to fill up for the five-hour ride to Lilongwe. No petrol. Shit! I now remembered there was a petrol shortage in Malawi. We arrived at a second petrol station. No petrol. Shit! We went to a third petrol station. Yes, it had petrol; fancy that, a petrol station with petrol. I never knew I would be so happy to be at a petrol station that sold petrol. I patted myself on the back for taking the early bus as I knew that by lunchtime there would be no petrol left in Mzuzu. I didn't have the time or money for anything to go wrong.

I arrived in Lilongwe and went to the hostel where I had stored my bike helmet, carved wooden animals and the other miscellaneous stuff that I hadn't needed on the last part of my cycle journey to the lake. I bumped into an overland truck crew I had met earlier in my trip. They invited me to their barbecue for some beers to celebrate my final night in Africa.

The next morning I transferred Mandy's last $100, which she had kindly loaned me, into my debit account from our Australian joint account. I then got a taxi to the airport arriving four hours early, but I was still nervous. There's something nerve-racking about only having $100 to your name and no access to a credit card. There is no room for error, and in a continent where errors are a part of life and with the past week's track record, I had good reason to be nervous.

I entered the airport and walked up to the check-in counter where I put my carefully packed luggage on the ancient scales.

The check-in attendant said, 'Sir, you're 25 kilograms over your baggage limit.'

'Ummm, there must be a mistake. I had specifically organised with my travel agent to have my bike shipped and I was assured that everything had been confirmed.'

'Well, we have no confirmation of this. You will have to show us the receipt.'

After more begging and telling the lady how my travel agent

and I emailed back and forth sixteen times so this situation could be avoided, she still insisted on seeing a receipt. I left the counter to try to find somewhere with the internet and a printer. This was much harder than you would expect.

Luckily I finally found an office that had a printer. I asked the attendant if I could use the internet. He said his boss was very strict, so I told him I would give him 100 kwacha (60 cents). He said okay. I found the email from my travel agent with the receipt and printed it out on his 1980s Amiga 500 printer, the type that prints out streams of paper with little holes along the side.

I took it back to the check-in lady and she told me that it wasn't the official receipt. I thought, *Bloody Africa and its love for bullshit paperwork.*

'Sir, you will have to wait for my superior to come.'

'When does she come?'

'At 11.30 a.m.'

I knew that was only an hour and a quarter before my flight departed. That made me nervous.

At 11.45 the supervisor arrived. My plane was departing in an hour. My bike and bags were sitting behind the counter next to the conveyor belt. My heart sank as I set eyes on the superior. She was a large lady who walked with the arrogance of an African person in a position of authority. She talked to the check-in attendant who pointed to me. I smiled and tried to look charming, which is easier said than done when you look like Osama bin Laden, which I got told on a daily basis. Sometimes, on a good day, they told me I looked like Jesus.

The supervisor waddled off out the back with the urgency of someone going on an hour-long lunch break. After what felt like an eternity, she came back and confirmed what I was dreading.

'There is nothing on your ticket that says you have excess luggage.'

I pleaded and told her my situation but she didn't care. I asked her what my options were. She told me that they charge US$36 a kilogram for excess luggage and that I was 25 kilograms over, therefore I needed to pay US$900. I told her I only had $100 and my credit card had been stolen. She shrugged her shoulders and walked off. The gate was closing in 20 minutes.

I weighed up my options. I could leave my bike at the airport and never see it again, which didn't appeal as it was now my only asset in the world. I would have to use plan B: beg.

I went back to the check-in lady, and I begged like I have never begged before. She told me that her boss had told me what I needed to do. I put my head back, closed my eyes, breathed deeply, ran my hands through my hair and made one last attempt. I pleaded and begged and let all my helplessness and vulnerability pour out of me, doing everything except crying. That was plan C.

'I've had everything stolen in Tanzania. I've lost my credit card. I only have $100, I can't pay. I had organised all my luggage allowances with my travel agent especially so I would avoid this situation.' I pleaded that I'd been in Africa helping the people, volunteering, doing good. If she didn't let me on the plane I was going to be stuck here with nothing. I just had to get on that plane. With my hands in a praying position I kept begging, 'Please, please let me on. I'll do anything.'

She tentatively looked behind her to see where her supervisor was.

She exhaled. 'OK, if you can get rid of 15 kilograms, I'll let the luggage go through. You have ten minutes till the gate closes.'

I ran behind the counter and attacked my carefully packed bag with a set of keys, tearing the roll of tape and bungy cords apart. I ripped open my panniers and took out all the heavy stuff, wrapped the bungy cord around my poor excuse for a bag and put it on the scales.

'You're still 4 kilograms over.'

Shit. In a panicked frenzy I pulled more out, begging her not to close the gate.

I placed my now torn polyweave bag with tape hanging from it on the scales. She gave me a look that said, *My God, you are a pain in the arse.*

'OK.'

She processed my bag, which was now only just holding together with the bungy cord, and bike. I grabbed my ticket, and she told me to run. I ran—well, I ran as best as you can when you are carrying about 20 kilograms of gear that is hanging off you in the form of a backpack, two panniers, a dirty washing bag and a flimsy, falling-apart supermarket bag.

I cleared security; then with my array of bags I got to the staff who were checking carry-on baggage. The attendant flashed me a look that said *This Osama bin Laden guy can't be serious.* I emptied my pockets of all the Malawi money I had. I got through.

But as I headed onto the tarmac, stumbling with all my hand luggage, an official ran after me.

'Sir, our X-ray machine has broken down. Can you come with us so we can go through your checked luggage.'

I couldn't believe it.

I entered the baggage room and picked up my miserable-looking, broken polyweave bag. The officer looked surprised that the bag belonged to a *mzungu*. He gave it the once over, which involved me battling to undo the bungy cord, then he stopped me, telling me not to worry. Then he pointed to my bike box. I was thinking *You can't be bloody serious, that took three hours and three rolls of tape to pack, and I'm bloody sure that you don't have any tape for me to re-pack it, and the plane is waiting on me.*

I looked at him, and felt like saying, 'Mate, does it look like a bloody bomb?', but I decided to use a different four-letter B word, *bike,* and pointed to my bike helmet hanging off one of my bags. 'It's a bike.' I turned around and went back out to board the plane.

'Would you like a water or juice, sir?' asked the flight attendant, when I finally got on board.

'Two beers, please.'

A couple of hours later the plane touched down in Johannesburg. I had an eight-hour stopover which I spent lying on the airport floor. Then in another nine hours I would be on Australian soil in Perth. Five more hours after that I would be back in Melbourne. I would, wouldn't I?

I entered the Perth airport terminal later than expected due to a delay with the quarantine staff, who had a field day with me—a bicycle, camping gear and half of Africa's wooden souvenirs in my luggage. But I enjoyed it; at least the quarantine woman was friendly and chatty. It was good to be back in Australia.

Someone asked her the time and she replied, 'Four p.m.'

I said, 'What did you just say the time was?'

'Four p.m.'

Shit! I thought I had a four-hour stopover. It seemed that had been eaten up; my plane left in just over an hour and I knew from my time living in Perth that the domestic airport was at least a ten-minute drive away.

I stuffed all my gear back into the polyweave bag and bungy-corded it up, not worrying about doing a good job. I pushed my trolley into the airport meeting area with the urgency of a homeless person who hears there is a burger giveaway at McDonald's.

My luck of the past week continued. The free transfer bus had just left and the next one left in another 40 minutes. I went to the ATM and withdrew my last AU$100.

I caught a taxi and paid the driver $21 for the ten-minute ride. This was the same sum of money that I lived off for a couple of days when cycling in Africa. Ahhh, the real world. I went to get a trolley. Bugger me! Four dollars for a trolley! Although it did say it was a 'smart cart'—I'm unsure what a 'smart cart' did differently to a normal cart. But I had no other choice to move my bike, so I paid the $4. I remembered back to my African days where I could get five guys to carry all my stuff for that much and still have change to buy a Coke. Ahhh, the real world.

I arrived at the check-in counter with my smart trolley loaded like an African truck.

'Sir, our system says that you only have an allowance for 5 kilograms excess luggage, and you're 15 kilograms over.'

I looked to my trolley thinking, *If you're so smart, mate, how about you handle this?*

After showing the check-in attendant and her manager all the email correspondence between me and my travel agent, I got a look of pity from the manager.

'Sorry, I know that your bags have been checked through Malawi to Melbourne and that you have pre-organised everything, but my hands are tied. If I let you on with this I could lose my job. There's nothing in our system, sir. We have to close the gate in seven minutes.'

'Okay, can I leave my bike here?'

'Sorry, sir, you can't store it here. We charge $15 a kilogram for excess.' I thought to myself that that was a bargain compared to Malawi, where it was US$36 a kilogram.

Then I gave them my sob story, everything stolen, no credit card, I only had $100 to my name, which after the taxi and smart trolley was now $75. In return I did get a sorry look. I handed them my debit card knowing that I had just withdrawn my last $100, but hoped by some miracle that $225, the cost of the excess, had appeared on it.

'Declined, sir.'

The manager stepped in again. 'Sir, we are going to have to shut the gate soon.'

The check-in attendant asked me, 'Is there anyone else who can pay for you?'

Then I remembered I had a few phone numbers in my pocket notebook.

# The Final Continent

I asked the check-in attendant, 'Can I use your phone?'

'Sorry, sir, only internal calls.'

I turned to the guy standing beside me, 'Mate, can I use your phone please?'

'Yeah, but hurry. I'm on the same flight as you and it's leaving.'

I dialled my sister Jarnia's number, but got a funny signal. The guy had to leave. Shit.

I asked another guy who looked like he was in a rush. He gave me his phone.

I tried my last two contacts but all I got were chirpy answer machine messages.

'We're closing the gate, sir.'

I punched Jarnia's number one last time. 'Just wait, the phone's ringing,' I pleaded. 'Please, please don't shut the gate, if she doesn't answer then you can shut it.'

'Hello, Jarnia speaking.'

In a rapid-fire frenzied voice, I blurted out, 'Sis, Hap here. What's ya credit card details?'

'Hey, Happy, how are you? You still in Malawi?'

'Sis, not Happy at the moment. Emergency, about to miss my flight, got no money, what's ya credit card details?'

I passed the phone to the check-in attendant.

'It's accepted. You're really lucky.'

I pondered that for a moment: *I'm lucky.* I thought to myself that I have a lot of luck in very unlucky situations.

The manager gave me my boarding pass with a smile. 'You really need to hurry, the plane's waiting on you.'

I ran to security, threw my random collection of bags on the conveyor belt and emptied my pockets of my passport and debit card. I picked them up on the other side and ran up the escalator three steps at a time.

With *final call* flashing at the gate I made it, then I heard a thick Aussie accent shouting out from behind me, 'Eh, mate, ya forgot ya passport.' Shit.

I sprinted back but I couldn't find an escalator that went down. Stuff it. The only way to go down I could see was the up escalator. As I jumped off, my dirty washing bag unstrapped itself from my backpack and started going up the escalator. I jumped back on, grabbed it and ran back down the upward moving stairs.

The security people were holding out my passport and debit card as I sprinted to them.

'Cheers, fellas,' I shouted behind me as I headed back up the escalator.

I got to the gate. 'Boarding pass, sir.'

I handed it over. I made my way onto the full plane and slumped into my seat. I wondered if I should use my remaining $75 to buy a beer, but I refrained.

I arrived in Melbourne, spent $4 more for a smart cart, and hopped into a taxi with my $71. Home safe, knowing the fare to my friend's Matt and Linnley's was only $50.

It was 1 a.m. as the taxi pulled up outside their place.

The meter showed a total of $72.60! I couldn't believe it. The driver told me that after midnight there was a 'special rate'.

I pulled out my last $71. 'Will this do, mate?'

'No worries, mate, $71 is fine.'

Ah, it was good to be back.

I walked through the door of Matt and Linnley's apartment to clean comfy sheets, my mail from the last six months, Mandy's old Australian cell phone and an emergency loan of $100 from Matt and Linnley.

Matt appeared at my door, bleary-eyed and in his boxers. He asked, 'Hey bro, how was it?'

I told Matt about my last six days and he summed it all up. 'Sounds like you got chewed up and spat out.'

# EPILOGUE
## Marble Bar, Western Australia, June 2012

*Regrets over yesterday and worries about tomorrow
are the twin thieves that rob you of the moment.*
—Anonymous

Seven months ago I was standing on top of Mount Kilimanjaro. Now I'm back in Marble Bar, the hottest town in Australia. I'm working for the Western Australian government as a field assistant on a geological mapping project. It's just gone 5.30 a.m. and I'm sitting in a rundown hotel room that smells of smoke despite the 'No Smoking' sign. The hotel is attached to a petrol station, which has no petrol. I'm drinking instant coffee from a mug that I had to wash mouse crap out of. I've just taken my daily Fluoxetine tablet. Fluoxetine is an anti-depressant and I've been on them for three months now.

Here's how I ended up mapping rocks for the government on anti-depressants.

After sorting out the remaining stuff I had left in storage in Melbourne, I flew back to New Zealand. More precisely I arrived back at Mum and Dad's place in Nelson. Here I was, with my weathered, flag-covered pack that had been new and shiny like the 21-year-old who had boarded the plane for Korea nine years ago. I was now 30 years old, I'd worked more than twenty-five jobs on seven continents. I was single, I had no money, no house, no career and I'd just moved into my parents' spare bedroom and the total sum of my worldly possessions weighed 23 kilograms.

After getting home, I was briefly swept up in the euphoria of being around my family and the positive buzz surrounding the accomplishment of my goal. I did a bunch of interviews on radio and TV and there were a few articles in the local papers. All of them asked, 'What are you going to do now?'

I spent Christmas with my family. It felt odd because the last time we were all together Mandy was there. Her absence was felt, not just by me but by my family who loved Mandy dearly.

The feeling was the same over the New Year break, which I spent with a big group of my mates. Last time I was with them, Mandy was there. Again her absence was felt.

But I was getting used to that feeling, I'd had it for five months at that point. I found it funny that I hadn't tried to fill that void. There was a backpacker in Africa, but it meant nothing. It was a meaningless drunken blur that left me depressed, dejected, lonely and missing Mandy even more. My friends did the best thing they could. They supported me and they tried to match-make me, but I couldn't shake the feeling that there was only one match for me, and I had said goodbye to her at a bus station in Zambia.

And still everyone kept asking me, 'Hap, what are you going

# Epilogue

to do now?' That same bloody question I'd been hearing for the last couple of years.

I told them, 'I'm going to finish writing my book and then Sich and I are going to finish the documentary'. I thought this sounded pretty impressive, but every time I said it the answer felt hollow. The next question always came, 'So what are you going to do after that?' When the hell were people going to stop asking me that question? I knew the answer. They would stop asking me that question when I stopped asking it of myself.

With the holidays over I settled in at Mum and Dad's to finish writing the book. Every morning, I would hear my parents get up in their room above me, I could trace their footsteps as they prepared their breakfast. Then that moment would come when I would hear Dad's footsteps come down the stairs and then open my door to wake me up before he went to work. I appreciated that, but I didn't need waking up. I had usually been awake since 3 or 4 a.m., my mind unable to switch off. It was always the same things buzzing around in my head, *What am I going to do?* But that question always seemed to pale in significance with the other question that was floating around in my head: *Did I make the biggest mistake of my life breaking up with Mandy?*

I would then gradually pull myself out of bed. The mental effort required to get up made me feel like I was back on Kilimanjaro, at base camp about to start the summit climb. After showering I would start the gruelling climb up the stairs, slow steps, unenthusiastic. Once there, I'd sit in front of my laptop at the kitchen table. Since my laptop had been stolen, I was back on my old laptop, the one I had bought after falling off the swing, with a loan from my sister. I took the five minutes that it took to start up to make a coffee that I hoped would start me up.

With coffee in hand, I would then sit in front of the laptop. I had to write, I had a book deadline. But it was torture sitting there trying to write about the happy times with Mandy. I'd sit there for hours, usually not typing, just staring, but my mind whirring away thinking about Mandy. I would try to turn it off, but I couldn't. It just kept grinding away and I had no escape. I had to write this book, and this book was about Mandy.

What made it even harder was that I still loved Mandy. I had never stopped loving her. But I had broken it off. I had destroyed her trust in me and made a fool of her. The least I could do was stay true to my word—it was over. We had decided the best thing to do was not to talk, to cut all communication between us. But all I wanted to do was talk to her. Nothing had changed since I had made the decision to break up with her. I was still lost, walking aimlessly with no purpose. I couldn't contact her because I hadn't got my life sorted.

I found it funny; the major reason I had broken up with Mandy was because I wanted to get this cloud that had been following me out of my life. The dark cloud that had hung around over my head every now and then since Paraguay, the same one that had been around while I'd been preparing for Africa. The dark cloud that welcomed Mandy and I into Cape Town, and the one that seemed to be never too far away while I was in Katima.

That black cloud was the shape of a thief, that little bastard, the worries about tomorrow. I had thought that if I broke up with Mandy, I would rid myself of the cloud because I would no longer have the pressure and anxiety of what we were going to do. It seemed to me that if I broke up with Mandy I would be able to focus on me, and get to the bottom of the problem, to find an answer to that omnipresent question, *What am I going to do?*

But I had a dilemma: Mandy was out of my life, and the black-thief-shaped cloud was still here. Even scarier was that there was another black cloud on the horizon. As the other cloud got nearer it looked the same shape and size as the existing cloud. Then it came right over top of me and it was identical to the other black-thief-shaped cloud; they looked like they were

# Epilogue

twins. Now not only did I have my worries about tomorrow to deal with, I also had my regrets over yesterday to contend with.

I did the only thing I knew how. I kept pushing myself. I had a book to write. Every day I would trek up those stairs and sit in front of my laptop for a day of torture, all alone at the kitchen table. When it came to writing about our break-up, I had to relive the experience every day, and every day that new cloud of regrets would get bigger and darker until it eventually dwarfed the existing worry cloud.

Some days I would feel the tears coming and it would rain, rain like it had on the grey days cutting rocks in Tasmania.

I tried to figure it all out. Was this grief that had finally come to me? Was I grieving my loss of Mandy? Had grief of my break-up with Mandy finally caught up with me now that I didn't have a bike shop to set up, 100 kilometres to cycle each day or a mountain to climb?

Every day the effort of getting out of bed and the climb up the stairs became harder and steeper and the words on the screen fewer and fewer. Then the thunder started rumbling through my mind. The thunder kept booming Mandy's name, every waking hour of the night and day. I would go mountain biking and running, I was trying breathing exercises, I wasn't drinking, I was playing soccer twice a week, but still the thunder kept booming in my mind, and the tears of that menacing cloud kept running down my cheeks until eventually I couldn't go on.

My parents were really supportive and I had been talking with them about how I was feeling, but they didn't know the full extent of what I was going through in the lonely days at home. No one did—to everyone else I was lucky, I got to sit at home, drink coffee and write. Everyone saw the outward side of Hap—the success, writing a book about his amazing adventure. Well, Hap would have given up being a published author to have that carefree happiness back that he had loaded in his pack as he boarded that plane on the way to Korea as a 21-year-old.

## HAP WORKING THE WORLD

When the breaking point finally came, luckily I had my parents there to pick up the pieces, especially my father. He had been in this dark place before. I was about ten years old and he had been in his early forties. My aunty and uncle had come down to help Mum out while Dad was in his room in bed behind the closed door. He was sick, but he didn't have a limp, he didn't have a cough, he wasn't wearing a bandage, but he was sick. I didn't understand, I just hoped he didn't die.

But now as the thunder boomed, and the rained poured down, I was also sick. At this point, on the worst days I was unable to make decisions—the littlest things seemed so hard, deciding if I wanted jam or honey on my toast would send me into a tailspin. Luckily I had my parents to weather the storm with me.

I booked in to see a counsellor and I talked about nothing except Mandy. Every appointment I talked about Mandy and I cried. The inspiring young man that was interviewed on TV and writing a book about his amazing adventure of working on all seven continents of the world was sitting in a counsellor's chair crying about a girl he had dumped in the middle of Africa. If only the people who thought what I was doing was so amazing could see me now.

During one of these sessions, the counsellor looked at me as I was wiping the tears from eyes, his eyes summing me up, his serious counsellor face on, and he said, 'You're really sad.' Through the tears I managed a laugh and said it was ironic given my nickname was Hap.

He told me that he thought I was depressed, and I had probably been depressed for some time. He also suggested that because I was depressed I was making depressed decisions. Looking back, I knew he was right. The big moment had been in Paraguay, my meltdown, and from then on depression and anxiety had come through in waves, sweeping me off my feet. In Africa, I had been swept up in the wave and that was why I had broken up with Mandy.

# Epilogue

From that meeting with the counsellor, I made two important decisions. First, I decided to go and talk to a doctor about the possibility of going on anti-depressants. And second, it became apparent that by fighting my urge to talk to Mandy, I was locking myself up.

After the meeting, I made an appointment with the doctor for the next day then went to write an email to Mandy. I wanted to tell her that I was finding life tough, that I wasn't doing that well and if she wanted to, I would like to talk to her.

As fate would have it, Mandy and I were on the same wavelength. After nearly three months of no communication, there was an email in my inbox from Mandy. She wanted to know if I wanted to talk to her on Skype in the hope of moving in the direction of being friends.

The following day Mandy and I talked for the first time in three months. She had been back in Denver for seven months and was fully settled in. She had moved into a house with her best friend; it had the big kitchen she had been wanting. She was attending yoga every day and was back working as a high school Spanish teacher. She was doing really well and she looked great. She asked me how I was doing. I started to cry. I could tell she was shocked to see how low I had slumped.

Even though I had broken up with Mandy, I had been holding onto hope that we might get back together. It was ridiculous; I had broken up with her, but I had never stopped thinking about my future being with Mandy. I was planning on us living in South America, with Mandy working at an international school and me staying at home with the dog, looking after the kids.

I had been trying to figure out if what I was feeling was love, grief or depression. But after what Mandy told me next, it didn't really matter which one it was. I asked her how her dating was going. She went a little quiet. I could see that she was trying to decide whether to tell me something. I assured her it was fine.

She told me she had signed up to a dating website, and a guy got in contact with her whose username was 'kiwiguy'. Even though we were in different countries on the other side of the world, talking through our computers, she couldn't hide her happiness. She had met kiwiguy, they had listened to the music we used to listen to, they played the card games we used to play and they drank tea. She was happy. She had everything she wanted. She had her Kiwi guy, the house and the big kitchen. I was happy for Mandy. I had had my chance. I had broken up with her so I could sort my shit out and stop destroying her life with my uncertainty.

She asked me if I was OK. I said yeah, and told her that I had been holding on, and I told her that I knew it was stupid as nothing had changed in our situation—she was in America and I was in New Zealand and I still didn't know what I wanted to do.

Once the conversation was over I realised this was the best thing that could have happened. Now that Mandy had moved on I felt like it gave me my ticket to move on. I think I had been forcing guilt on myself, beating myself up for the hurt and sorrow I had caused Mandy, and that I wouldn't allow myself to be happy until I had suffered like she had. So, it had appeared I had put myself through three months of self-torture because I wasn't willing to call her.

That morning, I made myself a promise—I would get my mental health sorted out, get out of this dark hole I had dug for myself, rid myself of the twin thieves and move on. That afternoon I went to the appointment with my doctor and got a prescription for anti-depressants. It was time to move on.

# EPICLOGUE

## Nydia Bay, Marlborough Sounds, New Zealand, July 2012

*Appreciation over yesterday and excitement about tomorrow are the twin angels that give you the moment.*
—Hap Cameron

I'm back in the Marlborough Sounds at the top of New Zealand's South Island, home to Outward Bound, the place where I first committed to my goal of living and working in every continent of the world before I was 30. I'm back here now as a 30-year-old having lived that big, crazy dream. I have no regrets.

This morning I didn't wake up at 5.30 a.m., and I didn't take my anti-depressant, as I've now cut them down to one pill every second day and I will be off them completely within a couple of months.

Things have certainly changed. Nearly a year ago to the day

I was experiencing the saddest day of my life as I cried and waved goodbye to Mandy from my life, and in the months that followed I thought I would never find anyone as wonderful and loving as Mandy.

Well, I spent this morning with my fiancée, writing our marriage vows—one of which is 'to live an exciting and adventurous life together, to be wealthy in experiences, love and friends'. I haven't been this happy for years.

I know now that I went into my depression because I was trying to follow society's norms and get a career and normal job, but that just sucked my enthusiasm for life out of me. I was thinking that because I had turned 30, the adventure was over. But now I've realised that I was looking at it all wrong. I now have a fiancée who is willing to come on the adventure of marriage with me, and that is what I believe marriage is—an adventure, an aligning of two people's dreams. Already we are planning to travel, to learn to sail and live on a yacht, to do all those things that will make us excited about our lives together.

I know now that I had been looking at everything the wrong way with Mandy—I had been worrying about things that might go wrong in the future. But worries are just negative feelings based on things that haven't happened and probably never will happen. I had to go back to how I was in the early days of my working-the-world quest when I didn't have a worry in the world, when I was full of enthusiasm for life because I just turned up to another country and things going wrong didn't bother me. I have learnt the hard way that you can't control the future.

I have learnt more in the last year than I have over the entire rest of my life. I realise that one of the most important things you can do in your life is to find your purpose, that thing you are passionate about, the thing that you have the skills and talent for, the thing that makes you you. It has taken a while and it has been a tough road—a bloody tough road—but I have finally

# EPIClogue

found it. I want to inspire and entertain the next generation using my humour and honesty, to teach them all the stuff that I know now, that I wish I had known when I was boarding that plane as a 21-year-old. To help them find their own purpose in life, to let them know that their dreams don't have to be mere dreams, but can be their reality if they have the courage to pursue them.

Because I have finally found my purpose, therefore myself, I'm able to fully give myself as a husband and hopefully as a father. And so it is here I lie with my wife to be—and by the way, Wheels was right: she is a Scorpio. I'm nearly 31 and all my possessions are in my car, which is parked at the start of the track where we began our hike after I had proposed to her and committed the rest of my life to her. I committed to my working-the-world goal over ten years ago in the exact same spot. I'm back living out of my car, my fiancée and I are $60,000 in debt and I have no money. But we're getting married in three weeks and I have never been happier. I have a partner for life who supports me to live my dreams and fulfil what I believe is my purpose in life, who I love and never stopped loving.

Yesterday when I walked to the end of the jetty in Anakiwa outside the Outward Bound school, I finally got to say the five words that made me the happiest man in the world.

'Mandy, will you marry me?'

**HAP WORKING THE WORLD**

www.hapcameron.com

# SHOUTOUTS

It's my name on the front of this book, but I'm just a pretty normal guy who has been surrounded by amazing people. I wouldn't have achieved my goal if it weren't for the support and generosity of so many: family, friends, and strangers. Thank you.

I've decided to not write individual thankyous, in the chance that I may miss someone out. From all the countries I have travelled, places I've lived, jobs I've worked, there have been a lot of you. You have all shaped this journey into a memorable one. Please accept my sincere THANK YOU.

Some of you were probably expecting our time together to be mentioned in the book, and our own little adventures and fun we had to make an appearance. But you have to realise, this was ten years of my life, and when you are moving around every three months to a new city or a new country you meet a lot of people and share many an amazing experience. I remember them all, but I cannot share all the stories (and probably some stories are best left untold!). But thanks to every one of you for sharing in this journey and making it what it was.

I would also like to thank the people who *have* appeared in the book. I have changed the names and identities of most of you for privacy reasons, but you know who you are and that is the most important thing.

Just a few shoutouts:

Mum and Dad, thank you for giving me what every kid should have: support and encouragement to live my dream when all the other sons of the world were getting real jobs. You have set the bar high, I hope someday I can be half the parent that you are. Thank you, I love you.

Jarnia, cheers for all the support, the emergency loans over the years and for putting up with my 'little brotherness', and for the first proofread.

Aunty Jill, cheers for countless airport runs at random times of the day and night and for always making my re-introduction or departure from New Zealand enjoyable and memorable experiences that I always looked forward to. Thank you. (P.S. I'll finally take my snowboard bag out of your garage.)

To my talented musician friend Hazel, thank you for supporting me through my goal, and for even writing a song about it! (Check out Hazel's soulful goodness at www.hazelheights.com.)

To Nic and the Allen & Unwin team, thanks for seeing that skinny guy on TV and believing there was a story in him.

To Mandy Sue, thank you so much for all you have done for me. The book really should be titled *Hap and Mandy Working the World*. It's taken me a while but now I finally realise that I was the luckiest man alive when I bumped into you outside the toilet in that bar in Mexico. I can't tell you how lucky I feel. Thank you.

# SHOUTOUTS

I also want to take this opportunity to shine the spotlight on some worthy causes that you may not have heard of because they don't have the marketing budgets of some multinational charity organisations. If you have any spare money that needs a good home—and that won't be chewed up paying for some corporate bigwig, business trip or glossy brochure—then please check out these charities that were mentioned in the book.

Mission Mexico
www.lovelifehope.com

Bicycles for Humanity
www.bicyclesforhumanity.com

Bicycling Empowerment Network, Namibia
www.benbikes.org.za/namibia

For some amazing jaw-dropping polar photography, and to support a guy who has supported me, check out Sich's website www.richardsidey.com

If you want to buy a copy of the documentary *Bikes for Africa*, then please go to my website www.hapcameron.com

Nuthin' but love,
Hap